Dojo

Dojo

Using the Dojo JavaScript Library to Build Ajax Applications

James E. Harmon

✦✦Addison-Wesley

Upper Saddle River, NJ • Boston • Indianapolis • San Francisco
New York • Toronto • Montreal • London • Munich • Paris • Madrid
Cape Town • Sydney • Tokyo • Singapore • Mexico City

Many of the designations used by manufacturers and sellers to distinguish their products are claimed as trademarks. Where those designations appear in this book, and the publisher was aware of a trademark claim, the designations have been printed with initial capital letters or in all capitals.

The author and publisher have taken care in the preparation of this book, but make no expressed or implied warranty of any kind and assume no responsibility for errors or omissions. No liability is assumed for incidental or consequential damages in connection with or arising out of the use of the information or programs contained herein.

The publisher offers excellent discounts on this book when ordered in quantity for bulk purchases or special sales, which may include electronic versions and/or custom covers and content particular to your business, training goals, marketing focus, and branding interests. For more information, please contact:

U.S. Corporate and Government Sales
(800) 382-3419
corpsales@pearsontechgroup.com

For sales outside the United States please contact:

International Sales
international@pearson.com

Visit us on the Web: www.informit.com/aw

Library of Congress Cataloging-in-Publication Data

Harmon, James Earl.

Using the Dojo Javascript library to build Ajax applications / James Earl Harmon.

p. cm.

Includes index.

ISBN 0-13-235804-2 (pbk. : alk. paper) 1. Ajax (Web site development technology) 2. Java (Computer program language) I. Title.

TK5105.8885.A52H37 2008

006.7'8—dc22

2008021544

ISBN-13: 978-0-132-35804-0
ISBN-10: 0-132-35804-2
Text printed in the United States on recycled paper at R.R. Donnelley in Crawfordsville, Indiana.
First printing June 2008

Associate Publisher
Mark Taub

Acquisitions Editor
Debra Williams Cauley

Development Editor
Michael Thurston

Managing Editor
Kristy Hart

Project Editor
Chelsey Marti

Copy Editor
Language Logistics

Indexer
Lisa Stumpf

Proofreader
Kathy Ruiz

Technical Reviewer
Eric Foster-Johnson

Publishing Coordinator
Kim Boedigheimer

Cover Designer
Gary Adair

Senior Compositor
Gloria Schurick

This Book Is Safari Enabled

The Safari® Enabled icon on the cover of your favorite technology book means the book is available through Safari Bookshelf. When you buy this book, you get free access to the online edition for 45 days.

Safari Bookshelf is an electronic reference library that lets you easily search thousands of technical books, find code samples, download chapters, and access technical information whenever and wherever you need it.

To gain 45-day Safari Enabled access to this book:

- Go to http://www.informit.com/onlineedition
- Complete the brief registration form
- Enter the coupon code JBKT-NKCJ-BJ2U-RSIN-7TC8

If you have difficulty registering on Safari Bookshelf or accessing the online edition, please e-mail customer-service@safaribooksonline.com.

❖

With Love to My Family:
Sonia, Phoebe, and Nathan

❖

Contents at a Glance

Table of Contents

II: Dojo Widgets

III: Dojo in Detail

Foreword

If there is one lesson to be learned from the Dojo Toolkit, it is "Be careful what you wish for!" When we first started Dojo, we had the modest goal of creating a JavaScript toolkit that would be useful and would prevent expert JavaScript developers from having to reinvent the wheel. With the buzz and excitement that would soon follow with the emergence of the term Ajax, we quickly found ourselves as the creators of a toolkit used by thousands and thousands of developers and millions of users in a very short time.

In the case of any project or company that grows much faster than expected, there are growing pains along the way. It has taken Dojo nearly 18 months to address and solve most of the issues caused by its rapid success: performance, comprehension, ease of use, and documentation. Open source projects are notoriously bad at both marketing and documentation, and Dojo was initially no exception to the rule. With each release from Dojo 0.9 to 1.1 and beyond, documentation and API viewing tools have improved significantly and are now something we're proud to have rather than being a blemish to the project.

Above and beyond source code documentation, demos, and great examples is the need for great books. When learning something new, the most difficult things to learn are usually the questions you don't know how to ask. The vernacular and philosophy of Dojo is very powerful and efficient but often leaves developers new to Dojo not knowing where to get started. Dojo in particular and Ajax in general also have the learning curve of basically needing to understand a wide range of technologies, from server-side programming languages to JavaScript, CSS, HTML, and the DOM, plus the browser quirks and inconsistencies across each. Toolkits such as Dojo go to great lengths to rescue developers from the most common and egregious of these issues, but developers creating something new will inevitably run into trouble along the way.

There are numerous opportunities for developers and users of Dojo to solve their problems and get up to speed, from reading this book to online community support, and the commercial support provided by companies such as SitePen.

Dojo has thrived and succeeded because of its transparent and open development process. All code is licensed under the AFL and BSD, licenses which are focused on adoption rather than control.

Contributions have been received from hundreds of individuals and from companies such as AOL, Google, IBM, Nexaweb, Renkoo, SitePen, Sun, WaveMaker, and many more. We have a strict but low-barrier contribution policy that requires all source code contributions to be made through a Contributor License Agreement, ensuring that usage of Dojo will not cause legal or IP headaches now or in the future.

And we innovate and experiment more than any other toolkit, introducing features in DojoX that are far ahead of other toolkits.

I first met James Harmon at a conference when he was giving a talk about Dojo. The great thing about James' approach was that he did an amazing job of simplifying the message. Alex Russell and I have a tendency to beat people over the head with every feature and every possibility, whereas James was able to distill complex topics down to easy-to-follow concepts that help people quickly get up to speed with Dojo.

This book takes the same simple approach of clearly explaining how to create web applications and web sites with Dojo in a manner that should make it easy, even for developers who are not JavaScript experts, to quickly get up to speed and become effective with the Dojo Toolkit.

Dylan Schiemann
CEO, SitePen
Cofounder, Dojo Toolkit

Acknowledgments

It seems like a ridiculous conceit to put only my name on the cover of the book. I've learned that "it takes a village" to write a book and I'd like to acknowledge some of the members of my village who have been so helpful with their time and encouragement. First, thanks to my editor, Debra Williams Cauley, who began by not taking "no" for an answer (in the nicest way, of course) and continued by expertly guiding me through the process.

Also, thanks to Debra's team at Prentice-Hall, including those I worked with directly, Chelsey Marti, Chrissy White, Michael Thurston, and all those who toiled behind the scenes to get this book into the reader's hands. Eric Foster-Johnson also provided invaluable suggestions to the text.

No book on Dojo would have been possible without the Dojo Framework itself. Thanks to all who've contributed to the project and provided me with help and support along the way, including Dylan Schiemann, Alex Russell, Karl Tiedt, Adam Peller, Becky Gibson, Sam Foster, Ben Lowery, and James Burke. And to all the other contributors too numerous to mention that have made Dojo the great framework it is.

Also thanks to my personal network who gave lots of great advice: Ed Lance, Ted Rafacz, Max Rahder, Steve Meshner, Bob Phifer, and Will Provost. Thanks to my technical idols, Douglas Crockford, Jesse James Garret, and the guys at Ajaxian.com who got me interested in Ajax and JavaScript in the first place.

And special thanks to my wonderful wife, Sonia, who helped me carve out the time to write this book. I couldn't have done it without you. Your constant support is always an inspiration to me. I love you.

About the Author

James E. Harmon is the President and Senior Instructor at Object Training Group in Chicago. He is an experienced developer who spent a majority of his career building large scale online applications at Accenture and for several other Web-centric consulting firms. He now specializes in training Java Developers to be more productive by using the latest technologies and frameworks.

The book's web site is http://www.ObjectTrainingGroup.com/dojobook.

A Dojo Tutorial

1

Understanding Dojo:
A Tutorial

If you tell me, I'll soon forget. If you show me, I'll remember forever.

—Chinese Proverb

In the spirit of the quote that opens this chapter, I believe that a simple demonstration is one of the best ways to introduce a new technology. So I'm opening this book by providing a tutorial that will use the Dojo Toolkit to enhance a basic HTML form. This chapter introduces the tutorial, which continues through Chapter 5, "Processing Forms with Dojo," and comprises Part I, "A Dojo Tutorial."

1.1 Introduction to the Tutorial

Imagine that you are a web developer (which is probably not a stretch if you are reading this book) and you are being encouraged to add some Ajax features to a site you're working on. Maybe the originator of this request is your boss or your boss's boss, who is not even sure what Ajax is, let alone what kinds of features might be useful. And maybe you're not sure yourself. Imagine that your prior experience has mostly been on the server-side, developing in Java or some other server-side technology, and your experience with HTML and JavaScript has been fairly limited. This is the scenario we will explore over the next several chapters as you are introduced to the Dojo Toolkit.

To further flesh out the scenario, imagine that you've heard lots of things about how powerful the JavaScript programming language can be and that there are a number of JavaScript libraries and frameworks that can help you take advantage of that power. You've decided to use the Dojo Toolkit because some of the web sites and forums that you frequent to keep up with the ever-changing IT industry have recommended it. And you've already selected one of the most frequently used pages in your application to be the first candidate for being "Ajaxified."

This tutorial walks you through a number of steps to update the page with Ajax features. We will enhance the page in a number of small ways that each address a specific type of issue. Along the way, we'll see the kinds of features that Ajax allows us to add to web pages, and we'll see exactly how to implement those features using the Dojo Toolkit.

1.1.1 Goals for this Tutorial

The primary goal of this tutorial is to show you how to use the Dojo Toolkit to introduce some common Ajax features into your web pages. The tutorial provides instructions for picking the low hanging fruit. In other words, it focuses on the features that are fairly easy to implement and yet provide a substantial return in increased usability. This tutorial is not meant to demonstrate every feature of Dojo, nor is it intended to exhaustively cover the features that we implement together. You can think of this tutorial as addressing the first phase of web site enhancement.

Another main goal of this tutorial is to implement features in the plainest way. Although most Dojo features can be implemented either declaratively (in HTML markup) or programmatically (using JavaScript), we'll first focus on the declarative technique given that most web server-side developers are more familiar with HTML markup than with JavaScript. Of course, we will also use some JavaScript as the glue to tie things together.

1.1.2 Goals for Using Dojo

What do we hope to achieve by using Dojo? First and foremost, we expect that our pages will be more usable. This might manifest itself in a variety of ways. The page should be faster. It should be better looking. It should be easier to operate by the user. It should help the user enter the required information properly, and the page should be easier to navigate. Yet at the same time, we should not violate any of the user-interface conventions that users have come to expect when accessing web pages. We should make significant usability gains without sacrificing anything that the user already depends on.

How do we make these gains in usability? Dojo provides enhancements to the existing HTML form elements that provide additional functionality. These enhancements should make the current form elements behave in more useful ways.

Performance can be improved either by making things run faster or by making things appear to run faster. The ideal way to make a process appear faster is to have the process run while the user is doing something else rather than just having him wait for the process to complete. Ajax provides the ideal mechanism to support this technique. We'll use Dojo to allow a page to make data requests of the server asynchronously while the user is continuing to work. The page will appear to the user to be faster and more responsive.

Data validation can be improved by bringing the validation of data closer to the entry of data. Dojo supports the ability to send small validation requests to the server without requiring an entire form to be submitted. When appropriate, we might even want to adopt the desktop application paradigm of validating data on a keystroke by keystroke basis.

We also expect our features to be easy to implement. We want to be able to leverage what we know about HTML, and when we use JavaScript, the programming model should be consistent and powerful. We expect to write a lot less code than if we were developing the functionality by writing it all ourselves. Less code means less opportunity for error. As you learn Dojo, you can expect that what you learn will continue to be useful as you dig further into Dojo. And when things do become more complex, you will have tools to aid in debugging. In short, you can expect Dojo to provide a great programming environment.

Finally, we hope to be constantly surprised by the benefits we derive from using Dojo, obtained without any extra work on our part. For example, we expect that any features we add will work the same regardless of what browser our users are using. And we expect our visual elements to support Web Accessibility and Internationalization standards.

We've set quite a high bar for Dojo to cross over. We're asking for a lot and not expecting to sacrifice much to obtain it. Can Dojo really deliver? Let's find out. We start at the beginning by reviewing the page that will be the basis for our enhancements and identifying the kinds of problems we hope to solve.

1.2 A Standard HTML Data Entry Form

We begin by selecting a page from our application that will be the target for our Dojo enhancements (see Figure 1.1). This page comes from a hypothetical Customer Service application for a nation-wide cable company and allows a customer to create an account and to request service. The tutorial is going to be pretty vague about the operations of our "business" because, as you probably guessed, this form is being used to highlight some specific types of functions that many business applications possess. So, if you can suspend your disbelief for a little while, let's review the form.

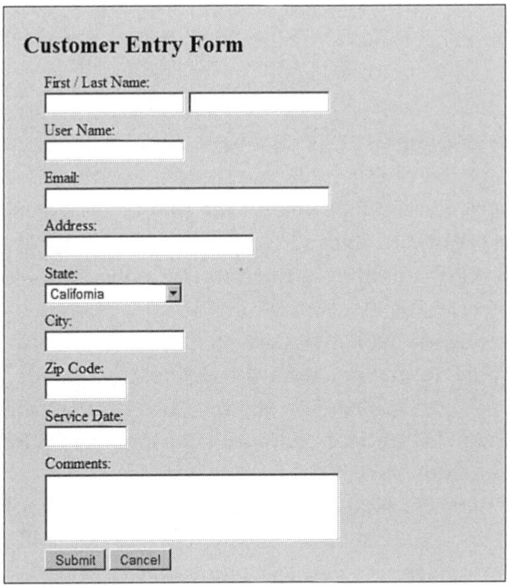

Figure 1.1   Standard HTML customer entry form

This page has a very basic design—almost no design at all. It uses only a small bit of styling and is about as plain as you can get. Your pages probably look much better than this, but we start with this minimal design to keep the examples as simple as possible.

Let's walk through each of the fields on this form and discuss the usability problems. A discussion of how Dojo can solve these problems then follows.

1.2.1 First and Last Name

The first data entry field is used to hold the customer's first name. Straightforward enough, yet we already have a problem. The label for the field says "First / Last Name:" and is followed by two text fields for input. Although the user can probably figure out what the page is asking for, it may be more difficult to understand for screen readers, which are used by those with visual impairment.

You could argue that from a usability perspective, this is already a bit confusing. All the other labels on the page refer to a single text box only, while this label refers to two text boxes. When a name is separated into two parts, should the last name be entered before the first name, or the other way round? These are good questions, but we'll have to wait for the answers. Remember, we're just identifying the problems now. We look at solutions later in the chapter.

Now let's examine the HTML markup for these fields.

```
<label for="firstName">First / Last Name: </label>
<input type="text" id="firstName" name="firstName" />
<input type="text" id="lastName" name="lastName" />
```

You might not have used the `<label>` tag before, but it can be helpful for improving your site's accessibility for the disabled. The tag is useful to screen readers when the label does not immediately precede the input field, such as when the label is in a different table cell. It also makes it easier to style all the labels with a single style when using Cascading Style Sheets (CSS). Another problem is that only one of the fields has a `<label>` tag.

Both the first name and last name fields are required. However, in our standard form, no JavaScript is being used, so how do we make the fields required? There is no HTML tag or attribute for this, so we'll depend on the server to do the validation. That means the user won't know the fields are required until after submitting the form and receiving an error message back from the server.

How will the error messages be displayed? Let's say that the user has entered some data in the form and pressed the "Submit" button. The browser will make a request to the server that will then validate the data and return the form back to the browser along with some error messages. Hopefully the server will also send back the data that the user entered so they don't have to re-enter it. Oftentimes, the error page will display all the error messages near the top of the page. The page with error messages might appear as shown in Figure 1.2.

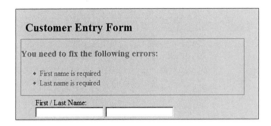

Figure 1.2   Typical error messages for a form

1.2.2 User Name

Our application will allow the user to sign in and manage his or her account, so we're asking the user to create a user name that will be used for that purpose. We ought to provide him with some guidance for creating a proper name, but that would require us to add quite a bit of text to the page, so we've decided not to. The form simply asks for a user name and provides a text field.

The HTML markup for this is quite similar to the "First / Last Name:" fields, just a `<label>` and `<input type="text">` tag as shown here.

```
<label for="userName">User Name: </label>
<input type="text" id="userName" name="userName" size="20" />
```

We've added a little client-side validation by specifying the `size="20"` attribute to ensure that the user can't enter a name longer than 20 characters.

A problem with this field involves validation. A user would like to create a short user name that is easy to remember, but because this is also the goal of every other user, it is possible that the name might have already been selected. How is the user notified of this? Again, validation can't be done until the user submits the page. The server will check the user name to see if it has already been assigned and, if so, will return a page that redisplays the form and shows the error message (along with any additional error messages associated with other fields). It might be helpful also to suggest some alternatives to the user so that he doesn't keep entering names that have already been taken. These suggestions should be based on the user's desired user name.

1.2.3 Email Address

We'd like to communicate with the user through email, so we'll ask for an address. A simple text box will be used to let the user enter the email address.

The HTML markup is shown here and is very similar to the other text fields on the page.

```
<label for="email">Email: </label>
<input type="text" id="email" name="email" size="45" />
```

Again, we've enabled some client-side validation by specifying the size of the field. But is there a way to tell if the email address is valid? There are two types of validation we could try. First, is the email address in the correct format? For instance, does it contain the "@" symbol? Does it end with a TLD such as ".com"? Second, is it an actual working email address? Unfortunately, there is no way to determine the latter without actually creating and sending an email. Though this might be useful for sending the user a password and letting her validate the user name, it is beyond the scope of what we want this page to do. So we'll just focus on confirming that the email address at least appears to be formatted correctly.

1.2.4 Address

We'll ask for the first line of the user's home address and use a regular text box to capture it.

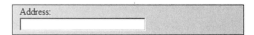

The HTML is similar to the previous fields.
```
<label for="address">Address: </label>
<input type="text" id="address" name="address"/>
```

This field should contain the first line of the customer's billing address, so we need to make sure it is entered. It is a required field, but again we'll have to depend on the server to perform that validation.

1.2.5 State

We need the user's state as part of the billing address. Because there are only a limited number of states, we can use a <SELECT> to provide a pull-down list of states, one of which can be chosen. A typical example of a pull-down list of states is shown in Figure 1.3.

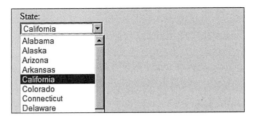

Figure 1.3   Pull-down list of states

HTML provides the <SELECT> form element, which can be used to supply a list of values. A snippet of the markup necessary to create the field is shown here.

```
<select name="state" >
        <option value="AL">Alabama</option>
        <option value="AK">Alaska</option>
        <option value="AS">American Samoa</option>
        <option value="AZ">Arizona</option>
    ... additional state values not shown ...
</select>
```

Because there is only a small set of values for state, they can all be shown. For this field, validation is not a problem, but behavior is. I live in Illinois, and I make frequent purchases on the Web, so I'm often faced with entering my billing address. When I come to the state selection field on a form, I first type an "i", and "Idaho" pops up on the list because it is the first state that begins with an "i." Fair enough—even though I don't live in Idaho. Next I type an "l" (a lowercase "L"), and "Louisiana" pops up. Now, many fine people live in Louisiana, but I am not one of them. The problem is that the <SELECT> tag interprets my typing as two distinct cases of typing the first letter of a word instead of just one case of typing the first two characters of a single word. When I type "il" I want to see all the states that begin with the letters "il", and only Illinois makes that cut. Unfortunately, this just isn't how a <SELECT> tag works—it displays "Louisiana" when I type the "l," assuming that I'm typing the first letter of the state again.

This isn't always a problem. Some browser versions do work as we'd like them to (interpreting the entire string "il" as the first characters of the state), but we need to have consistent behavior on our page regardless of what browser the page happens to be running in.

1.2.6 City

This is another required field. We'll use a text box to capture the value from the user.

The HTML will be the same as we've already seen for the other text fields.

```
<label for="city">City: </label>
<input id="city" name="city"/>
```

The basic HTML form will not provide any type of validation for this field. However, couldn't we have presented the user with a pull-down list of valid cities like we did for the state selection? There are only a finite number of cities for each state, but the number isn't small. Across the entire United States there are somewhere around 30,000 cities. So simply listing all of the values in our page would have increased the size of the page, making it slower to load. It is also not correct to list all the cities; we must list only the cities for the state selected by the user. We would need to create some JavaScript logic to do that, and we're trying to avoid JavaScript in our simple form.

The usability of the pull-down list would also be problematic. Because there are so many cities, many of them would start with the same letter. Typing the first letter of the city would only get the user to the beginning of a long list. The user would have to scroll down for quite a while to reach certain values—something that would get pretty tiresome.

1.2.7 Zip Code

Zip code is the final required field for the billing address. We'll use a text box to capture the data from the user.

The HTML is the same as for the other text fields.

```
<label for="zipCode">Zip Code: </label>
<input type="text" id="zipCode" name="zipCode" size="10" /></br>
```

Validation is required. Again, we'll depend on the server for making sure the field has been entered. The server will return a page containing the form, any data entered by the user, and any validation error messages that are created. Aside from making the field required, what other validations might be performed? Just like for the email address, there are two types of validation. Is the data in the right form? And is the data a valid value?

Zip codes take two forms in the United States. They can be five numeric digits long or five digits followed by a dash and then four more digits. This means that the entered data can either be five characters long or ten characters long. HTML does provide us with a technique for enforcing a maximum length by using the `size` attribute. However, there is no way in HTML to specify a minimum length. Nor is there a way to specify that a dash is required to separate the two parts of the long style of zip code. The server can perform all these checks but only after the user has submitted the form.

We could go even further. Like states and cities, the U.S. has a certain finite set of zip codes. Would we be able to list them in a `<SELECT>` list? And since we already know the state and city, could we list just the zip codes that apply? That logic is actually more complicated than you might think—some cities have multiple zip codes while some zip codes cross over city boundaries. Also if we expand our geographic reach beyond the boundaries of the U.S., we'll discover additional complexities. However, we'll stay within the U.S. borders for the sake of keeping our tutorial fairly simple.

We've introduced lots of problems with this field. Remember, solutions are suggested later in the tutorial.

1.2.8 Service Date

Our customers would also like to schedule the start of their cable service, so we provide a text box where they can enter the starting service date.

The HTML is the same as we have seen before for the other text fields.

```
<label for="serviceDate">Service Date:</label>
<input type="text" id="serviceDate" name="serviceDate" size="10"/>
```

What kinds of validation are required for the service date? Of course, it must be a valid date, but what format should the date be entered in? We're not giving the user guidance. This is clearly a problem. Beyond that, the date should be in the future and not the past. There might even be dates that should be blocked out such as non-business days.

Another usability problem with this field is that people can't easily calculate future dates. What is the date of the day two weeks from now? Do we just add 14 to the current date? Not if the current month ends before we reach that date. And what is the date of the first Monday three weeks from now? It can be very difficult for the user to calculate dates without having a calendar available.

1.2.9 Comments

Finally we come to the last field on the form—Comments. The user can enter free-form comments describing how she found out about our service and what kinds of shows she likes—or anything else she might want to tell us.

This is a multi-line text box that allows the use to enter as much or as little text as she would like. The HTML is shown here.

```
<label for="comments">Comments:</label>
<textarea name="comments" rows="3" cols="35" id="comments">
</textarea>
```

This is not a required field, so no validation is necessary. The HTML form element `<textarea>` provides some basic text editing capability. It will automatically wrap words when the user comes to the end of each line. Once the user enters more text than can fit in the visible portion of the box, a scroll bar automatically appears on the right-hand edge of the box to allow up and down scrolling. But that's the extent of its features. There are no formatting capabilities.

This completes our review of the original HTML form. Now that we've cataloged the many problems with this form, we can plan our strategy for addressing them with Dojo.

1.3 The Plan for Enhancing the Form

There is a lot of work to do to address all the problems we've identified. We need to create a plan of attack, and the first task is be to organize our problems into some broad categories. We'll start with the simplest changes first and gradually move up to more complicated ones. The categories are listed here. Each category will be a step of the tutorial.

1. Including Dojo in the form
2. Adding client-side validation
3. Adding server-side features
4. Using additional specialized Dojo widgets
5. Processing the form

Each topic is described in more detail in the following sections.

1.3.1 Including Dojo in the Form

The first step of the tutorial shows you how to add Dojo to a web page and is contained here in Chapter 1.

Dojo is a library of functions that we can access either programmatically or declaratively. We use it programmatically by writing JavaScript, which makes calls to Dojo functions, or declaratively by calling Dojo using HTML markup. But before we can make any calls to Dojo, we must make it available to our page. In other words, we must include Dojo in our web page. This step alone won't implement any of the many features available to us, but without it, we can't use Dojo at all.

1.3.2 Adding Client-side Validation

The second step of the tutorial focuses on client-side validation and is contained in Chapter 2, "Using Dojo for Client-side Validation."

Many of the usability problems we identified were things that could be solved by providing some validation in the browser. In this step we only address the validation that doesn't require communication with the server. Some developers might not even consider these features to be Ajax because there is no server request created. But that would not be quite accurate. After all, Ajax is a two-sided coin. One side is certainly asynchronous server communication without a page refresh, but the other side of the coin is all the interactivity and eye candy available by using JavaScript to manipulate the display.

One of the problems we solve in this step is the validation of required data. Rather than submit the form and asking the server to check that a required field has been entered, we use JavaScript to test for data *before* submitting the form. This will make the application seem faster because the user won't have to wait for a server response to find out about bad data.

1.3.3 Adding Server-side Features

The third step of the tutorial focuses on the classic definition Ajax—making calls to the server without refreshing the page that the user is working on. This topic is covered in Chapter 3, "Using Dojo to Work with the Server."

Some of the other problems with our form were caused by forcing a page submit to validate certain kinds of data. For example, the user name needs to be validated against existing user names on the server. There is no way to avoid checking the server—that's where the data is. But we don't have to request a whole new page. We can create an Ajax request just to check the user name, and the server will return just the validation information, not an entire new page. This will be quicker and won't interrupt the user's flow.

We'll also make requests to the server to get data based on values entered by the user. For instance, we can go get a list of cities from the server based on the state selected from the pull-down list. This step will require some additional scripts on the server to allow it to respond to these Ajax requests. I've created some simple JavaServer Page (JSP) scripts on the server to allow the examples to work. The scripts are over-simplified but serve the purpose of demonstrating the features that are discussed in the tutorial.

1.3.4 Using Additional Specialized Dojo Widgets

The fourth step of the tutorial demonstrates some of Dojo's powerful widgets and is contained in Chapter 4, "Using Dojo Widgets."

Eye candy is the term some designers use to describe cool visual effects. Drag–and–drop in Google Maps is at least partly an eye candy feature. Not only does Dojo allow us to enhance existing HTML form elements, but it also provides entire new visual elements called *widgets*, which provide new form elements not available in HTML. For example, one of the problems with service date was that the user really needs to see a calendar to pick the date. We can add the Dojo Date Picker widget, which causes a calendar to display right on the page. We can also replace the simple `<textarea>` element with a full-blown rich text editor widget.

1.3.5 Processing the Form

The fifth and final step of the tutorial demonstrates form processing and submission and is discussed in Chapter 5.

The final step of the tutorial deals with treating the form elements as an integrated whole. We look at how to verify that all the client-side validations have been performed before the form is submitted, and we see how to submit the form. I hate to ruin the end of the movie, but here goes (spoiler alert): Dojo will submit the form data as through it were a regular HTML form. In other words, we won't have to modify the component on the server that processes the form data. The server won't even know that the form has been "Dojo-ized." That will save us some work on the server.

1.4 Getting and Running the Source Code

Each step in the tutorial is fully described in this book. However, you might want to play along at home. All the source code required for the tutorial is available at the web site for the book, which includes starting code for each step along with the final code for each step. You can download the starting code and make the changes yourself—or just download the final code for each step and run it.

You can use whatever editor you like to modify the code. For some of the steps, you do not even need a web server. However, this is a web application, so some of the features do require a server. I've created some server components using Java Server Pages (JSPs). These server components are sufficient only to run the examples and are not suggested or recommended for production systems use.

To run the server code you need a web server that provides a JSP container. I'd recommend Tomcat, available at the Apache Software Foundation web site.[1] Tomcat is free. However, any web server which supports JSPs will do. The web site for the book also provides support for running the code along with corrections to the book's text. Please check out the website and feel free to contact me.[2]

---

[1] You can download the Tomcat web server from the following address: http://tomcat.apache.org/.

[2] The web site for this book can be found at the following URL:
http://www.objecttraininggroup.com/dojobook.

1.5 Tutorial Step 1—Including Dojo

The purpose of the first step of this tutorial is to make the Dojo Toolkit functions available to our web page. For now, we can think of Dojo as a JavaScript file that must be included on our page (and on each page that will use Dojo). This is a simplification. The Dojo Toolkit actually consists of many files organized in a directory structure. We explore that in later chapters, but for now we can pretend that Dojo is just a single JavaScript file.

We include Dojo in our page using the same technique that we would use to include any JavaScript source file. We will use the `<script>` tag, which is explained in more detail shortly.

1.5.1 Download or Create the Source Files

Before we can modify the form to include a `<script>` tag, we must first create the form. Just in case any problems have been identified since this book was published, you might want to check the book's website. You can also download the source files there. You'll need two files: "form.html" and "form.css." The source code for each file is also included here in the text.

Following is the code for the form itself. This file should be named "form.html."

```
<?xml version="1.0" encoding="utf-8"?>
<!DOCTYPE html PUBLIC "-//W3C//DTD XHTML 1.0 Transitional//EN"
   "http://www.w3.org/TR/xhtml1/DTD/xhtml1-transitional.dtd">
<html xmlns="http://www.w3.org/1999/xhtml" xml:lang="en" lang="en">

<head>
  <!- Dojo Tutorial - Step 1 (form.html) ->
  <meta http-equiv="Content-Type" content="text/html;charset=utf-8" />
  <title>Customer Entry Form</title>
  <!- CSS ->
  <link rel="stylesheet" href="form.css" type="text/css" />
</head>
<body>

<div class="formContainer">
<form action="submit.jsp" method="get" name="custForm">

   <div class="formTitle">Customer Entry Form</div>

   <div class="formRow">
   <label for="firstName">First / Last Name: </label>
   <input type="text" id="firstName" name="firstName" />
   <input type="text" id="lastName" name="lastName" />
   </div>
```

```
<div class="formRow">
<label for="userName">User Name: </label>
<input type="text" id="userName" name="userName" size="20" />
</div>

<div class="formRow">
<label for="email">Email: </label>
<input type="text" id="email" name="email" size="35" />
</div>

<div class="formRow">
<label for="address">Address: </label>
<input type="text" id="address" name="address" size="32"/>
</div>

    <div class="formRow">
  <label for="state">State:</label>
      <select name="state" >
            <option value="AL">Alabama</option>
            <option value="AK">Alaska</option>
            <option value="AZ">Arizona</option>
            <option value="AR">Arkansas</option>
            <option value="CA" selected="selected">California</option>
            <option value="CO">Colorado</option>
            <option value="CT">Connecticut</option>
            <option value="DE">Delaware</option>
            <option value="DC">District of Columbia</option>
            <option value="FL">Florida</option>
            <option value="GA">Georgia</option>
            <option value="HI">Hawaii</option>
            <option value="ID">Idaho</option>
            <option value="IL">Illinois</option>
            <option value="IN">Indiana</option>
            <option value="IA">Iowa</option>
            <option value="KS">Kansas</option>
            <option value="KY">Kentucky</option>
            <option value="LA">Louisiana</option>
            <option value="ME">Maine</option>
            <option value="MD">Maryland</option>
            <option value="MA">Massachusetts</option>
            <option value="MI">Michigan</option>
            <option value="MN">Minnesota</option>
            <option value="MS">Mississippi</option>
            <option value="MO">Missouri</option>
            <option value="MT">Montana</option>
            <option value="NE">Nebraska</option>
            <option value="NV">Nevada</option>
```

```
                  <option value="NH">New Hampshire</option>
                  <option value="NJ">New Jersey</option>
                  <option value="NM">New Mexico</option>
                  <option value="NY">New York</option>
                  <option value="NC">North Carolina</option>
                  <option value="ND">North Dakota</option>
                  <option value="OH">Ohio</option>
                  <option value="OK">Oklahoma</option>
                  <option value="OR">Oregon</option>
                  <option value="PA">Pennsylvania</option>
                  <option value="PR">Puerto Rico</option>
                  <option value="RI">Rhode Island</option>
                  <option value="SC">South Carolina</option>
                  <option value="SD">South Dakota</option>
                  <option value="TN">Tennessee</option>
                  <option value="TX">Texas</option>
                  <option value="UT">Utah</option>
                  <option value="VT">Vermont</option>
                  <option value="VA">Virginia</option>
                  <option value="WA">Washington</option>
                  <option value="WV">West Virginia</option>
                  <option value="WI">Wisconsin</option>
                  <option value="WY">Wyoming</option>
          </select>
      </div>

      <div class="formRow">
      <label for="city">City: </label>
      <input id="city" name="city"/>
      </div>

      <div class="formRow">
      <label for="zipCode">Zip Code: </label>
      <input type="text" id="zipCode" name="zipCode" size="10" />
      </div>

      <div class="formRow">
      <label for="serviceDate">Start Service:</label>
      <input type="text" id="serviceDate" name="serviceDate" size="10"/>
      </div>

      <div class="formRow">
      <label for="comments">Comments:</label>
      <textarea name="comments" rows="3" cols="35" id="comments">
      </textarea>
      </div>
```

```
       <input type="submit" value="Submit" id="submit" />
       <input type="reset" id="reset" value="Cancel" />

</form>
</div>

</body>

</html>
```

This form refers to a CSS file that can provide some simple styling. This CSS file, which should be named "form.css," follows.

```
/* - - - - - - - - - - - - - - - - - - - -
 File        : form.css
 Description : Dojo Tutorial
 Last Updated : March 1, 2008
 - - - - - - - - - - - - - - - - - - - -
*/

.formContainer {
        margin: 2px auto;
        background: #DBE4FF;
        width: 500px;
        border-width: 1px;
          border-style: solid;
          border-color: purple;
        padding: 10px;
}

.formTitle {
        font-size:24px; font-weight:bold;
        padding: 10px;
}

form {
        margin-top: 5px;
        width: 480px;
}
.formRow {
        position:relative;
        padding: 4px 0.75em 2px 10em;
}

.formRow label {
        position: absolute;
        left: 0.75em;
```

```
    float: none;
    width: 10em;
    display:block;
    margin: 0;
}
```

1.5.2 Include the Code for the Dojo Toolkit

Now we need to add a reference to the Dojo Toolkit to our page. Usually we would do this by downloading the source from the Dojo web site and putting it on our own site then linking to it. But one of the goals of this tutorial is to be as simple as possible, so we're going to take advantage of a cool technique for referencing the Dojo source files on the Internet without requiring us to have the source on our own web server.

AOL provides a facility it calls the *Content Delivery Network* (CDN), which is a "worldwide geographic edge caching" mechanism for the Internet. This allows super fast delivery of files to web users from AOL servers that are geographically close to them. The files are also compressed, which further improves the download speeds. AOL has generously made this facility available to developers and end users. For more information on the AOL CDN and Dojo, visit http://dev.aol.com/dojo.

So we can just provide a link to the Dojo files on AOL CDN and do not need to download them to our site at all. Include the following code in the <head> tag in "form.html." Please put this below the ending </head> tag so your code is consistent with the rest of the tutorial.

```
<script type="text/javascript"
    src="http://o.aolcdn.com/dojo/1.1.0/dojo/dojo.xd.js"
    djConfig="parseOnLoad: true"></script>
```

There are a few caveats. The link provided in the code was for the current version of Dojo at the time this book was published. A more recent version may be available for you. If you choose to use a later version, check this book's web site to see if the source code has changed.

You don't have to use the AOL CDN. You can download Dojo to your own server. This might be a preferable approach, especially during development. It allows you to look at the Dojo source code and to work offline in case you don't have an Internet connection.

Downloading Dojo is easy. You simply point your browser to Dojo's web site, http://www.dojotoolkit.org, and look for the download link. The download page contains links to the current version and to older versions. While new versions might provide you with additional features, they might not necessarily work with the source code for this tutorial. Just check this book's web site for updates.

If you choose to download Dojo, the <script> tag for the link will be different. The following code snippet assumes that you have downloaded the Dojo zip file and unzipped it to the same directory as your form.

```
<script type="text/javascript"
    src="dojo-release-1.1.0/dojo/dojo.js"
    djConfig="parseOnLoad: true"></script>
```

The attribute `djConfig="parseOnLoad: true"` tells Dojo to search the HTML on your page for any Dojo widgets you may have added. For this to work, we need to include the Dojo parser. This is accomplished by adding some JavaScript code to our page. Include the following code in the `<head>` tag after the `<script>` tag that linked to Dojo.

```
<script type="text/javascript">
    dojo.require("dojo.parser");
</script>
```

> **NOTE**
>
> This is important—the preceding code containing "dojo.require" must *follow* the link to Dojo, *not* precede it.

1.5.3 Include Dojo Style Sheets

Throughout the tutorial, we add various Dojo widgets to our page. The "look" of the Dojo widgets is defined through styles specified on a few style sheets that must be added to our page. The Dojo team has separated the "look" of the widgets into separate style sheets. This is an outstanding feature of Dojo widgets. It means that you can easily style the widgets to match the look of your website by overriding the default styles. You're not limited to whatever out-of-the-box style that the widgets come with.

The first style sheet, "dojo.css," overrides some of the styles of standard HTML page elements such as `<body>`, `<div>`, and `<form>`. There are just a few styles, and they're meant to set the style to a plain vanilla look.

The next file, "tundra.css," defines the style for components of many of the standard Dojo widgets. The "tundra" theme is one of the three built-in themes available in Dojo. Why the name tundra? A tundra is the cold, treeless area just below the icecap of the arctic regions. It consists of the permanently frozen subsoil populated with mosses and small shrubs. Dojo's "tundra" theme is meant to be reminiscent of that barren landscape and provides a minimal palette for the widgets. The "noir" theme is darker ("noir" is a genre of film that emphasizes starkness and often is filmed in black and white). And the "soria" theme is brighter (Soria is a city in the sunny north-central region of Spain).

Add the following code to the `<head>` section of the page to style our widgets and provide the Dojo tundra theme. Order is not important.

```
<style type="text/css">
  @import "http://o.aolcdn.com/dojo/1.1.0/dojo/resources/dojo.css";
  @import
    "http://o.aolcdn.com/dojo/1.1.0/dijit/themes/tundra/tundra.css";
</style>
```

The code just given only makes the styles available to the page. Now we must actually apply the theme to the page by adding a `class` attribute to the `<body>` tag as the code that follows demonstrates.

```
<body class="tundra">
```

1.5.4 Review All the Code Changes

We've made quite a number of changes to the page, and it might be a little confusing as to exactly what the page should now look like. Following is a new listing of the top part of the page so that you can see all the changes.

```
<!- Dojo Tutorial - Step 1 (form.html) ->
<?xml version="1.0" encoding="utf-8"?>
<!DOCTYPE html PUBLIC "-//W3C//DTD XHTML 1.0 Transitional//EN"
   "http://www.w3.org/TR/xhtml1/DTD/xhtml1-transitional.dtd">
<html xmlns="http://www.w3.org/1999/xhtml" xml:lang="en" lang="en">

<head>
  <!- Dojo Tutorial - Step 1 (form.html) ->
  <meta http-equiv="Content-Type" content="text/html;charset=utf-8" />
  <title>Customer Entry Form</title>
  <!- CSS ->
  <link rel="stylesheet" href="../form.css" type="text/css" />

  <!- CSS ->

  <style type="text/css">
    @import "../dojo-release-1.1.0/dojo/resources/dojo.css";
    @import "../dojo-release-1.1.0/dijit/themes/tundra/tundra.css";
  </style>

  <link rel="stylesheet" href="../form.css" type="text/css" />

  <script type="text/javascript"
  src="../dojo-release-1.1.0/dojo/dojo.js.uncompressed.js"
  djConfig="isDebug: true, debugAtAllCosts: true"></script>

  <script type="text/javascript">
```

```
    dojo.require("dojo.parser");
</script>

</head>

<body class="tundra">
```

Once all these changes are made, we can run the new page to see what it looks like.

1.5.5 Run the New Page

The new page appears as shown in Figure 1.4.

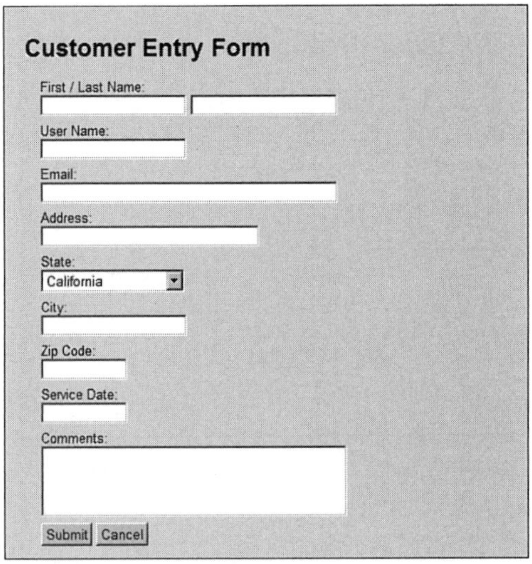

Figure 1.4 HTML Customer Entry Form with link to Dojo

Hopefully you're not too disappointed—the page appears to look almost the same as the original form. There are some subtle style changes, though, such as the font for the labels and form title—but nothing dramatic. That is ok. We really haven't started using Dojo yet. We've just made it available to our page. In the next chapter, we continue on with step 2 of the tutorial where we implement the client-side validations, which is when we start to see some exciting stuff.

Summary

We explored Dojo by starting a tutorial that will demonstrate some of its basic features. The tutorial consists of five steps:

Step 1—Including Dojo (Chapter 1)

Step 2—Adding client-side validation (Chapter 2)

Step 3—Adding server-side features (Chapter 3)

Step 4—Using additional specialized Dojo widgets (Chapter 4)

Step 5—Processing the form (Chapter 5)

We started out by implementing step 1 of the tutorial in this chapter by placing references to Dojo within our HTML page.

The next chapter continues the tutorial. Now that we've made Dojo available to our page, we can start to use it to do some client-side validation on our text fields.

Using Dojo for Client-side Validation

To err is human…

—Alexander Pope (1688–1744)

We all make mistakes, so input forms must anticipate that users will inadvertently enter bad data. Identifying and correcting these mistakes is an important job of an HTML form, and this chapter describes Dojo features that allow you to easily add validation.

2.1 Validating Form Fields

Validating input data on web pages is usually a function performed by the server. The web page allows the user to enter data, and when the Submit button is pressed, the browser wraps up the data into an HTTP request and sends it to the server. The server checks each data field to make sure it is valid, and if any problems are found, a new form along with error messages is sent back to the browser. Wouldn't it be much more useful if problems could be detected in the browser before a server request is made? This approach would provide two primary advantages. It would lighten the load on the server, and, more importantly, it would notify the user of a problem with a data field almost immediately after he or she entered the bad data. This supports the truism that errors are cheapest to fix the closer the detection is to the original creation of the error. For example, if there is a problem with a zip code field and the user is notified just after he enters the bad zip code, then he is still thinking about zip code and can easily make the correction. If the user isn't notified until the server response comes back, he's already stopped thinking about zip code—his mind has moved on to other concerns. This problem of context switching is especially difficult when the server returns errors for many different fields.

How can we drive validation closer to the entry of the data? There are two primary techniques available. The first technique involves trying to prevent the error from being entered at all. For example, if the form requires the user to enter a field that must contain a numeric value of a certain length, we can use the `size` attribute available in HTML to specify the maximum amount of characters the user can enter. So the user is prevented by the browser from entering more characters than are allowed. Following is an example from our form for the zip code field.

```
<label for="zipCode">Zip Code: </label>
<input type="text" id="zipCode" name="zipCode" size="10" /><br>
```

This initial validation markup gives us more optimism than is deserved. We might be hoping for many other attributes to provide some kind of client-side validation. Unfortunately, the `size` attribute is basically the extent of HTML-based validation techniques. There are no markup tags or attributes for minimum size or for data type. Nor is there a way in HTML to designate that a field is required.

That brings us to the second type of validation available to us in the browser. We can use JavaScript. Given the power of JavaScript, the sky is the limit in terms of types of validations we can perform. We can trigger a JavaScript function to run after the user enters a field, and that function can check to see if data is entered, check for a minimum or maximum length, or even perform sophisticated pattern matching using regular expressions.

Problem solved, correct? Not quite. The problem with depending on JavaScript as our validation technique is that we have to write lots of code to implement the checks. JavaScript code is required to perform the validation. Other JavaScript code tells the validation when to run. And even more JavaScript code is needed to display the error messages back to the user. Code, code, and more code. Suddenly, this approach doesn't seem as desirable anymore.

But this is where Dojo can come to the rescue. In this part of the tutorial, we explore how Dojo can help us with validation by combining the two techniques we've discussed. In other words, we'll be able to turn on validation by using simple HTML markup, but we'll let Dojo provide the complex JavaScript code automatically. Let's get started.

2.2 Tutorial Step 2—Adding Client-side Validation

In this step of the tutorial, we use Dojo to provide basic client-side validations. We look at a number of useful techniques within the context of making real enhancements to our form. One by one, we examine the fields that these techniques are appropriate for.

2.2.1 Validate the First Name Field

Let's look at the "First Name" field first. What are the validations that we need to apply? The data on this form feeds into our billing system, so the customer's name is very important—the field must be required. Are there any other validations? Not only do we want to get the data, but also we'd like it to be in a consistent format. Possibly the data should be stored in all capital letters. Or maybe we want to ensure that the data is *not* in all capitals. Let's choose the latter—but we'll still want to make sure that at least the first letter is capitalized. As in many of the issues related to validation, things are more complicated then they might first appear. For example, are we allowing enough room to enter long names? Will single-word names such as "Bono" be allowed? For our purposes, we'll keep it simple.

We turn on validation by using special attribute values in the HTML markup for these fields. The following code will add validation to the fields.

```
<label for="firstName">First Name: </label>
<input type="text" id="firstName" name="firstName"

    dojoType="dijit.form.ValidationTextBox"
    required="true"
    propercase="true"
    promptMessage="Enter first name."
    invalidMessage="First name is required."
    trim="true"

/><br>
```

The code is formatted to be more readable by using line breaks. To summarize what has happened: All we've done is add some new attributes to the `<input>` tag for the field. Each of the new attributes affects the validation in some way.

Notice the following line of code from the preceding example:

```
dojoType="dijit.form.ValidationTextBox"
```

This attribute is not a standard HTML `<input>` tag attribute. Depending on which editor you are using to modify the file, it may even be highlighted as an error. The `dojoType` attribute is only meaningful to the Dojo parser, which was referenced in step 1. Remember the code we needed to include the parser? It is shown here:

```
dojo.require("dojo.parser");
```

The parser reads through the HTML and looks for any tag that contains `dojoType` as one of its attributes. Then the magic happens. The parser replaces the element with the Dojo widget specified by `dojoType`. In this case, the widget `dijit.form.ValidationTextBox` is substituted for the Document Object Model (DOM) element created from the `<input>` tag.

How does Dojo know what to replace the tag with? That is determined by the specific widget. Each widget behaves a little differently. HTML markup and JavaScript code is associated with the widget in its definition, and that is how Dojo knows what to replace the original element with—which brings us to the missing piece of the puzzle. We need to tell Dojo to include the code for the widget by specifying the widget in JavaScript. To do that, we include the following JavaScript code after the link to Dojo and after the reference to the Dojo parser.

```
dojo.require("dijit.form.ValidationTextBox");
```

Notice that the name of the widget specified as the value for the dojoType attribute is the same as the argument for the dojo.require call. This is the linkage that allows Dojo to associate the HTML markup with the JavaScript code for that widget.

To emphasize this process, let's review the HTML markup specified in the original page and then compare it to the HTML markup after the parser runs. To see the original markup, we merely have to view the source of the file form.html. Seeing the new markup is a bit harder. The browser converts the original HTML into a DOM tree representing the various tags. The Dojo parser modifies the DOM elements using JavaScript, but the original source for the page is untouched. We need some tool that will convert the DOM (the browser's internal representation of the page) back into HTML for our review. The Firefox browser provides a DOM Inspector to do just that. An excellent add-on to Firefox, called Firebug, also allows the DOM to be inspected. Firebug also provides a number of excellent tools for developing web pages such as its DOM inspection capabilities we can use to inspect the DOM after the Dojo parser has run—so we can see exactly what it does. But before we see how the DOM changes, let's first review the original <input> tag for the first name field.

```
<input
    type="text"
    id="firstName"
    size="20"
    dojoType="dijit.form.ValidationTextBox"
    required="true"
    propercase="true"
    promptMessage="Enter first name."
    invalidMessage="First name is required."
    trim="true"
/>
```

The code has been reformatted to make it more readable by adding some line breaks. The attributes from dojoType through trim are not valid HTML attributes. They are meaningful only to the Dojo parser and drive some features of the Dojo widget they pertain to. Now let's see what the HTML looks like after the parser runs.

```
<input
  type="text"
  tabindex="0"
  maxlength="999999"
  size="20"
  class="dijitInputField dijitInputFieldValidationError dijitFormWidget"
  name="firstName"
  id="firstName"
  autocomplete="off"
  style=""
  value=""
  disabled="false"

  widgetid="firstName"
  dojoattachevent="onfocus,onkeyup,onkeypress:_onKeyPress"
  dojoattachpoint="textbox,focusNode"
  invalid="true"
  valuenow=""

/>
```

The preceding code has also been reformatted for readability, adding line breaks and changing the order of the attributes a little. Notice that a number of valid HTML attributes have been added to the `<input>` DOM element such as `tabindex`, `class`, `autocomplete`, and `disabled`. And additionally, a number of Dojo-only attributes have been added such as `widgetid`, `dojoattachevent`, `dojoattachpoint`, `invalid`, and `valuenow`. We look at these in more detail in Part II, "Dojo Widgets," but for now it's enough just to point out that the parser is rewriting our HTML. The parser is doing even more work that we can see here. It is associating various event handler functions to events that might occur on this DOM element. For instance, when the user enters or changes the value in the field, Dojo functions get called, which perform validation. And Dojo even creates objects that correspond to the HTML tags. We can't tell that this is happening just from seeing the HTML markup, but behind the scenes, that is exactly what Dojo is doing.

Let's review the other special Dojo attributes. Each Dojo widget has a set of properties that control its behavior. These properties are set by various Dojo widget attribute values.

- The `required="true"` attribute setting tells Dojo that this field must be entered.
- The `propercase="true"` attribute setting tells Dojo to reformat the field value entered by the user. In this case, the setting for `propercase` tells Dojo to make sure that the first letter is capitalized and subsequent letters are in lowercase. In other words, Dojo will put the entered value into the format for a typical proper noun.

- The `promptMessage="Enter first name."` attribute setting tells Dojo to display a message next to the field to instruct the user on what kind of data can be entered into the field. The prompt message displays while the field is in focus.

- The `invalidMessage="First name is required."` attribute setting causes Dojo to display a message next to the field if it fails the validation. In our case, if the user does not enter a value, then a message will appear.

- The `trim="true"` attribute setting tells Dojo to remove any leading or trailing spaces from the entered value before sending it to the server.

Now let's run the page and see how it behaves. Because this is the first field on the page, the field gets focus, and the cursor immediately is placed on the input area for the "First Name" field.

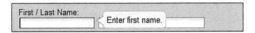

Notice that we get a message box that says "Enter first name." Dojo calls this a *Tool Tip*, and it has dynamic behavior. It is only displayed when the field has focus (the cursor is in the field), and once the field loses focus, the message disappears. The message appears on top of any visible element below it, so there is no need to leave room for it when designing your page.

Try entering different values in the field and then press `<tab>` to leave the field. For example, enter " joe " and watch it be transformed into "Joe" with leading and trailing spaces removed and the first letter of the name capitalized.

> **NOTE:**
>
> You might not agree with the various validations I have chosen. For example, one early review of this text pointed out that "LaToya" would be a hard name to validate. You could probably make a case for different validations, and I could probably agree with you. But I've chosen the ones I have not only to represent my example application, but also to highlight certain Dojo features—so I'm sticking to them!

2.2.2 Validating the Last Name Field

The last name field has the same validations as the first name field does. There is nothing extra to do for this field and nothing new to learn. Just replace the `<input>` tag for Last Name with the following code.

```
<input type="text" id="lastName" name="lastName"
    dojoType="dijit.form.ValidationTextBox"
    required="true"
    propercase="true"
    promptMessage="Enter last name."
```

```
    invalidMessage="Last name is required."
    trim="true"
/>
```

2.2.3 Validating the User Name Field

We are going to allow the user to manage his or her own account information in our application. To provide some security we need the user to make up a user name that he or she can use later to sign on to the system. This field will be required, and we'd like it to always be entered in lowercase. To validate this field, we'll use the same Dojo widget that we've already used, `dijit.form.ValidationTextBox`, but we'll use a new attribute called `lowercase` to force the transformation of the entered data into all lowercase letters.

There are some additional validations we'd like to do on this field. For instance, is this user name already assigned to someone else? We could check the server for existing values. However, because this validation requires interaction with the server, we'll save it for step 3 of the tutorial and focus on only the client-side validation right now.

The following HTML markup is needed to enable validation for this field.

```
<input type="text" id="userName" name="userName"
    dojoType="dijit.form.ValidationTextBox"
    required="true"
    promptMessage="Enter user name."
    trim="true"
    lowercase="true"
/>
```

2.2.4 Validating the Email Address Field

We need to communicate with our customers so we'll get their email addresses. This will be a required field. We'll also make it all lowercase for consistency. In addition, we'd like to make sure that the value entered in this field is also in the correct format for an email address. There is no way to know if it is a working email until we actually try to send something to it, but at least we can make sure that it contains a "@" character and appears to reference a valid domain.

How can we specify the desired format? By using a specialized pattern matching language known as *regular expressions*, we can specify a pattern of characters to check the value against. We need to build a regular expression to validate for email addresses. At this point in our discussions, let's not go on a long detour to discuss the building of these expressions.

> **NOTE:**
> Some great information on building regular expressions can be found at the Mozilla Developer Center at http://developer.mozilla.org/en/docs/Core_JavaScript_1.5_Reference: Global_Objects:RegExp.

The following is regular expression that can be used to validate most formats of email addresses—*most* because it is surprisingly difficult to validate for *all* possible email addresses. This is because of some of the unusual variations such as domains longer than four characters such as ".museum" or addresses consisting of a sub-domain. But the following regular expression will work for most.

```
[\b[A-Z0-9._%+-]+@[A-Z0-9.-]+\.[A-Z]{2,4}\b]+
```

> **NOTE:**
>
> For more information on validating email addresses, the following link will get you to a Dojo Forum article describing a regular expression for email: http://dojotoolkit.org/forum/dijit-dijit-0-9/dijit-support/text-validation.

The `ValidationTextBox` contains a special property for validating against regular expressions. The attribute to use is `regExp`—just specify the regular expression as its value. Replace the `<input>` tag for email with the following code in "form.html" to specify validation for the email address field.

```
<input type="text" id="email" name="email" size="30"
    dojoType="dijit.form.ValidationTextBox"
    required="true"
    regExp="\b[a-zA-Z0-9._%-]+@[a-zA-Z0-9.-]+\.[a-zA-Z]{2,4}\b"
    promptMessage="Enter email address."
    invalidMessage="Invalid Email Address."
    trim="true"
/>
```

Validating email addresses is a really interesting subject. There are quite a few variants to the simple `name@company.com` format that we often see. For a really thorough discussion of email, you should review the RFC rules. The following link will get you to the Wikipedia page that describes email, from which you can link to the official RFC documents: http://en.wikipedia.org/wiki/E-mail_address.

2.2.5 Validating the Address Field

The address field will contain the first line of the user's mailing address. We'll make it required. We will use the `ValidationTextBox`, and we have seen all of the attributes already. Replace the `<input>` tag for address with the following code.

```
<input type="text" id="address" name="address" size="30"
    dojoType="dijit.form.ValidationTextBox"
    required="true"
    promptMessage="Enter address."
    invalidMessage="Address is required."
    trim="true"
/>
```

There are many additional validations that can be performed on address data, the most important being to ensure that the address is an actual address. Standard abbreviations such as "St" for "Street" could also be allowed. These additional validations could be done by a number of web services available from the U.S. Postal Service, but that is really outside the scope of this tutorial.

2.2.6 Validating the City Field

The city field will contain the value for the city in the user's mailing address. We'll make it required. We will use the ValidationTextBox. Replace the <input> tag for address with the following code.

```
<input type="text" id="city" name="city" size="30"
    dojoType="dijit.form.ValidationTextBox"
    required="true"
    promptMessage="Enter city."
    invalidMessage="City is required."
    trim="true"
/>
```

2.2.7 Validating the Zip Code Field

The zip code field is part of the mailing address and is required. There are some additional validations we can apply. Our hypothetical company is a U.S. corporation and only provides service to U.S. customers, so we'll limit our address to valid U.S. addresses, which means that the zip code must be in one of two forms. Either it is a 5-digit number, or it is a 5-digit number followed by a dash and then followed by a 4-digit number. If we can come up with a regular expression to test for either format, then we're golden!

Replace the <input> tag for zip code with the following to enable Dojo validation for this field.

```
<input type="text" id="zipCode" name="address" size="30"
    dojoType="dijit.form.ValidationTextBox"
    trim="true"
    required="true"
    regExp="\d{5}([\-]\d{4})?$"
    maxlength="10"
    promptMessage="Enter zip code."
    invalidMessage="Invalid zip code (NNNNN) or (NNNNN-NNNN)."
/>
```

An interesting feature of the preceding code is that we've got two overlapping validations. The maxlength attribute prevents the value from being over 10 digits, but so does that regular expression. What are the implications of this? One could argue that it is inefficient because both validations will be executed. But they each operate differently on the page, which might justify using both. If the user tries to enter a zip code that is 12 digits long, he will be notified as he tries to type the eleventh digit, rather than after typing all 12 digits and pressing tab to leave the field. By using both techniques, the error is detected sooner.

> **NOTE:**
>
> This chapter has stopped short of describing validations for the "Start Service" and "Comments" fields. This is because we will use more advanced Dojo widgets to validate these fields, which are described in Chapter 4, "Using Dojo Widgets."

Summary

The Dojo widget `dijit.form.ValidationTextBox` provides many common client-side validations. Include the `ValidationTextBox` by referencing it in the `<input>` tag for the field that needs the validation.

```
dojoType="dijit.form.ValidationTextBox"
```

Remember to tell the page that it needs the JavaScript code for the widget by coding a call to the `require` method somewhere after the call to the Dojo parser.

dojo.require("widget dijit.form.ValidationTextBox");

Additional attributes in the `<input>` tag specify behavior for the `ValidationTextBox`. A few are listed here:

`require="true"` makes the field required.

`trim="true"` removes leading blanks.

`lowercase="true"` converts field to all lower case letters.

We've now completed step 2 of the tutorial. The changes we've implemented have added client-side validation to our form. We were able to add validation almost exclusively through modifying the HTML—only a small amount of JavaScript was necessary to include the Dojo validation code. Client-side validation is an extremely powerful capability and makes our page much more usable. Yet by using Dojo, we obtain this power without the corresponding cost of writing a lot of JavaScript.

In this chapter we've focused on functionality that doesn't require a call to the server. In the next chapter the server will play a role. We'll make calls to the server using the `XMLHttpRequest` to get data and perform validations. Now that's Ajax!

Using Dojo to Work
with the Server

You're gonna have to serve somebody.

—Bob Dylan

This chapter describes how we can use Dojo to communicate with a server. Two of the primary purposes that the server can fill are to run processes and provide data. Examples of both of these are provided in this part of the tutorial.

3.1 Adding Server-side Features

Although Dojo calls itself a JavaScript library, it is often categorized as an Ajax library instead. Though the characterization might not be accurate, it is understandable. Because there is no "International Organization For the Definition of Ajax," the term has been used in a variety of ways. In general, it's used to refer to web pages that access the server without benefit of a full page refresh and that perform some snazzy manipulation of the DOM to make the site more interactive than stodgy old HTML alone can. But still, for some, we're only using real Ajax when we're making server requests.

This chapter deals with making Ajax requests of the server. We examine two kinds of requests. The first type of request is to ask the server to perform some processing. In this case, we'll ask the server to validate user name. The second type of request is to ask the server to provide some data, which we will then add to the DOM so it is visible to the user. Our data request will be for a list of cities in a given state.

> **NOTE**
>
> There are two primary reasons for communicating with the server: (1) to perform validation and (2) to get data. This part of the tutorial is split into two steps to correspond to each of these reasons for using the server. The first step, 3a, describes server-side validation. The second step, 3b, describes getting data from the server.

3.2 Tutorial Step 3a—Adding Server-side Validation

In this step of the tutorial we use the server to validate some data entered by the user. A number of interesting questions are addressed. How do we capture the data? At which point should the server request be made? What should the application do while waiting for the server to return? How should the server response be handled? As simple as this scenario might appear, it does introduce a few complexities. Dojo provides flexibility in coding for these issues, and some common patterns and best practices will emerge.

We can validate that a user name entered by the user is not already assigned to another customer. Many applications allow a user to specify a name by which they are known to the application. This user name allows the user to login to the application to do things like edit his or her account or see transaction history. The user name must be unique for each user across the entire system; therefore, it requires server-side validation to ensure that it hasn't been assigned to another user. The use case for this scenario might seem rather simple, but still it introduces some interesting complexities.

3.2.1 Assign Event Handler Function

The process begins with the user entering a desired user name. The user types the characters and at some point is finished. But how do we really know that the user is done entering data? Is it when the individual stops typing? If so, how long does the application wait before deciding that the user is done? We could even perform the validation after each keystroke. However, this approach has a number of drawbacks. The load on the server would be needlessly increased. And the user might be subjected to a flurry of messages describing the intermediate validations. It would be more useful to perform the validation just once, when the user has completed entry of the data.

A better approach might be to wait until the user exits the field by pressing the Tab key or even the Enter key. The problem with pressing Enter is that the browser might interpret this as a form submission (the default behavior for a standard HTML form). By pressing the Tab key or using the mouse to place the cursor into another field, the user would be signaling that he is done entering the user name field and wishes to enter data for a new field. We'll use this condition as the right time for the validation to be performed.

Now we need to translate the logical event we wish to capture (the user exiting the field) into an actual event monitored by the browser. JavaScript provides us with two possible candidate events, `onblur` and `onchange`. The `onblur` event is triggered when the focus leaves the field, which normally means that the user has pressed the tab key to move to the next field or used the mouse to click on another field. The onchange event does almost the same thing. The difference is that if the data did not change, onblur would still be called anyway, but onchange would not. The first time the user enters this field, the difference is moot. But if the cursor passes through the field again without the user changing the data, then the event will be triggered again, and an unnecessary call will be made to the server. So the most efficient event to use would be onchange. We need to create a function that will handle the onChange event and we need to call that function when the event occurs.

At this point we need to discuss the difference between regular JavaScript events and Dojo events. JavaScript provides a way to assign an event handler (function) to an event on a DOM element. The code that follows presents an example of this by setting the onChange attribute to a value of userNameOnChange(). This will cause the userNameOnChange function to execute when the browser detects that the value of the field has been changed.

```
<input
    type="text"
    id="userName"
    name="userName"
    size="20"
    dojoType="dijit.form.ValidationTextBox"
    onchange="userNameOnChange()"
/>
```
The same technique using Dojo appears in the following code.
```
<input
    type="text"
    id="userName"
    name="userName"
    size="20"
    dojoType="dijit.form.ValidationTextBox"
    onChange="userNameOnChange"
/>
```

Notice that we are not using the standard function calling syntax in the second example. In other words, Dojo uses a reference to the function, *not* a call to the function. We can tell this because the first example uses double parentheses at the end of the function name, while the second example does not. Another difference is that the attribute has a different case—although the spelling is the same, the "C" in the second example is capitalized. As you might guess, Dojo is intercepting the browser events and calling its own events. We go into more detail on exactly what Dojo is doing in Part II, "Dojo Widgets." But for now, we only have to recognize that Dojo has a slightly different syntax than regular JavaScript for specifying event handler functions.

Let's put the handler function into a completely separate JavaScript file. This isn't necessary but will allow us to keep our JavaScript separate from the original HTML file and will make our code easier to read. Create a new JavaScript file called "userNameValidation.js" with a function called userNameOnChange. The following code contains the contents of our new JavaScript file. We enhance it as we progress through this step of the tutorial.

```
// define function to be called when username is entered
function userNameOnChange() {
    return;
}
```

We also need to reference the JavaScript file in our page, so we'll have to add a new <script> tag to our HTML page to include the new file. The code the follows should be placed in "form.html." The order isn't important, but to facilitate good organization of our code, we should put it after the <script> tag for including Dojo.

```
<script type="text/javascript" src="validateUserName.js">
</script>
```

The first thing you might notice is that the onChange function is called when the form is first displayed, even before the user has entered any data in the field. The field doesn't even have focus yet. This is because the default behavior for a form widget (of which our widget is a subclass) calls the onChange function when it first sets the value of the element. So we'll want to remember to skip our validation if there is no data in the form yet, as is shown in the following code. The additional code has been bolded for emphasis.

```
// define function to be called when username is entered
function userNameOnChange() {
    var userName = document.getElementById("userName").value;
    if (userName == "") {
    console.log("userName is empty");
        return;
    }
    return;
}
```

Notice that we are using the console.log function to display messages in a special browser console that is separate from the web page. Logging is a useful technique during development so that we can see what the program is doing without having to use JavaScript alert boxes or write to the web page itself. We dig deeper into debugging in Dojo in Chapter 17, "Testing and Debugging."

3.2.2 Make a Call to the Server

We've placed the hook into the page so that when the user enters or changes the value of the user name, our handler function will run. But our function is merely a stub—it doesn't really do anything. Now, let's flesh out the function and do the work that needs to be done. We need to perform the following steps:

1. Get the data entered by the user.

2. Send the data to the server along with a request for the server to validate it.

3. Handle the response from the server.

Additionally, we'll need to handle the response on the server and then process the results that come back from the server but that can wait a bit. Let's concern ourselves with that at a later stage and start with getting the data.

3.2.2.1 Get the Data Entered by the User

Dojo provides a number of techniques for getting the value of entered data from a widget. But to understand them, it might be helpful to remind ourselves of how we can get data from form fields without Dojo, just using plain old JavaScript and the DOM. The DOM automatically builds references to form elements, and we can use that to get a value.

```
var userName = document.form.custForm.userName.value
```

Another technique is to use the id property of the DOM elements to find the correct form element. Of course, this will only work if we've assigned id properties to the elements (as we have in our form).

```
var username = document.getElementById("userName").value
```

Dojo provides some additional techniques. The DOM gives us a single object to get data from—the object corresponding to the DOM element for the field. But when using Dojo, there are two possible objects we could use to get the value. The first object is the DOM element, as with plain old JavaScript, but Dojo provides a shortcut for referencing that object. Notice the `dojo.byId` function in the following code.

```
var username = dojo.byId("username").value
```

The second object that Dojo provides is one that is not part of the DOM. It is a separate object that contains additional properties and functions that don't exist in the DOM element—the Dojo widget object. Every Dojo widget object corresponds to a set of DOM elements that describe that widget. We need a different Dojo function to access the widget object.

```
var userName = dijit.byId("userName").getValue()
```

Notice in the preceding code that we are referencing a different namespace (that is, `dijit.byId`, not `dojo.byId`). The function `dojo.byId` returns a reference to a DOM element. The function `dijit.byId` returns a reference to the "shadow" object corresponding to each Dojo widget.

Alright already! We've got lots of ways to get the data. Which one should we use? "In for a penny, in for a pound," as Ben Franklin use to say. Because we're using Dojo, let's really use it. We'll write our code against the Dojo object whenever possible so we'll use the last version discussed—getting the value from the Dojo widget object using the `dijit.byId` function.

Let's add the new code to our userNameOnChange function. We'll replace the existing code that assigns `userName`. The new code is bolded.

```
// define function to be called when username is entered
function userNameOnChange() {
    var userName = dijit.byId("userName").getValue();
    if (userName == "") {
    console.log("userName is empty");
        return;
    }
    return;
}
```

3.2.2.2 Send the Data to the Server

Now we'll send the data to the server. We need to use the `XmlHttpRequest` (XHR) object. But rather than use it directly, we'll take advantage of the function wrapper provided by Dojo. By using the `dojo.getXhr` function, we'll be using the XHR object indirectly and letting Dojo handle the housekeeping for us. Our code will be simpler that way.

```
// define function to be called when username is entered
function userNameOnChange() {
    var userName = dijit.byId("userName").getValue();
    if (userName == "") {
    console.log("userName is empty");
        return;
    }

    dojo.xhrGet( {
        url: "validateUserName.jsp?userName=" + userName,
        handleAs: "json",
        handle: userNameValidationHandler
    });
}
```

The `dojo.xhrGet` function has a very interesting signature. It takes a single object as an argument, but that object might have a number of properties. And it is specifically which properties we set and their assigned values that determine how the XHR call is made. We go into much greater detail in Chapter 15, "Ajax Remoting," but let's take a cursory look at the function now. It might be helpful at this juncture to remind ourselves of how we would use the XHR directly using JavaScript.

```
var xhr = new XMLHttpRequest();
xhr.open("GET","validateUserName.jsp?userName=" + userName);
xhr.onreadystatechange = function() {userNameValidationHandler;}
```

How does our call to `dojo.xhrGet` differ from the standard usage for XHR? First, and most obviously, we aren't creating a new XHR object. The new object does get created eventually—somewhere deep in the internals of Dojo (actually not that deep but more on that later). But we have a simpler syntax using an existing Dojo function.

Second, rather that pass the HTTP message type as a parameter, it is built into the name of the function. To do an HTTP GET, we use `dojo.xhrGet`, while to do a POST we use `dojo.xhrPost` instead.

Third, and finally, we pass the callback function, `userNameValidationHandler`, as a property of our argument object, not by setting an XHR property. There are some benefits that aren't obvious from viewing this code. When using XHR directly, our callback method has to test the `state` and `status` properties of the XHR object before it can safely execute the handler code. When using `dojo.xhrGet`, Dojo will perform the checks before calling our handler, allowing us to write simple handler code. The less code we write, the less the potential for error. That's a good thing, as Martha Stewart might say.

3.2.2.3 Handle the Response from the Server

The server receives our request, processes it, and returns the response back to the browser. The browser executes a callback function internal to Dojo. Dojo, in turn, calls the function that we specified as the callback, `userNameValidationHandler`, in the `dojo.xhrGet` function call. All we have to do is code that function. What must this function do? At a minimum, it should display an error message stating that someone else has already taken the user name. The following code will display an error message.

```
function userNameValidationHandler(response) {

  // Clear any error messages that may have been displayed
    dijit.byId("userName").displayMessage();

    if (!response.valid) {
    var errorMessage = "User name already taken";
        // Display error message as tooltip next to field
        dijit.byId("userName").displayMessage(errorMessage);
    }
}
```

Note that we're making sure to clear the error message first. This is necessary to get rid of the error message if the user is entering this field a second time after having failed to enter a valid user name the first time.

There is at least one thorny issue left. What if the call to the server to validate user name takes a long time—maybe 20 seconds or more? The user might already be entering the next field. We don't want to interrupt what the person is doing by switching focus back to the user name field. But what will they think when an error message suddenly appears next to a field they aren't even working on? We could block the user from working while the validation is being done by making the XHR call synchronous, but that could also be frustrating for the user. We'll discuss this issue further in Part II when we explore Dojo widgets in more detail.

Our example rests on the assumption that the server can validate the user name. To do that we're traveling past the boundaries of Dojo. We assume that there is some resource on the server called "validateUserName.jsp." This resource takes the user name as a parameter and returns a JavaScript Object Notation (JSON) string, defining an object with a property called `valid` that might either be true or false. Dojo doesn't care how you write this resource or what kind of server it is running on, just so long as the server can talk HTTP. Following is a simple JSP page that would validate the user name with a hard coded check to see if the value is "olduser." As long as it isn't, then the user name would be considered valid. This will allow our example to work, but obviously the server program should be more sophisticated.

```
<%@ page contentType="text/plain"%>
<%
    try {

                System.out.println("UserName  : " +
                request.getParameter("userName"));
                if (request.getParameter("userName").equals("olduser")) {
                    out.println("{valid: false}");
                        System.out.println("To Browser  : false" );
                } else {
                    out.println("{valid: true}");
                        System.out.println("To Browser  : true" );
                }

    } catch (Exception ex) {
                out.println(ex.getMessage());
                ex.printStackTrace();
    }
%>
```

The code will return the following JSON string for invalid user names.

```
{valid: false}
```

And for valid user names, the following JSON string will be returned instead.

```
{valid: true}
```

You might be wondering how our page can receive JSON and yet never have to convert it to an object. In our callback function we are able to use the object by referencing `response.valid`. We're taking advantage of some Dojo magic. By specifying the `handleAs` property and giving it a value of `json`, we are telling Dojo to expect to receive a JSON string from the server and to create the object from the JSON string and pass it to our callback method. Now that really saves us some coding!

3.3 Tutorial Step 3b—Retrieving Data from the Server

In this step of the tutorial we use the server to return some data back to the browser. We need to send a state value to the server so that it can determine the cities within that state. The server will send back the cities, and then we'll populate the city select list. The user will be able to select a city from the newly populated pull-down select list. This approach will work most of the time, but there is a small problem. There are a lot of cities in the U.S., and it is just possible that we've missed one or that a new one has been incorporated. Therefore, it would be useful to allow the user to type the value of a city just in case it isn't in our list. The regular HTML `<select>` doesn't allow for this but, fortunately, the Dojo version does.

Let's summarize the steps.

1. Select the appropriate Dojo widget to replace the HTML `<select>` for city.

2. Get the value of state and send it to the server.

3. Process the response from the server

Now let's drill into the details for each of these steps.

3.3.1 Select Appropriate Widget for the City Field

In the original HTML form for entering customer information, the "City" field is a textbox in which the user can enter the city by typing it in. Some city names can be rather long and require a lot of typing, making the entry time consuming and prone to spelling errors. We could improve the user interface by providing an auto suggest facility that would list the cities corresponding to the letters typed by the user. For example, if the user typed "ch," they would be presented with a list of cities beginning with those two letters as shown in the following example.

Figure 3.1   Proposed City Section

An additional refinement would be to list only the cities of the state the user selected from the "State" field. Shall we congratulate ourselves on such a wonderful solution? Well, let's not throw a party quite yet. After all, there is no standard HTML widget that provides the features we so ardently seek. Luckily, we are using Dojo, which just happens to have a widget called the ComboBox that contains just the features we are looking for.

Let's replace the standard textbox for city with the Dojo ComboBox. We must make sure that the code for the widget is included by using the `dojo.require` statement. Add the following code to the `<script>` tag containing the other require statements.

```
dojo.require("dijit.form.ComboBox");
```

Then the Dojo widget must be attached to the DOM by adding the `dojoType` attribute to the `<input>` tag for the "City" field. The following code shows how to replace the standard textbox with the new Dojo widget. The new code is in bold.

```
<input type="text" id="city" name="city" title="city"
    dojoType="dijit.form.ComboBox"
    autoComplete="true"
    forceValidOption="false"
/>
```

The `dojoType` attribute tells the Dojo parser to attach the widget to the DOM. The `autoComplete` attribute tells the widget to automatically include the full text for the first matching value based on the characters entered by the user. So if the user enters "ch," and the first matching city is "Chicago," then the user can leave the field, and the widget will assign the entire city name to the field value. This saves the user significant typing, especially for long city names.

The `forceValidOption` attribute setting of `false` allows the user to enter a value that isn't included in the select list. This behavior is quite different from a regular select list, which only allows the user to select one of the listed values. If you want that behavior, simply set the `forceValidOption` attribute to true. However, in this case, we get some useful functionality setting it to false because it is possible that the user's city is not in our list.

The Dojo `ComboBox` widget is a great replacement for the standard `<select>` list. So why not use it for the "State" field also? Let's do that! We'll just make a few changes. Because the list of possible states is well-known, we'll force the user to select one from the list rather than being able to enter a new one. This will require setting the `forceValidOption` attribute to `true`. This widget also provides a neat technique for entering data, which solves a problem we've already discussed. When you type the letters "il" in the standard `<select>` list, the state of "Louisiana" is selected because most browsers treat each letter as the first letter of the state, even though you would have already typed an "i." Instead, the Dojo `ComboBox` uses the entire string to properly select the intended state of Illinois.

Following is the code to replace the standard select list for state with the new Dojo widget. The new code is in bold.

```
<input type="text" id="state" name="state" title="state"
    dojoType="dijit.form.ComboBox"
    autoComplete="true"
    forceValidOption="true"
/>
```

3.3.2 Get the Value of State and Send to the Server

Now that we've got the appropriate widgets for both state and city, we need to focus on getting the correct data. As we've discussed already, we could pre-populate the city list with all the possible cities in the U.S. The problem is that there are nearly 30,000 of them, and loading them all would make our page unnecessarily large. The better approach is to get from the server only the cities found in the specific state selected by the user.

This introduces a few challenges. First, we must decide how and when to capture the value of state. Second, we must then make a request to the server to get some city data. And third, we must populate the city list with just those cities. Let's just tackle each of these problems in turn.

Every time the user selects a state, we should repopulate the city list. We've already dealt with this kind of issue for the user name field. We'll use the onChange event for the state select list. By assigning an event handler to the event, we'll be able to capture the new state value and submit it to the server at just the right point. We've already discussed the issues related with event handlers in step 2 of the tutorial. For more detail go back and read that step.

Let's add an event handler to the state field so that every time the value changes, we'll call an event handler function that will populate the city list. Let's name our event handler populateCity, And let's associate it with the onChange event for the "State" field using the following code by setting the onChange attribute for the state ComboBox to the name of the event handler function. The new code is in bold text.

```
<input type="text" id="state" name="state" title="state"
    dojoType="dijit.form.ComboBox"
    autoComplete="true"
    forceValidOption="true"
    onChange="populateCity"
/>
```

Now whenever the user selects a new state value, the event handler will be called. This will also work the first time that the user selects a state. The correct event handler will be called, but what should it do? It needs to get city values, but what is the correct approach for achieving this? We need to get the value of the state and then send it to the server. Getting the value of the state is pretty straightforward. We just need to run the getValue method for the widget, and it will return the selected value.

Once we get the value, life gets more complicated. Our intuition might tell us that we've already solved this problem. In the prior step of the tutorial, we created an XHR call to the server. We could use that same technique again. However, this time we're populating a Dojo widget that has some data coming back from the server, so our solution can be simpler. Some Dojo widgets are "bound" to server data. What this means is that the widgets will automatically make an XHR call to the server and automatically populate themselves with the data returned by the server. This can save us lots of coding. And fortunately for us, the ComboBox widget happens to be one of these data bound widget types.

Although the coding for using data bound widgets can be simpler, it does require us to understand a new Dojo concept, that of *data stores*. A former professor of mine was fond of saying that any problem in Computer Science could be solved simply by wrapping it in an abstraction. That philosophy certainly applies when using Dojo data stores, which provide a wrapper around various underlying types of data. The data that an application might use could exist in many places or in many formats. Typically, we would be getting data from a server, but we might be getting it from a web service instead, or a legacy application in Cobol, or even a Directory Service. Additionally, the data might exist in many different possible formats such as XML, JSON, raw text, or some other proprietary format. It would be very difficult for the Dojo team to create different widgets for all these possible scenarios, so instead Dojo has provided an abstraction layer between the widget and the data source called the *store*.

The store provides a consistent set of method calls, or API, which allows the widgets to communicate with the data source without knowing exactly what kind of data source they are dealing with. The Dojo team has provided documentation necessary to write a data source layer because they can't anticipate all the different data sources that an application might communicate with.

However, there are some data sources already defined for us. One of these is the JSON data source. If your server is providing data in JSON format, you can use the JSON data source as a way of connecting to that data. How do you use this data source? The following steps are necessary to bind a data source to a Dojo widget using the data store layer.

1. Expose the data through an HTTP request on the server.

2. Define the data store Dojo object on the client.

3. Bind the data store to the Dojo widgets that use it.

Now that we know about the existence of data stores, let's use one.

3.3.2.1 Expose the Data Source

To use some data, we must have access to it. In other words, the server must be able to provide the data. We'll expose the data by creating a server resource, which can be called through either an HTTP GET or POST request and that will return some data in JSON format. The server resource can use parameters passed in the request to dynamically build the data that is being requested.

For our tutorial, we'll create a server resource called `getCities.jsp`, which will take a state as a parameter and return a list of cities in that state. To make our code simpler, we'll only return a list of cities for the state of Illinois. All the other states will just return a single city called "Anytown." And for the state of Illinois, we'll only provide a small number of the actual cities. Following is the JSP page we need to create to expose our city data.

```
<%@ page contentType="text/plain"%>
<%
response.setHeader("Cache-Control","no-cache"); //HTTP 1.1
response.setHeader("Pragma","no-cache"); //HTTP 1.0
response.setDateHeader ("Expires", 0); //prevents caching at the proxy server
%>
<%
String state = request.getParameter("state");
if (state == null) { state = "";}
if (state.equals("Illinois")) {
%>
{identifier:"name",
items: [
    {name:"Champaign", label:"Champaign"},
    {name:"Chicago", label:"Chicago"},
    {name:"Naperville", label:"Naperville"},
    {name:"Wheaton", label:"Wheaton"}
]}
<%
} else {
%>
{identifier:"name",
items: [
{name:"Anytown", label:"Anytown"}
]}
<%
}
%>
```

This is fairly primitive code. The web site for this book contains some additional examples that show more complete techniques for returning all the cities from all the actual states.[1]

The data that comes back from the server for Illinois appears as follows.

```
{identifier:"name",
items: [
    {name:"Champaign", label:"Champaign"},
    {name:"Chicago", label:"Chicago"},
    {name:"Naperville", label:"Naperville"},
    {name:"Wheaton", label:"Wheaton"}
]}
```

If this data format seems strange to you, it might be that you have not worked with JavaScript Object Notation (JSON) before. JSON is a technique for representing complex data objects as text strings. Think of it as XML for JavaScript. This JSON string is

---

[1] The web site for the book can be found at http://www.objecttraininggroup.com/dojobook.

representing an array with four elements, one element for each city. Further, each element of that array is also an array that consists of two elements containing values for the city select list.

Each element corresponds to one option in the <select> list. The object has a property called "name," which contains the string for the value attribute of the <option> element, which defines each of the items in the select list. This is also the value sent to the server. The label property contains the string that displays to the user. In this case both values are the same, but they can be different.

This is the format for JSON data necessary to feed the widget properly. This widget needs elements with two values where the first value is the value sent to the server when an item is selected and the second value is the value displayed for the user in the select list. Part II describes the data format used by various other data enabled Dojo widgets. For more information on using JSON, see Chapter 13, "Strings and JSON."

3.3.2.2 Define the Dojo Data Store

For Dojo to be able to automatically use the data from the server, we must create an object within the browser to represent the data. This object is known as a Dojo data store. We can get the Dojo parser to create the object for us by declaring the store using HTML. Although this is the simplest approach, it is also possible for us to create the object using JavaScript. Because we will create a new data store each time a different state is selected, we'll use the programmatic technique for creating the store object.

We'll add JavaScript code to the "populateCity.js" file referenced as our event handler. As before, when we create a new JavaScript file, be sure to reference the file using a script tag as shown in the following code. Place the code after the <script> tag for including the "validateUserName.js" file.

```
<script type="text/javascript" src="populateCity.js">
</script>
```

Now we must create the new file and define the handler function.

```
function populateCity() {

    // Get the new value of state
    var selectedState = dijit.byId("state").getValue();

    // Build URL to make XHR call to server
    var url = "getCities.jsp?state=" + selectedState;

    // Build new data store
    cityStore = new dojo.data.ItemFileReadStore({url: url});

    return;
}
```

The data store is now created but does not make an XHR request yet. That will only occur after we bind the data store with the widget.

3.3.2.3 Bind the Data Store to the Widget

To actually cause the data store to get the data from the server, we need to associate it with the widget that will use the data. All we have to do is assign the value of the `store` property of the widget to the data store, and Dojo does all the rest.

We need to add additional code to our event handler to get a reference to the widget and to assign the new property value. Add the following code that is in bold to your handler function.

```
function populateCity() {

    // Get the new value of state
    var selectedState = dijit.byId("state").getValue();

    // Build URL to make XHR call to server
    var url = "getCities.jsp?state=" + selectedState;

    // Build new data store
    cityStore = new dojo.data.ItemFileReadStore({url: url});

    // Create a reference to the city widget
    var city = dijit.byId("city");

    // Clear out any existing values in the widget
    city.setDisplayedValue("");

    // Assign new data store which will force a new XHR request
    city.store = cityStore;

    return;
}
```

This is all that is necessary. By building a new data store to ask for the selected state and then assigning that data store to the widget, Dojo automatically creates an XHR object to get data from the server and then populates the widget with that data. With just a few lines of code we've implemented a powerful server lookup feature in our form.

> ### Summary
>
> Dojo can be used to call server resources, which can perform processes or retrieve data.
>
> The Dojo `xhrGet` and `xhrPost` functions can be used to provide a wrapper around the `XMLHttpRequest` (XHR) object, which can perform a call to the server.
>
> Data stores provide a wrapper around external data retrieved from the server.
>
> Some Dojo widgets can bind with a Dojo data store to automatically retrieve data from the server and populate the widget.

This chapter provided insight into a few of the standard Dojo widgets and showed how to use them to call server processes and to get data. The client-side functionality of the Dojo widgets was much more powerful than the standard HTML widgets, but we can go even further. Although communicating with the server is an important Ajax feature, the flip-side of the Ajax coin is the ability to create impressive visual elements in the browser. The next chapter focuses on a few very powerful and visually impressive widgets available in Dojo.

Using Dojo Widgets

There is nothing worse than a sharp image of a fuzzy concept.

—Ansel Adams

For better or worse, the Web is a strong visual medium. A web page is a collection of visual elements that allow the user to view and manipulate information whose best presentation fits the right widget to the right data. In other words, the information cries out to be displayed in the correct form. Unfortunately, standard HTML only provides a small set of options for displaying data. Dojo expands our possibilities by providing a robust set of visual elements, called widgets, which offers us a much richer palette to choose from for bringing the data and features of our applications to life.

4.1 Adding Dojo Widgets to the Page

Web developers are looking for ways to apply Ajax techniques to their web pages. But what exactly is Ajax? The original acronym was capitalized as AJAX and stood for Asynchronous JavaScript and XML. But the meaning has evolved over time. Let me give you a more current meaning.

Ajax can be described as a two-sided coin. One side of the coin is the ability to communicate with the server asynchronously without refreshing the page—also known as the XHR object. This, in many ways, is the essential feature of an Ajax web site because this is the new paradigm on which many Web 2.0 interfaces are built. The other side of the Ajax coin is the rich user interface that most Ajax applications provide. To many, this is the real hallmark of an Ajax application, regardless of how server requests are made under the hood. A JavaScript library might address either side of this coin, but Dojo addresses both. We've already covered the XHR object, so in this part of the tutorial we focus on the ability of Dojo to provide the rich user interface through its set of advanced widgets.

4.1.1 Dijit—The Dojo Widget Module

Dojo uses the term *dijit* to describe its features related to creating and using widgets. Not only is this a conceptual term, but Dojo also physically organizes these features into a subdirectory called `digit`, which is at the root of the `dojo` directory. Also `dijit` is the namespace used to reference widget-related functions. We've seen some examples of the use of the `dijit` features already, but now we can explore them in a little more detail. The Dojo team had a number of goals in creating the widget features:

- Create a set of visual widgets that provide useful features beyond the standard HTML elements.

- Expose the technique for creating Dojo widgets so that developers can extend existing Dojo widgets or create entirely new widgets based on the same techniques.

- Make the widgets look the same in all the different browsers.

- Ensure that the widgets can support accessibility features for impaired users.

- Provide internationalization support for all the widgets so they can support multiple languages.

As you work with the Dojo widgets, you will discover that Dojo has achieved these goals and given developers a powerful toolbox for creating visually sophisticated web sites. Part II, "Dojo Widgets" explores individual Dojo widgets in greater detail. For now, let's explore how to use a couple of the most powerful Dojo widgets by adding them to our web page.

4.2 Tutorial Step 4—Using Dojo Widgets

In this step of the tutorial, we use Dojo widgets to replace some of the standard HTML widgets on our page. We've already done this in prior steps of the tutorial, so the technique should be familiar. Our approach will be to add a special attribute, `dojoType`, to the standard HTML tag that will be read by the Dojo parser and will cause the Document Object Model (DOM) element to be enhanced with additional features. That was a mouthful. More simply, we are just telling Dojo to replace the single DOM element representing the standard HTML widget with a more complex set of elements. This new group of elements, when acting together, provides the functionality for our Dojo widget. Additionally, Dojo will create a JavaScript object that is not part of the DOM that will be associated with the new widget. This "shadow" object will contain properties and methods not available in the DOM elements.

> **NOTE:**
>
> Because Dojo widgets can consist of multiple DOM elements, you'll want to be sure to access them using `dijit.byId()` instead of `document.getElementById()`.

4.2.1 Use the Dojo DateTextBox Widget

Let's start with the "Service Date" field. This is the date on which the user wishes service to start. We haven't seen this field since step 1 of the tutorial, so you might want to take a look at the original form in Figure 1.1 to refresh your memory. In the original form the user is presented with a text box containing no validation. As we discussed earlier, a number of problems exist with this approach, the most obvious of which being that the user does not know what format in which to enter the date. Beyond that, it is difficult for people to determine dates without access to a calendar. So it seems obvious that this widget, the standard HTML textbox, does not fit the function of the data the user needs to enter.

A more appropriate graphical user interface (GUI) element would provide the user with a calendar from which he or she could select a date. That would address the format problem because the user wouldn't need to enter the date as text. And it would allow the user see the data in the form most useful for them: a calendar.

Let's see how we can quickly add this widget to the page. Then we can discuss it in more detail.

We simply need to add the `dojoType` attribute to the `<input>` tag for the element. We'll also add a few additional attributes that aren't required but will provide some useful functionality. The following code shows the attributes to add to the tag. New attributes are bolded.

```
<input type="text" id="serviceDate" name="serviceDate" size="10"
    dojoType="dijit.form.DateTextBox"
    required="true"
    promptMessage="Enter service date."
    invalidMessage="Invalid date."
/>
```

The new attributes tell the Dojo parser to replace the standard HTML `<input>` tag with the Dojo `DateTextBox` widget. However, Dojo needs to know where to get the code for the new widget, so an additional step is necessary. We tell Dojo where to get the code by including a `dojo.require` function call passing the widget name as a parameter. Add the following code to the top of the "form.html" file to the existing group of `require` function calls.

```
dojo.require("dijit.form.DateTextBox");
```

Notice that the value of the `dojoType` attribute `dijit.form.DateTextBox` is the same as the parameter passed to the `dojo.require` function. This is the link that allows Dojo to associate the widget in the `<input>` tag with the code and additional HTML associated with the widget.

When we first run the form after making our code changes, it appears that nothing has changed. Next to the "Service Date" label, what looks like a simple text box is still displayed.

However, as soon as we place the cursor in the field, a calendar is automatically displayed from which we can select a date.

Figure 4.1

Service Date Field With DateTextBox WidgetNot only does a calendar appear, but also the current date is highlighted. In the preceding example, October 24 is selected, as shown by the dark background behind that date on the calendar. The user can flip through the calendar by clicking the back and forward arrows in the upper left and right of the calendar. When the desired date is visible on the calendar, the user can select it simply by clicking on the desired day, and the calendar widget automatically fills the text field with the correct text value for the date.

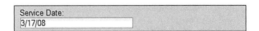

We've now added an extremely useful widget to our page with very little effort. But let's get a little greedy. What other useful features can take advantage of in this widget? Let's consider some additional business rules. For example, the user should not be able to schedule a date in the past. How can we accomplish this? It turns out that there is an attribute called `constraints` that can be used to define valid values for the date. By setting a minimum constraint to the current day, we are excluding prior dates. This can be done using the constraint attribute as shown in the following code. The new code is bolded.

```
<input type="text" id="serviceDate" name="serviceDate" size="10"
       dojoType="dijit.form.DateTextBox"
       required="true"
       promptMessage="Enter service date."
       invalidMessage="Invalid date."
       constraints="{min:'2007-10-24'}"
    />
```

Even through the value of '2007-10-24' appears to be hard-code, you could generate this dynamically when creating the page on the server so that the current date is
always supplied. Now when the widget appears on the page, prior dates are crossed out
as shown here.

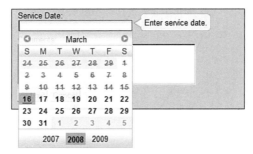

We could go even further. For example, we could exclude weekends. However, we
must be careful. Even if we include business rules for service date in the browser, they
must be re-validated on the server. The server should never trust data from the browser.
A better approach might be to create an XHR request to validate the selected date once
the user enters it. This would allow us to keep the business logic on the server and yet
still give the user the benefit of instant validation without having to submit the entire
form. A number of other useful attributes to control the behavior of the calendar exist
and will be explored in more detail in Part II.

4.2.2 Use the Dojo Rich Text Editor Widget

Now let's turn our attention to the comment field. This field allows the user to enter
multi-line text comments using the `<textarea>` HTML tag. This standard HTML tag
provides some simple features such as automatic word wrapping at the end of each line.
But that is about all it offers. If we want to do anything fancy such as changing the font of
the entered characters, making them bold, or putting them in a bulleted list, then we are
out of luck. The standard widget just doesn't allow for it. Wouldn't it be nice to have a
powerful text editor that we could insert right into the page? Yes, it would. And Dojo provides one. It is called `dojo.editor`, and it provides quite a robust set of default features.

Before exploring the details, let's just put the default widget onto our page by replacing the existing `<textarea>` tag. As with the prior widgets, all we really need to do is
add the `dojoType` attribute in the existing HTML tag. Then we need to make sure the
widget code is included in the page by referencing the widget using `dojo.require`.
First let's change the current HTML tag so that the Dojo Rich Text Editor Widget will
be used in its place.

```
<textarea id="comments" name="comments" height="100px"
      dojoType="dijit.Editor"
 >
```

Notice that the widget name is a little different than for the other Dojo widgets we have used. The Editor is not part of the `form` package, so we don't include `form` in the widget name.

Now we need to make sure that the code for the widget is available to the Dojo parser for substitution into the DOM. Add the following code to the top of the "form.html file" to the existing group of `require` function calls.

```
dojo.require("dijit.Editor");
```

Now when we run the page, we see the new widget. By clicking just below the widget toolbar, we can enter some instructions regarding service. Figure 4.2 shows the widget along with some user-entered text concerning the types of service that the person wishes to purchase.

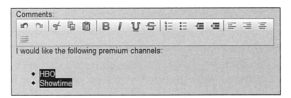

Figure 4.2   Text editor widget

As you might have noticed in using the widget, it is hard to figure out exactly where the text area for the widget begins and ends. To improve the look of the widget, we'll enclose it within a `div` and assign a style to it. We'll add a solid border around the widget and make the text area have a light background, as shown here. The new markup code is in bold.

```
<div style ="border: 1px solid #9B9B9B; background: #FFFFFF;">
  <label for="comments">Comments:</label>
  <textarea id="comments" name="comments" height="100px"
         dojoType="dijit.Editor"
  />
</div>
```

Now we get a clearer idea of where text can be entered, as shown in the following screen shot.

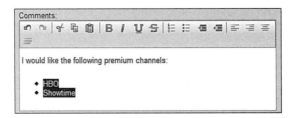

Notice how it is now much easier to see where the text area of the widget is.

The toolbar at the top of the widget displays a number of icons that can be used to provide formatting features. In the given example, the items "HBO" and "Showtime" were converted into an unordered list by selecting them and then clicking the unordered list icon. The various icons are explained in Table 4.1.

The default Editor widget provides a number of formatting tools represented by the icons on the toolbar. But you might not want to make all of the editing features available to the users of the page. It is possible to specify which tools you would like the editor to make available by setting the `plugins` property of the widget, which contains a list of editing features that should be displayed in the toolbar. Also you might notice that a vertical bar separates some features. This allows related icons to appear together as a group. The "|" character is used as a separator by default, but any character is allowed.

Following is the definition for an Editor widget that only allows three editing features (bold, italics, and ordered list/unordered list) with a separator after italics.

```
<textarea id="comments" name="comments" height="100px"
        dojoType="dijit.Editor"
    plugin="['bold','italic','|','insertUnorderedList']"
>
```

Notice that the widget now has a different toolbar and is showing only the features that we have specified.

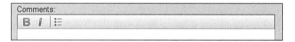

Each of the editing features has an icon and a name that can be used in the value for the `plugins` attribute. The following table lists the available editing features along with their corresponding icons.

Table 4.1   **Rich Text Editor Icons**

Icon	Attribute Value	Description
	undo	Undo last edit.
	redo	Redo last edit.
	cut	Cut selected text.
	copy	Copy selected text.
	paste	Paste text at cursor.
	bold	Make selected text bold.
	italic	Make selected text italicized.
	underline	Underline selected text.
	strikethrough	Strike through selected text.
	insertOrderedList	Turn selected text into an ordered list.

Table 4.1   **Continued**

Icon	Attribute Value	Description
	insertUnorderedList	Turn selected text into a numbered list.
	indent	Indent selected text.
	outdent	Outdent selected text.
	justifyLeft	Left justify selected text.
	justifyRight	Right justify selected text.
	justifyCenter	Center justify selected text.
	justifyFull	Justify selected text on right and left.

We can specify any combination of editing features in any order.

Summary

Dojo provides a rich set of graphical widgets that can be added to web pages.

Dojo widgets can be placed on a page by adding the `dojoType` attribute to the HTML tag for the DOM element to contain the widget.

```
dojoType="dojo.form.ValidationTextBox"
```

The Dojo parser reads through the HTML and replaces the DOM element with the specified Dojo widget everywhere that it finds a `dojoType` attribute.

The Dojo parser is included in the page by including the following JavaScript code:

```
dojo.require("dojo.parser")
```

The Dojo parser needs to know where the code is for every widget it needs to place on the page. A call to the `dojo.require` function is required for each type of widget on the page.

```
dojo.require("dojo.form.ValidationTextBox")
```

In this step of the tutorial we added two very powerful widgets to our page. Dojo contains many more widgets then we've seen so far. And although each widget has certain unique features, all widgets follow a similar structure. The techniques provided here to manipulate and work with widgets apply to the other Dojo widgets as well. We explore more Dojo widgets in Part II.

In the next chapter we put the finishing touches on our form and see how we can submit the form to the server.

Processing Forms with Dojo

The job's not done until the paperwork is complete.

—Anonymous

This chapter finishes up the tutorial. We've already added validation, server-side processing, and widgets, but there are a few finishing touches required before we can call our work complete. This chapter describes the remaining problems with the form and shows us how we can use Dojo to fix them.

5.1 Using Dojo to Process Forms

We are almost done upgrading our form to use Dojo. To some extent, we are done—we could declare victory and go home or at least submit our changes to production so that the users could benefit from our wonderful changes. We've addressed most of the problems identified in our analysis of the original HTML page. However, there are a few remaining issues that are still in need of remediation.

For example, what happens if the user tries to submit the form before entering information into all the fields? The way we've coded our validations so far requires that the user actually visit each field. We now need to consider the fields as a whole by making sure all the validations have been applied before we allow the entire form to be submitted to the server. A plain vanilla HTML form would make a server request once the user clicks the submit button without regard to the additional validations that could be performed. We'll use Dojo to intercede in the processing so that it can perform those useful client-side validations before making an unnecessary request to the server.

A slightly subtler problem involves exactly how the page makes the server request and also what resource on the server is necessary to respond to that request. A standard HTML form is submitted to the server when the user clicks the submit button. The browser knows which server resource to call based on the `action` attribute of the form

element. In our example, our form calls the `submit.jsp` resource on the server as designated in the code snippet here taken from the form.

```
<form action="../submit.jsp" method="post" name="custForm">
```

The browser not only needs to call the correct server process, but it also needs to
wrap up the data entered in the form and send it also. Fortunately, the browser can do
that automatically. The browser iterates through each of the form elements and creates a
name/value pair containing the element's name and its value at the time the form was
submitted. If the form method is "POST," then these name/value pairs are hidden in the
body of the HTTP request, and if the form method is "GET," then the name/value pairs
are appended onto the end of the URL request made to the server. The data will be
URL encoded—the spaces and other special characters have been replaced with their
decimal equivalent. The field name is first and then separated from the value by the "="
character. Also name/value pairs are separated from each other by the "&" character.

What else do we have left to worry about? For instance, once we upgrade the page
with Dojo, will there be an effect on the data being sent to the server? Will we have to
rewrite some server code to deal with the new data? The short answer is, "No!" In other
words, the same program on the server that currently handles the request can continue
to handle the request once we add Dojo to the page. That will minimize the impact on
adding Dojo to our application.

However, suppose we are willing to do some work on the server by rewriting our
response processes. Could we achieve any benefit by this? We could submit an XHR
request to the server and receive back the response from the server without doing a page
refresh. This might be useful but would require that we create a server process that simply sends back the error messages instead of trying to replace the entire screen along
with error messages embedded in it. This technique might not be as useful when the
form submission succeeds because we would likely be moving onto an entirely new page
anyway. But as a general technique, this could be very useful. We could submit the form
as an XHR object and process the response without a full page refresh. For the purposes
of this tutorial, we will not rewrite any server processes, so we'll leave XHR form submission for a later chapter when we study Remoting in Chapter 15.

5.2 Tutorial Step 5—Processing the Form

In this step of the tutorial we deal with the issues related to the entire form and not just
to individual fields. The first thing to do is convert the standard HTML form into a
Dojo Form widget.

5.2.1 Creating a Dojo Form Widget

We've already defined a form on the HTML page. Now we need to convert it to a Dojo
Form widget. It is easy enough for us to do now that we're familiar with the general
technique for creating Dojo widgets. We simply add the `dojoType` attribute to the form
element as the following code illustrates (with our required changes in bold).

```
<form action="../submit.jsp" method="get" name="custForm"
      dojoType="dijit.form.Form"
  />
```

Of course, we also need to make sure that the Dojo code for the widget is available to the parser. We'll add another `require` statement to our list.

```
dojo.require("dijit.form.Form");
```

That's all there is to it. We've now converted the standard HTML form into a Dojo Form widget.

5.2.2 Intercept Form Submission

The form is now a Dojo widget and possesses some new super powers. It gives us the ability to intercept the request when a user clicks the Send button so that we can perform our own processing. By specifying a special attribute, we can cause the browser to pass control to a function instead of submitting the request to the server. We'll set the value of the `execute` attribute to the name of a function that we will use to handle the form submission.

```
<form action="../submit.jsp" method="get" name="custForm"
      dojoType="dijit.form.Form"
      execute="processForm"
  />
```

We need to create a new function called `processForm`, and we need a place to put it. So we'll create a new file called "processForm.js," and we'll include it in our page by using the `<script>` tag. Add the new `<script>` tag to the current set of `<script>` tags at the top of the page as shown as follows.

```
<script type="text/javascript" src="validateUserName.js"></script>
<script type="text/javascript" src="populateCity.js"></script>
<script type="text/javascript" src="processForm.js"></script>
```

For now, let's just create the stub for the form handler function. Create a file called "processForm.js" and place it in the same directory as our form. Following is the code for the stub function.

```
// Process form
function processForm {
    // Re-validate form fields
    // Place focus on first invalid field
    // If all fields are valid then submit form
}
```

We're now ready to implement the function.

5.2.3 Check That All Form Elements Are Valid

What should we do in our form handler? We need to validate the fields in the form and notify the user by performing the following actions.

1. Re-validate each of the fields in the form.

2. If an invalid field is found, then display an error message and place the cursor in the field.

First we need to identify a technique for iterating through the form fields. On each field, we'll check to see if the field is valid. This can be easily accomplished by calling the isValid() method on the form element. This method will return a true if the field is valid or a false otherwise.

Iteration should stop on the first field that is not valid, and we should display an error message and place focus on that field. Displaying an error message turns out to be something that happens automatically. Simply by calling the isValid() method on the element, the message text specified in the invalidMessage message attribute in the elements tag will appear. Placing the field in focus is accomplished by executing the focus() method on the element.

We've now walked through the necessary code for implementing the form validation. Let's see what it looks like altogether in the following code snippet. Our changes to the function are shown in bold.

```
// Process form
function processForm {

    // Re-validate form fields
    var custForm = dijit.byId("custForm");
    var firstInvalidWidget = null;
      dojo.every(custForm.getDescendants(), function(widget){
          firstInvalidWidget = widget;
            return !widget.isValid || widget.isValid();
      });

    if (firstInvalidWidget != null) {
          // set focus to first field with an error
            firstInvalidWidget.focus();
      }

}
```

Now all that is left is to submit the form in the case where all the fields are valid.

> **NOTE**
>
> The example provided introduces a new function, `dojo.every`. This is a special Dojo function that takes an array of objects as its first parameter and a function as its second parameter. The function is then run once for every object in the array with the object being passed as the argument to the function.

5.2.4 Submitting the Form to the Server

The next step is to submit the form to the server. Our risk here is to be too smart for our own good. What I mean is that we should not over-think things. Based on what we now know about Dojo, our intuition might suggest that we need to iterate through the field elements, collect the element values, convert them to JSON, and use `xhrGet()` to create an XHR request to the server. While that is certainly an elegant and workable approach, it is much more complex than is really needed. We can take advantage of the fact that the browser does all those tasks already when a form is submitted. So all we have to do is let the browser continue with its normal process of form submission that we so rudely interrupted.

JavaScript provides us with a direct method for submitting a form. In the DOM, form objects have a `submit()` method, which can be used to cause the browser to perform its normal form submission process. The following code would work.

```
document.forms.custForm.submit()
```

However, we can do a little better. Because we are using Dojo, we should use a Dojo method when one is available. Although not required in this particular case, the Dojo object that acts as a companion object to the DOM object for this form also contains a `submit` method. In general, we should use the Dojo method when available because it might be providing some extra functionality or performing some cross-browser incompatibility checking. So we'll use the following code instead.

```
custForm.submit();
```

And now we've submitted the form. But just for completeness, let's see the `processForm` method in its entirety with the final piece of required code in bold.

```
// Process form
function processForm {

    // Re-validate form fields
    var custForm = dijit.byId("custForm");

    var firstInvalidWidget = null;
      dojo.every(custForm.getDescendants(), function(widget){
          firstInvalidWidget = widget;
            return !widget.isValid || widget.isValid();
```

```
        });

    if (firstInvalidWidget != null) {
            // set focus to first field with an error
            firstInvalidWidget.focus();
    } else {
        custForm.submit();
    }


}
```

The browser will package up the form element values and create an HTTP request to be sent to the server. This request will not be an XHR request, so we're expecting that the server will be sending an entire new page back to the browser. Because we are using the browser to submit the request, the format of the data is exactly the same as it would have been before we "Dojo-ized" the form. So we don't have to modify the server process in any way, which minimizes the code changes necessary to implement our new features. As the page works now, the server forwards the user to a completely new page if the form submission is successful. Eventually, we may decide that we would like to evolve the server process to return the error messages or submission status only instead of an entire new page. At that point, we would need to change our form to submit an XHR request instead and to handle the response on the page. But for now let's leave that effort for another day and declare victory on our new form!

Summary

The `dojo.form.Form` object can be used to replace the standard HTML form object by adding `dojoType=" dojo.form.Form"` to the form tag.

We can interrupt the normal form submission performed by the browser by using the execute attribute of the Dojo form to name a method to be called when the user submits the form.

To have the browser submit the form, use the `submit()` method of the Dojo form object.

Now that we've seen the general techniques for adding some neat widgets to our web page, it would be interesting to see all of the kinds of widgets that Dojo provides. Part II, "Dojo Widgets," describes many of the widgets available to us right out of the box with Dojo. We also explore how we can modify and extend the widgets and even create brand new widgets of our own.

Dojo Widgets

6

Introduction to Dojo Widgets

Pay no attention to that man behind the curtain!
—The Wizard of Oz

We aren't going to follow the advice of this quote. In this chapter we pull back the curtain on Dojo widgets and reveal their secret inner life. It is a life of purpose and utility achieved with simplicity and yet, like a duck furiously paddling just beneath the water line, there is lots going on under the surface. We explore the internal workings of Dojo widgets and acquire a foundation of knowledge for using them effectively.

6.1 What Are Widgets?

Describing exactly what a widget is (and isn't) turned out to be harder to do than I thought it would be at first. As I did a little research I came across a wonderful definition in, of all places, some Red Hat Linux documentation. The definition describes a widget as "a standardized onscreen representation of a control that may be manipulated by the user. Scroll bars, buttons, and text boxes are all examples of widgets."[1] What a great description.

> **Note**
> Another interesting fact is that "widget" is short for "window gadget"—who knew?

1. *Red Hat Linux 6.2: The Official Red Hat Linux Getting Started Guide*: http://www.redhat.com/docs/manuals/linux/RHL-6.2-Manual/getting-started-guide/ch-glossary.html.

Let's tease out each of the elements of the definition and see what it means for us.

- **A widget is an onscreen control**—Widgets are visual elements on the page that provide a way for the user to manipulate some data or functionality of the application. One of the simplest widgets is an HTML check box. It appears on the page, and by checking it, the user is setting some data values that will eventually be sent to the server. And though a widget must be on the page, it doesn't necessarily have to be visible. It may sometimes be temporarily hidden.

- **A widget is standardized**—The widget should work the same way everywhere and should have some intuitive or obvious behavior. Also the widget should follow generally accepted patterns of usage and behavior. Within the Ajax world, this criteria is not always met. Some widgets are used in such a limited role or are so new that standardized behavior hasn't been defined yet.

- **A widget can be manipulated by the user**—The purpose of a widget is to allow the user to set some data or control the functionality of the system in some way. So just because there is a visual element on the page doesn't mean that it is a widget.

- **A widget contains data**—Although this isn't in the definition, it is also a crucial fact in understanding widgets. A widget contains some state that can be manipulated. For instance, an image isn't a widget even though it is an element on the page. However, a slide show of images is a widget because not only can the user manipulate it, but it also contains state information (the current image in focus, for example).

Are the existing standard HTML controls such as check boxes and radio buttons also widgets? I would argue that they certainly are. However, the small number of widgets provided by HTML don't give us enough variety. A really good widget matches itself to the functionality the user expects for a given feature of an application. An excellent example of this is the "crop" widget in Photoshop. The icon shows a picture of an actual physical cropping tool used in film-based photography. The icon also allows the user to set the crop area in a fashion similar to the real tool. However, there is no "cropping" widget in HTML. Nor are there widgets to match much of the functionality we'd like to provide in current browser-based applications. There are too many missing widgets in HTML. Dojo provides some of these "missing widgets" that HTML should have given us.

6.2 What Are Dojo Widgets?

We just discussed a general definition for widgets, but we can further ask exactly what Dojo widgets are. First a short definition: A Dojo widget is a collection of DOM elements and JavaScript objects that work together to provide a single control for manipulating the application. They are combinations of DOM elements on the web page that act together to provide a visual component that provides the widget characteristics that we've already discussed. The great thing is that you don't have to write code for them. Dojo has provided everything you need to add your widget to a web page and start using it. Although you probably understand what a widget is now and probably already knew before we defined it, we discuss one of Dojo's most popular and most complicated widgets here, the Rich Text Editor. Here's a picture—which is not only worth a thousand words but will let you edit a thousand words as well!

Figure 6.1   Dojo Rich Text Editor widget

This editor is really an HTML `<textarea>` widget on steroids. It allows you to create multi-line text and apply various styles to it. It's like having a word processor built right into your web page.

So Dojo widgets are simple to use, are they? We just "add" them to a page? Exactly how do we do that? Following is an example of HTML markup that places a Dojo widget on a web page.

```
<input
    type="text"
    dojoType="dijit.form.TextBox"
/>
```

See, it *was* simple! The only "magic" (if you can even call it that given how simple it is) is to include the `dojoType` attribute and name the desired widget. There is one other small step, and that is to include the code for the widget by putting a `dojo.require("dijit.form.TextBox")` statement somewhere in the JavaScript. And of course, this example doesn't take full advantage of customizing the widget. It is also possible to set properties of the widget by using additional attributes in the `<input>` tag.

Note

Notice how the code is referring to "dijit"? This is the module, known as Dijit, that contains the code and other artifacts for creating Dojo widgets.

There is also a technique for creating Dojo widgets using JavaScript that is quite simple also. We just create an object using the desired constructor and then add it to the DOM for the page. Following is an example of how to add a Dojo `TextBox` to a web page (this example assumes there is a DOM element named `placeHolder` to which we can attach the widget).

```
new dijit.form.TextBox({}, dojo.byId("placeHolder"));
```

The first parameter is an object containing properties of the widget to be created. Although we're not setting any in the example, there certainly are many possible properties that can be used to customize the widget. Also the second parameter is a DOM element to which we can attach the new widget. Without a reference to an existing DOM node, the new widget would be created but wouldn't be part of the page. This is a common mistake to make when you're first learning to work with widgets.

Now that we've described Dojo widgets in a top-down fashion, if you're like me, let's dive into and explore the technical details. We'll drill down to the atomic level and see what elementary substances make up a widget.

6.3 Components of a Dojo Widget

Every Dojo widget consists of three elements, as follows.

- The structure defined in HTML tags
- The look defined in CSS styles
- The behavior defined with events and event handlers in a JavaScript object

Let's walk through each of these elements in more detail using an actual widget from Dojo as an example to clarify these areas further.

6.3.1 Widget HTML

A Dojo widget is a collection of DOM elements created from the HTML tags that describes its structure. The HTML for each widget is contained is a separate file and saved in a special directory. The following example will describe one HTML file and identify its location. The example will explain the general technique that all widgets use to define their structure in HTML.

Let's start with one of the simplest widgets, a text box. This widget replaces the standard HTML text field. Following is an example of a simple text field that would allow the user to type in an address.

```
Address: <input type="text" name="address" />
```

This field in this example is preceded by a label that describes the field on the web page. Figure 6.2 shows how this field would display on a page (in the absence of additional styling).

Figure 6.2   Standard HTML text box

We're going to replace this standard HTML widget with the Dojo equivalent, using the declarative method. This means we'll use HTML markup within the body of the page to define the widget. The alternative is to use the programmatic method that uses JavaScript. The following HTML markup would build the Dojo widget.

```
<br><br>(Plain HTML ) Address:
<input type="text" name="address" />


<br><br>(Dojo Widget) Address:
<input type="text" name="address" dojoType="dijit.form.TextBox"/>
```

I also added some additional HTML to include the regular widget, the Dojo widget, and just a bit of formatting. Figure 6.3 shows how the original HTML text box and the Dojo text box would appear.

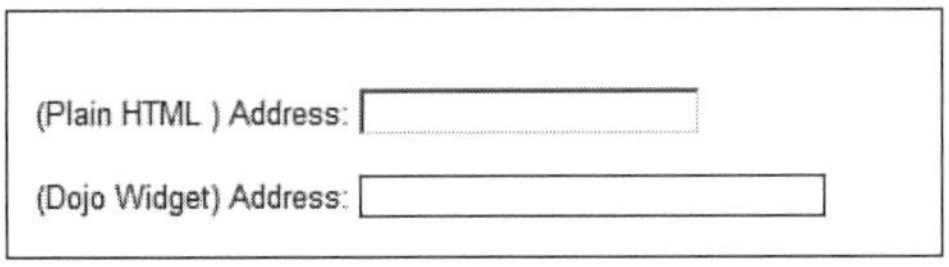

Figure 6.3   Dojo text box compared with standard HTML text box

Remember, for the example to work, we've got to make sure we've included Dojo, started the parser, and included the widget code. We'll repeat the code for this here, but for more detail, see the tutorial in Part I, "A Dojo Tutorial."

```
<script type="text/javascript"
    src="../dojo-release-1.0.2/dojo/dojo.js"
    djConfig="parseOnLoad: true"></script>


<script type="text/javascript">
    dojo.require("dijit.form.TextBox");
</script>
```

There are some obvious differences between the plain HTML widget and the Dojo widget. For instance, the background color for the Dojo widget is yellow. Why do these differences exist? To answer that question we need to examine the actual DOM elements that have been created. We'll use the Firebug plug-in for Firefox to see the DOM elements represented as HTML.

```
<br/><br/>(Plain HTML ) Address:
    <input type="text" name="address"/>


<br/><br/>(Dojo Widget) Address:

<input
    id="dijit_form_TextBox_2"
```

```
class="dijitTextBox"
type="text"
autocomplete="off"
dojoattachevent="onmouseenter:_onMouse,
    onmouseleave:_onMouse,
    onfocus:_onMouse,
    onblur:_onMouse,
    onkeyup,onkeypress:_onKeyPress"
name="address"
dojoattachpoint="textbox,focusNode"
tabindex="0"
widgetid="dijit_form_TextBox_2"
value=""
aaa:valuenow=""
aaa:disabled="false"
style=""/>
```

Firebug looks at the DOM after it is modified by the JavaScript on the web page and converts the DOM back to the equivalent HTML. You might expect that the HTML displayed from Firebug should be the same as the HTML we created in the original source for the page. And in the case of the HTML for the plain text widget, it is. However, the Dojo parser looks for Dojo widgets defined in HTML and replaces them with additional DOM elements and attributes. That is why the HTML we see from Firebug for the Dojo widget seems so much different from the HTML we typed into the source page.

Why are the differences there? The obvious answer is that Dojo put them there. But how? Dojo does it by replacing the entered HTML with alternate HTML, which it calls a template. The template contains most of the replacement HTML with a few hooks where Dojo can add some additional information.

Let's review the HTML template for this widget. First we have to find it. The HTML markup containing the structure of a widget (its template) can be found by looking for its "template" directory in the path corresponding to its package name. Our widget is in the package "dijit.form," so we should look for the template subdirectory at "dijit/form/template" as shown in Figure 6.4. The figure shows only the relevant directories and files, and your directory structure may be slightly different depending on the version of Dojo you are using.

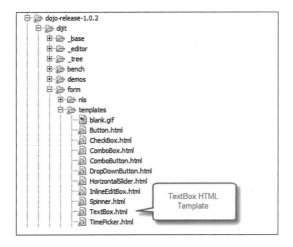

Figure 6.4   Location of templates directory in `dijit.form` package

Below is the code in the "TextBox.html" file. It's been reformatted by adding some line breaks to make it more readable. Otherwise, the code shown is exactly as what is in the file.

```
<input
    class="dojoTextBox"
    dojoAttachPoint='textbox,focusNode'
    name="${name}"
    dojoAttachEvent='
        onmouseenter:_onMouse,
        onmouseleave:_onMouse,
        onfocus:_onMouse,
        onblur:_onMouse,
        onkeyup,onkeypress:_onKeyPress'
    autocomplete="off"
    type="${type}"
/>
```

Now we can see why the HTML from Firebug looks different than what we entered in the source file. It has simply been replaced by the preceding template file. However, there are a few differences—a few places where Dojo has changed the value in the template. The first difference is in the following line from the template file.

```
name="${name}"
```

Compare this to the same line from Firebug:

```
name="address"
```

How did "${name}" from the template get replaced with "address" in the final HTML? This was done by the Dojo parser, which looks for values in the template and replaces them with attributes from the actual HTML. The "$" character is a special symbol used to name a variable in the template file that will be replaced with an attribute value from the HTML markup with the same name. In other words, the name attribute from the HTML markup in the source was used. Remember, the name attribute was in the original HTML as shown as follows in bold.

```
<br><br>(Plain HTML ) Address:
<input type="text" name="address" />


<br><br>(Dojo Widget) Address:
<input type="text" name="address" dojoType="dijit.form.TextBox"/>
```

This value replacement is a general purpose process that can be used to substitute any attribute value into the template. It is a way of passing data from the HTML markup to the template. The same mechanism is used to pass type="text" into the template as well for the assignment of the type="${type}" line.

The id and widgetid attributes in the template are created automatically by Dojo. They can be assigned by setting the value of these attributes in the markup. In this case, Dojo made up some values based on a simple naming scheme.

There are also some new attributes that don't seem to come from the template. These are autocomplete, tabindex, and value. They have also been added automatically by Dojo for this widget type. Different widget types also have some unique properties added. We explore these in later chapters when we examine individual widgets.

We now have a much better idea how Dojo is updating the DOM for this widget. However, there are still some open issues. For example, why does the text area for the Dojo widget appear longer and with a slightly different border? We need to examine how Dojo applies styles to widgets.

6.3.2 Widget Styles

You may have noticed that the Dojo TextBox widget does not look the same as the standard HTML text box. This is because Dojo has applied some special styling to the widget. One of the three primary elements of every Dojo widget is the set of styles associated with it. How does the style get applied? We can answer that by examining one of the attributes in the DOM element for the widget we've been discussing. The following code comes from the HTML defined in the template file for the TextBox Dojo widget.

```
class="dojoTextBox"
```

The class attribute is used to associate various styles to the DOM element. The specific styles are unique to each widget. The TextBox widget uses only a single style, but many Dojo widgets use multiple styles. The various Dojo widget styles are defined in CSS files, which can be found in the Dojo directory structure.

Inside the subdirectory "dijit/themes" we can find the file "dijit.css." This file contains the styles for most of the Dojo widgets. Additionally, Dojo also provides a number of alternative themes that can be used to apply additional styling beyond the default.

Figure 6.5 shows a screen shot of the directory structure used to hold the various style sheets including images used by the styles.

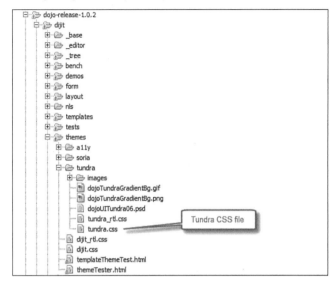

Figure 6.5   Location of Dojo widget styles files

We'll look inside the "dijit.css" file and see if we can find the style information related to this widget. With just a bit of searching, we can find the following style definitions.

```
.dijitTextBox,
.dijitComboBox,
.dijitSpinner {
        border: solid black 1px;
        width: 15em;
}
```

This code assigns a solid black border to any DOM element whose class is either `dijitTextBox`, `dijitComboBox`, or `dijitSpinner`. It also assigns these elements a default width of 15em. The "em" is a unit of measure roughly equivalent to a character at the current font size.[2]

You can customize the style of a Dojo widget by adding properties to the appropriate style. For instance, if we wanted the `background` color of all TextBox widgets to be yellow, we could simply add the background property to the `dijitTextBox` style.

2. For a more detailed explanation of "em," you can read the Wikipedia explanation at
http://en.wikipedia.org/wiki/Em_%28typography%29.

```
<style>
.dijitTextBox {
        background: yellow;
}
</style>
```

Of course, you'll probably want to include this in a separate CSS file so that you can use it from all your pages. This would allow you to create your own style on top of the Dojo default style. Dojo has done some of this work for us already. They've provided an additional style called Tundra that you can use as a base or as a model for your own themes.

We're heading toward a complete understanding of Dojo widgets. Are we there yet? Not quite. There is one more element we need to review to complete our understanding of Dojo widgets. Now we'll look at the JavaScript code associated with each widget we create.

6.3.3 JavaScript Component of a Widget

A widget is a control that possesses behavior. But where does all that behavior reside? The functionality of a widget is provided by a JavaScript object associated with the widget that contains properties and methods not contained in the DOM element.

The JavaScript object is created from a constructor function defined for each widget. In the example we've been following for `dijit.form.TextBox`, we can find that constructor function in a file within the "dijit/form" subdirectory. Notice how the widget package name corresponds to a subdirectory in the Dojo directory structure. Figure 6.6 is a screenshot of the directory structure for `TextBox` showing only the files relevant for our example.

Figure 6.6   Location of Dojo widget JavaScript file

When we open up the "TextBox.js" file we will find the following code near the top of the file.

```
dojo.declare(
        "dijit.form.TextBox",
        dijit.form._FormWidget,
```

The `dojo.declare` function will be described in more detail in Chapter 12, "Objects and Classes," when we discuss Object Orientation, but here's a brief description of it now. The `dojo.declare` function creates a constructor function that can be used to build new objects. The first parameter is the name of that constructor function. The next parameter defines the super class for the object being created. The new object will inherit all the properties and methods from the super class. Additional code (not shown) describes properties and methods in the object created by the constructor. To create a new object after `dojo.declare` has been defined, you just use the standard JavaScript technique for object creation using the `new` keyword.

```
newWidget = new dijit.form.TextBox();
```

The variable `newWidget` will now reference a JavaScript object. This object is not the DOM element itself, but a separate object associated with the Dojo widget. Like the wave/particle duality of light, Dojo widgets also have a dual nature existing as both a DOM element and a JavaScript object. As we've already discussed, there are two ways to create a Dojo widget—declaratively by including HTML markup or programmatically by using the `new` keyword as the preceding example shows. When we're creating the widget using HTML markup, the Dojo parser automatically creates the widget object for us. So in both cases, the widget object is built from the constructor, but when using HTML markup, we don't have to write the code ourselves.

What kinds of properties and methods are included in the constructor code? It all depends on the specific functionality of the widget. Each widget constructor is different, but there are some common characteristics. They all contain the following types of properties and methods:

- **Attributes**—An attribute is a property of the object that is used to specify some behavior or characteristic of the widget. It can be set by passing a parameter when calling the constructor function or by setting an attribute value in the HTML markup when declaratively creating the widget. In general, it is set only when the object is created. However, some widgets allow these properties to be modified by using special methods following the setter/getter naming convention. For example, an attribute called `value` could be set by calling a method named `setValue` and passing the new value of the property. This technique is familiar to Java programmers who use JavaBeans. You should use these methods when they exist and avoid setting properties directly in the widget objects.

- **Behavioral Methods**—These are the functions that define the specific behavior of the widget. These are different for each widget depending on what the widget does.

- **Extension Points**—These are really just methods, but they have a special role. They are meant to be overridden by developers to change the default behavior of the widget. This is a very powerful feature of Dojo widgets. You don't have to just take what you get. Dojo widgets are built with the expectation that you can modify and extend them. These methods are not called directly but instead are called by other methods at a certain point in the lifecycle of the object—for example, when a widget object is created or deleted. The default implementation of the methods (the code inside them) usually does nothing. They just provide the developer with a place to add functionality to the object.

We talk about the specific properties and methods for Dojo widgets when we review each widget in subsequent chapters. But there are some specific examples of these components that all widgets share, which we can discuss now.

6.3.4 Dojo Widget Hierarchy

There are many different kinds of Dojo widgets available to us. And although each type of widget is unique, they share many common features. To understand how a widget acquires these shared features, we need to understand a little about an object-oriented programming concept called *inheritance*. This is the idea that we can build new objects by inheriting the capabilities of existing objects. All Dojo widgets have some similarities. One of the most important ways they are similar is that they all descend from a few classes from which they inherit a number of special properties and methods. In object-oriented programming languages, these special ancestor objects are knows as *abstract objects* because they can't be built into usable objects themselves.

They are not standalone widgets but act as placeholders for inheritable properties and methods.

Let's review Figure 6.7, which allows us to visualize the various widget classes and their relationships.

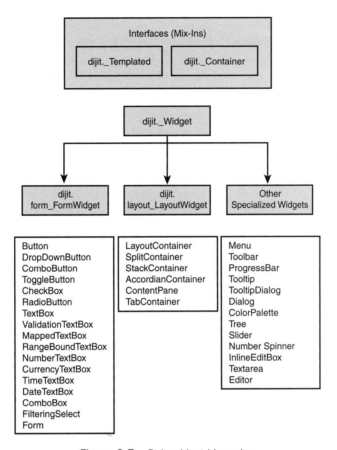

Figure 6.7   Dojo widget hierarchy

The diagram shows the overall relationship between the major widget classes. The diagram only shows a highly selective and abbreviated description of the class hierarchy for widgets. We'll drill down more into these in later chapters. But I think it would be helpful now to at least get a brief description of some of the classes shown in the diagram.

- **`dijit._Widget`**—This is the root class for the hierarchy. Every widget is a subclass of this class.

- **`dijit._Templated`**—This class provides methods for subclasses that can be built from templates of HTML code. Java programmers are accustomed to single inheritance, but Dojo provides a type of multiple inheritance by allowing an object to inherit from more than one class. Another way to think of this class is as an interface.

- **dijit._Container**—This class provides methods for objects that can contain other widgets as children. This class can also be thought of as an interface.
- **dijit.form._FormWidget**—This is the root class for widgets that will appear on a form.
- **dijit.layout._Layout**—This is the root class for widgets that provide some kind of a layout mechanism that can contain other widgets.
- **Specialized Widgets**—This isn't an actual Dijit class, but I'm using it as a placeholder for all the Dojo widgets that are not part of the Form or Layout package.

Figure 6.7 contains many other widget classes besides those just described. We discuss these in detail in Chapters 7, 8, and 9, but we should describe some of them now. We'll start with the most important class, dijit._Widget.

6.3.4.1 dijit._Widget

The abstract class dijit._Widget is the root class from which all widget objects descend. Notice a few characteristics of the class name that give us hints about its purpose. One is the use of the underscore character in the name. This tells us that this is a class to be used internally by Dojo—we won't create instances of this class ourselves as Dojo users. The other hint is that there is no subpackage name, which tells us that this class applies to all widgets. So this class is the "mother" of all widgets. It has properties and methods that are shared by every Dojo widget object that we will create. Table 6.1 shows some of the important ones.

Table 6.1   **Key Properties of** dijit._Widget **Object**

Property	Description
id	This is a unique identifier for the widget that can be assigned by Dojo or by the developer.
class	HTML class attribute.
style	HTML style attribute.
title	HTML title attribute.
srcNodeRef	Reference to the DOM element in the page associated with this widget prior to processing by the Dojo parser.
domNode	This is the root-level DOM element representing this widget. This is the node that is added to the DOM. This node may exist without actually yet being associated with the DOM.

Table 6.2 shows some of the methods in dijit._Widget.

Table 6.2   **Key Methods of** `dijit._Widget` **Object**

Method	Description
create	This function creates the widget.
postCreate	This is a stub function that you can override to modify take actions after the widget has been placed in the DOM. There is no requirement to call this function.
startup	This is a life-cycle function that can be called after the all the widget's children have been created but not yet displayed. This is a stub function containing no code. There is no requirement to call this function.
postMixInProperties	This is a life-cycle function that can be used to over-ride properties in the widget. It is a stub function containing no code. There is no requirement to call this function.
buildRendering	This function actually creates a DOM element for the widget. This function can also be overridden by code in the `dijit._Templated` object, which builds the DOM element from a template of HTML code. This function does not add the element to the DOM for the page.
destroyRecursive	Destroy this widget and its descendants.
getDescendants	This function returns all the children of this widget.
connect	This function is used to associate an event handler with a function within the widget.
disconnect	This function is used to remove an event handler from the widget. It is the reverse of `connect`.

It isn't enough just to know what methods are available in `dijit._Widget`. We also need to know when they are called and how. In other words, what are the lifecycle methods for each and every widget? Fortunately for us, it is pretty easy to create a good idea of the important methods by looking at the `create` method for `Widget`. This is the method that is called when a widget is created, either by the parser as it works through the HTML or by the constructor function of the widget we are building programmatically.

Following is the main code from the create method. The code has been reformatted and some additional comments added to further explain the comments you have read in these sections.

```
//mixin our passed parameters
if(this.srcNodeRef && (typeof this.srcNodeRef.id == "string")){
    this.id = this.srcNodeRef.id;
}
```

```
if(params){
    dojo.mixin(this,params);
}

this.postMixInProperties();

if(!this.id){
    this.id=dijit.getUniqueId(this.declaredClass.replace(/\./g,"_"));
}

dijit.registry.add(this);

this.buildRendering();

// Copy attributes listed in attributeMap into
// the [newly created] DOM for the widget.
. . .

if(this.domNode){
        this.domNode.setAttribute("widgetId", this.id);
}

this.postCreate();

// If srcNodeRef has been processed and removed
// from the DOM (e.g. TemplatedWidget) then delete it to allow GC.
if(this.srcNodeRef && !this.srcNodeRef.parentNode){
        delete this.srcNodeRef;
}
```

Let's walk through each section and describe the key processing steps.

Table 6.3   Key Methods Called as Processing Steps During Widget Creation

`postMixInProperties:`	A stub function that you can override to modify variables that may have been naively assigned by the `mixInProperties#` widget is added to the manager object here.
`buildRendering`	Method which performs UI initialization including attachment of additional DOM nodes to the root DOM element for the widget.
`postCreate`	A stub function that you can override to modify take actions after the widget has been placed in the UI.

6.3.4.2 `dijit._Templated`

This is an interesting class from which many widgets descend. I think of it like an interface in Java. This provides special properties and methods that allow a widget to be created from a template (a string of HTML) rather than instantiated programmatically.

6.3.5 Visual Overview of Dojo Widgets

At this point it would be useful to see some of the widgets. This will give you a good idea of the breadth of the Dojo widget set. The widgets are divided into general categories that correspond to the way the widgets are packaged. Most of these widgets have numerous properties that can be set to enable additional functionality. We only show the simplest version of each widget just to give you an idea of what they do. We drill down into each widget in subsequent chapters and see their full power.

Many of these examples are modified versions of test pages available in the Dojo distribution directory at "dijit/tests."

6.3.5.1 Form and Data Widgets

These widgets appear in the form package. Their basic purpose is to display some data and provide the user with a way of modifying that data that is appropriate for the data type.

Table 6.4   **Examples of Form Widgets**

Description	Example
Button This replaces the standard HTML button. It looks nicer and has a slightly better effect on rollover.	
DropDownButton When this button widget is clicked, it will display whatever widget is defined as its child. In the example, the leftmost widget is the widget before it is clicked. The rightmost example shows the same widget after it has been clicked. It displays its child widget, which in this case is a ColorPalette but could be any valid widget (menus are very typical).	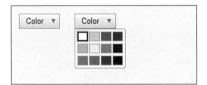

Table 6.4   **Continued**

Description	Example

ComboButton

This widget combines a regular Button
widget with a DropDownButton widget,
hence the name ComboButton. The
leftmost example shows the widget before
the down arrow is selected. The rightmost
example shows the widget after the down
arrow icon has been checked. The user
can click either on the down arrow icon or
on the button itself.

ToggleButton

This button looks the same as a regular
Button but behaves differently. When the
button is clicked, the button CSS as well
as the icon CSS can change.

CheckBox

This replaces the standard HTML checkbox.
It looks nicer and has a better check icon.

RadioButton

This replaces the standard HTML checkbox.
The advantages are a nicer look and a
better checked icon.

FilteringSelect

This widget is an enhanced version of the
HTML `<select>` tag. One improvement is
that when text is typed in the field it will be
used to "filter" possible values from the
full list of data. In this example, typing **i**
causes the widget to only display states
that begin with "I." The data list could be
static (provided in the HTML page) or could
be acquired from the server using Ajax.

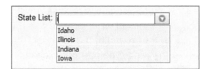

Table 6.4   **Continued**

Description	Example

NumberSpinner

This is really just a text box for entering numbers but with a special feature: Up and down arrow keys can be used to increase or decrease the value instead of the person having to type it directly.

Slider

This widget is also a replacement for a simple numeric text value, but instead of entering the number directly you drag an icon (the slider) across a bar of values. The value for the widget is determined by the position of the slider on the bar.

Textarea

This widget is a replacement for the standard HTML `<textarea>` tag. The primary additional feature of this widget is that it "grows" vertically instead of "scrolls" vertically. As you type, the size of the box expands to hold the text rather than displaying scroll bars to the side.

TextBox

This widget is a replacement for the `<input type="text">` HTML tag.

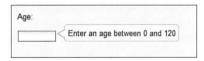

ValidationTextBox

This widget extends TextBox and adds various kinds of validations including those for dates, times, and numbers. Messages and prompts are automatically displayed.

Table 6.4   **Continued**

Description	Example
DateTextBox This widget extends TextBox by providing the user with a calendar metaphor for selecting a date. The widget looks like a TextBox on the page, but when the field is in focus, a pop-up calendar appears. This is a complex widget possessing a number of controls that allow the user to sequence through days, weeks, or years. And, of course, the look is easily customized by the developer.	

6.3.5.2 Layout Widgets

These widgets appear in the layout package.

Table 6.5   **Examples of Layout Widgets**

Description	Example
LayoutContainer This widget provides a technique for dividing the page into separate areas for placing content. The areas can be aligned to the "top," "bottom," "right," or "left." Think of this widget as a replacement for using a table to provide layout.	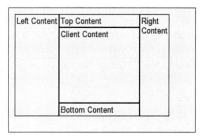
SplitContainer This widget allows the user to define different areas, either vertically or horizontally, that can contain content. Between the areas is a border dragged to change the relative sizes of the panes. Any content within a pane can be automatically reformatted. The callout is not part of the widget.	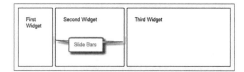

Table 6.5   **Continued**

Description	Example

StackContainer

This is a container that has multiple children but only displays a single child at a time. It usually depends on some external control (like the prior page and next page buttons in this example) to allow the user to trigger the display of a different child. Otherwise, it looks like a typical ContentPane.

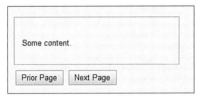

AccordianContainer

This widget acts as a container for its children. Only one child at a time is displayed (as with the StackContainer). However, the controls are built into this widget and display as pane titles with an arrow icon that can be used to collapse the displayed content and expand the hidden content.

ContentPane

This widget that acts as a container for other widgets and includes the capability for dynamically loading content using Ajax.

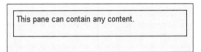

TabContainer

This widget acts as a container for its children and only displays a single child at a time. However, just like the AccordianContainer, its controls are built in and appear as tabs. By selecting a particular tab, the content associated with that tab is displayed.

6.3.5.3 Other Specialized Widgets

These are other widgets.

Table 6.6   **Examples of Other Specialized Dojo Widgets**

Description	Example
InlineEditBox This widget displays text that will be highlighted when the user places the mouse over it. Clicking the highlighted text causes it to be replaced with a different widget that can be used for editing. In this example, the user clicks the word "running" in the first line, which is then replaced with a TextBox that the user can enter a new value in.	
Menu This widget displays a popup menu that can be nested as deeply as the developer wants. Menu items can be separated with a line icon or disabled.	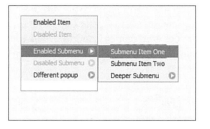
Toolbar A toolbar presents a series of options or icons that can display additional content (including submenus) or trigger some process to occur.	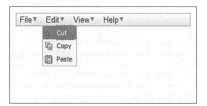
ProgressBar This widget is used to represent the completion state of a process. In this example, the current state of the widget is shown as a number (i.e., 10%), and the bar is partially filled in at the left.	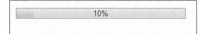

Table 6.6   **Continued**

Description	Example
Tooltip This widget displays a popup.	
TooltipDialog Pops up a dialog that appears like a Tooltip. It may contain any content including a form. The page behind the widget is still active.	
Dialog This widget provides a pop-up dialog containing content that may include a form (as shown in the example). When the dialog appears, the original page is disabled. This is sometimes known as a *modal dialog*. The page does not become active until the dialog is dismissed.	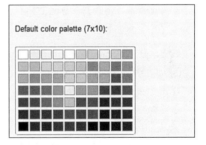
ColorPalette This widget displays color swatches that can be selected by the user. The widget will automatically convert the selected color into its RGB value for use inside the page.	Default color palette (7x10):
Tree This widget displays data in a hierarchical tree with nodes that can be expanded or collapsed. You can specify an icon for each node. One of the major features of the tree widget is the ability to build itself from data on the server by making Ajax requests when either the tree is first built or when nodes are expanded.	⊟-Rocks ├Igneous ⊞-Metamorphic └Sedimentary

The visual guide provides a quick introduction to many of the widgets available to you in Dojo. However, there are some we didn't cover, which we review in subsequent chapters. Also remember that Dojo is constantly being improved, and new widgets are becoming available all the time.

6.3.6 Building Your Own Widgets

Dojo widgets are highly customizable. You can change the way they look by changing their style properties. You can control their behavior by setting properties and by providing overrides to the various life-cycle methods. However, sometimes you may just want to build your own widget. The various base classes such as `dijit._Widget`, `dijit.form._FormWidget`, and `dijit.layout._LayoutWidget` are perfect starting points for creating new widget classes of your own.

Summary

The `dijit` module in Dojo provides a toolbox of widgets that can be easily added to a web page.

Dojo widgets can be created declaratively by using HTML tags with the `dojoType` attribute. For example

```
<input type="text" dojoType="dijit.form.TextBox" />
```

Dojo widgets can be created programmatically by using JavaScript by creating new objects with the Dojo widget constructors (don't forget to add the object to the DOM). For example

```
new dijit.form.TextBox({}, dojo.byId("placeHolder"));
```

Be sure to include the `dojo.require` statement so that the Dojo parser knows how to get the code for the widgets you are using on the page. For example

```
dojo.require("dijit.form.TextBox");
```

Widgets have three primary components that make them very easy to customize:

- HTML for their structure
- CSS for their styling
- JavaScript for their behavior

Dojo provides many useful widgets right out of the box. See the visual guide in section 6.4 for a quick walkthrough.

Dojo widgets are highly customizable, but you can also build your own using the existing Dijit base classes such as `dijit._Widget`, `dijit.form._FormWidget`, and `dijit.layout._LayoutWidget` as a starting point.

Now that we've seen how Dojo widgets work in general (and we've seen some examples of specific widgets), we can begin a detailed study of the various widgets available in Dojo. The next chapter explores each of the Form widgets in detail.

7

Dojo Form Widgets

...and the world was without Form...

—Genesis

As with creation, there was a point when the World Wide Web itself was also without form, `<form>` tags that is. But we certainly have them now, and they are the primary technique for gathering data from the user. Standard HTML provides a number of useful form widgets such as text boxes, radio buttons, check boxes, and select lists. However, these widgets are limited and a bit primitive especially considering that users today are clamoring for Rich Internet Applications with user interfaces rivaling those of some desktop applications. Dojo provides replacements for these standard widgets along with many new widgets that can be used in forms to collect information from the user of our pages. This chapter drills down into the details of the Dojo form widgets.

7.1 Standard Forms and Dojo Form Widgets

To begin our discussion of form widgets, let's go back to first principles for a moment. Why do we need forms at all? We need them so that we can capture data from the user and send it to the server for processing. But we don't really send forms to the server; we send the individual data elements. Remember what a query string looks like in a URL? Here's an example of something you might see in the address bar of the browser:

```
submit.jsp?name=Joe&id=123&type=new
```

In this example we have three data fields being sent from the browser (name, id, and type) along with their values ("Joe," 123, "new"). But where is the form? The form is the aggregation of the data but doesn't appear as a distinct component in the URL. However, within the HTML for the page, it certainly has a distinct identity and its own tag: `<form>`. We need it so we can specify characteristics of the entire form such as the action (server resource to be requested) and the method type ("GET" or "POST"). So we need a form widget, and Dojo provides one for us that allows us to treat the form as a Dojo object and gives us a few additional methods that make it easier to use.

However, the real meat in this chapter is in the form *element* widgets. These are the components that capture the actual data and associate it with a logical name to be used on the server. To make this more concrete, let's look at just one of the name/value pairs from the prior URL example.

```
id=123
```

From this we can tell that there is a field (or variable) called "id," which was given a value of "123" by the user. This doesn't tell us anything about how the user entered the value. Did they do it by typing it in, selecting it from a pull-down list, or maybe even just checking a radio button that was associated with the value. The server doesn't know, and it doesn't care—and it shouldn't. The server just cares about the data value. But for the user, the "how" is very important. They need a widget that makes it easy and intuitive for them to enter the right value. And that is why we need a number of form widgets—to present different metaphors to the user for entering and validating data. So for us, a form widget is simply a visual component of the page that captures a single data value but does it in a way that corresponds to the user's understanding of the data. For example, the technique for selecting a data value for a date should be different than that of selecting an RGB value for color. Each should have its own unique visual metaphor, and Dojo provides snazzy widgets for both!

Now let's explore the technical details of the Dojo form widgets.

7.1.1 The `dijit.form._FormWidget` Class

Form widgets are used to capture entered values from the user so that the data can be submitted to the server. The simplest examples of these widgets are the replacements for the standard HTML form elements such as text fields, multi-line text fields, radio buttons, check boxes, and select lists. Each acts as an individual data element on a form. Dojo provides us with souped-up versions of these HTML elements along with some new widgets that have no HTML counterparts.

Although there are many different Dojo form widgets, they have many common features. The Dojo widgets are built using an object-oriented approach, which implies that a new widget should be able to inherit properties from more general widgets. The most general widget of all is `dijit.form._FormWidget`, which can be described as "the mother of all form widgets." In other words, any Dojo widget we create in the form package inherits properties and methods from this class. Remember, inheritance is additive. A form widget will possesses all the properties and methods in its own class *plus* any from the `dijit.form._FormWidget` class. And also remember that in Chapter 6 we studied the base class for all widgets: `dijit._Widget`. The form widget `dijit.form._FormWidget` is a subclass of `dijit._Widget`, so any individual form widgets would also inherit all `dijit._Widget` methods and properties.

Let's review the properties and methods that all widgets have in common by studying the members of the `dijit.form._FormWidget` class. We'll review the key properties and methods. To see a full list of every property and method, you should review the source code for the widget.

7.1.1.1 Properties in `dijit.form._FormWidget`

You may notice that many of the properties have a null value in `FormWidget`. This is because they are common properties of all form widgets, but each specific widget must assign its own value for the property. The reason that they don't need values in `FormWidget` is that we will never build a `FormWidget` object directly. We'll build one of its subclasses. That makes `FormWidget` an abstract class.

Table 7.1   `dijit.form._FormWidget` **Properties**

Property	Default	Description
baseClass	null	CSS class for this widget used to associate styles.
alt	null	Used to assign the alt attribute of the HTML <input> tag associated with the widget.
value	null	Used to assign the value attribute of the HTML <input> tag associated with the widget. This is the most important property of the widget: its data value.
name	null	Used to assign the name attribute of the HTML <input> tag associated with the widget.
tabIndex	"0"	Used to assign the tabIndex attribute of the HTML <input> tag associated with the widget. This determines the order in which the cursor moves through the fields.
disabled	false	Determines whether the user can interact with this widget. A value of true turns the widget off, but it is still displayed (usually with a different style) while a value of true makes the widget usable.

We seem to be missing some important properties. For instance, where is the `style` property that defines styles for a DOM element? Remember, `dijit.form._FormWidget` inherits from `dijit._Widget`, and it is `dijit._Widget` that contains the definition for the `style` property.

7.1.1.2 Methods in `dijit.form._FormWidget`

Here are the key methods for `dijit.form._FormWidget`. Again, these aren't all the methods, just the ones I felt were important. There are more in the source code.

Table 7.2 `dijit.form._FormWidget` **Methods**

Method	Description

`setDisabled (disable)`	Turns the widget on or off based on the argument `disable`. Both the DOM element and the widget object are disabled (or enabled). Following is the key line from the method:
	
	`this.domNode.disabled =`
	`    this.disabled = disabled;`
	
	Notice that both the DOM element and the Dojo widget have a `disabled` property that is set to the value of the argument to this method.

`isFocusable()`	Returns `true` if focus can be placed on the widget (it is enabled and visible), otherwise returns `false`.
`focus()`	Places the widget in focus. This places the cursor on the widget.
`onChange(newValue)`	This is the method that you would override to add your own behavior to the widget when the user enters some new data. If you look at the code for this method, you'll notice that it doesn't do anything. It is a stub method that can be replaced by your own code—although you don't have to.
`setValue(newValue)`	Programmatically change the value of the widget to `newValue`. This is run automatically when the user enters data.
`getValue()`	Returns the current value of the widget.
`undo()`	Resets the value of the widget to the last value passed to the `onChange` method. This method allows the developer to back out a change to `setValue` without having to write code to store the old value.

7.2 The Dojo Form Widget Explained

This section provides a detailed write-up, usually two pages long, describing each of the form widgets in a standard format. But first, the following are some suggestions on how to use these write-ups, and a description of each of the categories in the write-ups.

Table 7.3   **Legend for Dojo Widget Documentation**

Widget Name	This is the full name of the widget including the package name. For example, `dijit.form.TextBox` is the `TextBox` widget in the package "dijit.form". Sometimes you'll see references to only the name of the widget, but that isn't completely correct. However, in this version of Dojo, widget names are unique within a package but also across all the packages.

Table 7.3   **Continued**

Super Classes	Widgets inherit properties and methods from their super classes. This shows the class hierarchy for the widget. There are some missing pieces here. Some of the classes that act as interfaces aren't shown, such as `dijit._Templated` and `dijit._Container`. Almost all widgets use these, so showing them would take more space without really adding any value. When you really need to be sure if these classes are used by a widget, check the source code.
File Location	This contains the location of the file containing the JavaScript source code for the widget. You don't need to look at the source code, but here's some advice: Don't be afraid to look at the source code. It is very well written and very instructive. A wise developer once said that a programmer who doesn't read the source code is really no better than one who can't read the source code. Let's not be *that* developer.

This section also contains the JavaScript code necessary to include this widget in your page. Declaring the widget in the HTML is not enough. |
Usage	This describes when you might use the widget and describes the behavior of the widget.
Display Examples	This shows you some examples of what the widget would look like on your page.
HTML Markup Examples	This shows the HTML that you would need to include in your page to create the widget. Remember, you can create the widget either in HTML or JavaScript. The HTML markup method is also known as the *declarative method*.
JavaScript Constructor Examples	This shows the JavaScript code you would need to create your widget. This is the programmatic method of creating the widget. When you create a widget this way, it is not automatically included in the DOM; you need to explicitly attach it; otherwise, it won't be usable.
Key Properties	These are some of the important properties of the widget. I usually only show properties unique to the class and not the ones that are inherited from super classes. However, sometimes the really important properties are the inherited ones so they are listed.
Key Methods	These are some of the important methods of the widget.
Key Styles	Need explanation from Jim.
Key Events	These are some of the important events of the widget.
Notes	This contains additional items of interest about the widget.

One final note before we begin the form widget write-ups. The write-ups do not attempt to document every aspect of each widget. They provide a summary of each widget. These write-ups balance completeness versus succinctness. When you really need all the details you should go to the Dojo site to review documentation, the API, and the forums. You should also dive into the source code.

Also there are a few form widgets that are more complicated and specialized. I've chosen to put those in Chapter 8, "Dojo Layout Widgets." These include the Slider, Number Spinner, InlineEditBox, Textarea, and Editor.

Table 7.4   **Explanation of Dojo Form Widgets**

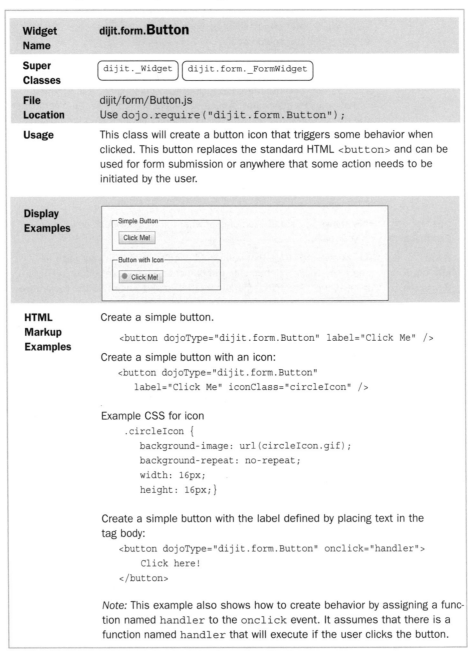

Widget Name	dijit.form.**Button**
Super Classes	`dijit._Widget` `dijit.form._FormWidget`
File Location	dijit/form/Button.js Use `dojo.require("dijit.form.Button");`
Usage	This class will create a button icon that triggers some behavior when clicked. This button replaces the standard HTML `<button>` and can be used for form submission or anywhere that some action needs to be initiated by the user.
Display Examples	Simple Button Click Me! Button with Icon ⬤ Click Me!

HTML Markup Examples	Create a simple button.
	`<button dojoType="dijit.form.Button" label="Click Me" />`
	Create a simple button with an icon:
	`<button dojoType="dijit.form.Button"`
	`   label="Click Me" iconClass="circleIcon" />`
	
	Example CSS for icon
	`.circleIcon {`
	`    background-image: url(circleIcon.gif);`
	`    background-repeat: no-repeat;`
	`    width: 16px;`
	`    height: 16px;}`
	
	Create a simple button with the label defined by placing text in the tag body:
	`<button dojoType="dijit.form.Button" onclick="handler">`
	`    Click here!`
	`</button>`
	
	Note: This example also shows how to create behavior by assigning a function named `handler` to the `onclick` event. It assumes that there is a function named `handler` that will execute if the user clicks the button.

JavaScript Constructor Examples	Constructor for creating a new `Button` with a label of "Click me": `new dijit.form.Button({label: "Click me"}, dojo.byId("form1");` This code automatically adds the widget to an existing widget in the DOM whose id is "form1". If you don't specify a node for attaching the widget, it will not appear on the page.

Key Properties	**Property**	**Default**	**Description**
	`label`	`null`	Button text
	`showlabel`	`true`	Label text to be displayed on button
	`iconClass`	`null`	CSS class containing icon for button

Key Methods	**Method**	**Description**
	`setLabel(label)`	Change the button label to new value label. This function must be used to change the label once the button has been created.

Key Styles	**Style Name**	**Description**
	`dijitButtonText`	Style for button label text.

Key Events	**Event Name**	**Description**
	`onClick`	Clicking the button will cause this event handler to run. Although this method is really part of `dijit.form._FormWidget`, it is included here on `dijit.form.Button` because it is the primary method you typically use for this widget.

Notes	You can also attach an `onClick` event to the widget using JavaScript so that there is a clear separation between the structure (HTML markup) of your widget and the behavior (JavaScript). This example assumes there is a function named `handler`, and the id of the button is `btn1`. `dojo.connect( dojo.byId("btn1"), "onclick", handler);`

Widget Name	dijit.form.**DropDownButton**
Super Classes	`dijit._Widget` `dijit.form._FormWidget` `dijit.form.Button`
File Location	dijit/form/Button.js Use `dojo.require("dijit.form.Button");`
Usage	This class creates a button icon that displays its child element when clicked. The child element can be any widget type. This widget is named as it is because it makes the creation of drop-down menus very simple. By default, the displayed content appears just below the button.
Display Examples	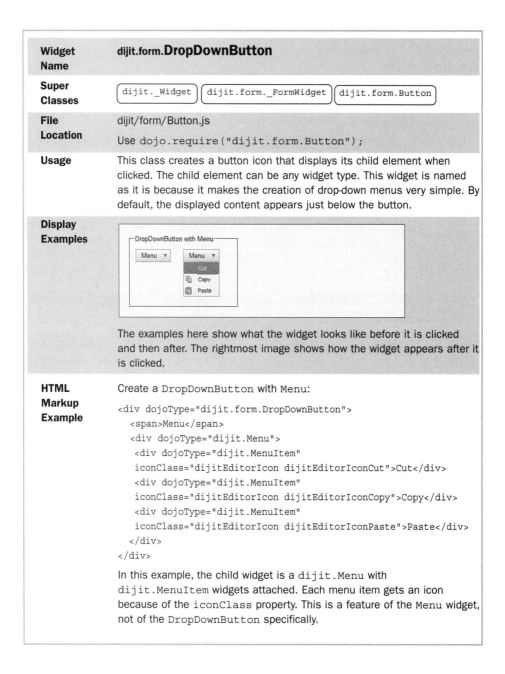 The examples here show what the widget looks like before it is clicked and then after. The rightmost image shows how the widget appears after it is clicked.

HTML Markup Example	Create a `DropDownButton` with `Menu`:
	
	 ``html
	<div dojoType="dijit.form.DropDownButton">
	  <span>Menu</span>
	  <div dojoType="dijit.Menu">
	   <div dojoType="dijit.MenuItem"
	   iconClass="dijitEditorIcon dijitEditorIconCut">Cut</div>
	   <div dojoType="dijit.MenuItem"
	   iconClass="dijitEditorIcon dijitEditorIconCopy">Copy</div>
	   <div dojoType="dijit.MenuItem"
	   iconClass="dijitEditorIcon dijitEditorIconPaste">Paste</div>
	  </div>
	</div>
	``
	
	 In this example, the child widget is a `dijit.Menu` with `dijit.MenuItem` widgets attached. Each menu item gets an icon because of the `iconClass` property. This is a feature of the `Menu` widget, not of the `DropDownButton` specifically.

JavaScript Constructor Examples	Constructor for creating a new `DropDownButton` with a label of "Menu":
	`btn1 = new dijit.form.DropDownButton({label: "Menu"};`
	This code creates the widget, but it must be attached as a child of some DOM element to be visible on the page.
	For this widget to be useful you must also attach a child widget that will be displayed when the button is activated. Let's say that you've already created a `Menu` widget with items on it (see the description for `dijit.Menu` for details on how to create menus), and the object name is menu. The `DropDownButton` provides a special property to attach the widget to the button.
	`btn1.dropDown = menu;`
	This is necessary because a bit of processing needs to be done to make the widget hidden, so just adding the new widget as a child of the button using `addChild()` wouldn't be sufficient.

Key Properties	Property	Default	Description
	`dropDown(child)`	`null`	Reference to `child` widget to be displayed when button is clicked. Don't use `addChild()`.

Key Methods	There are no additional public methods for this widget, just those that have been inherited from its super classes.
Key Styles	There are no additional public key styles for this widget, just those that have been inherited from its super classes.
Key Events	There are no additional public events for this widget, just those that have been inherited from its super classes.
Notes	The power of this widget comes from its ability to display any other widget on activation, but its most typical use is to display menus.

Widget Name	dijit.form.**ComboButton**
Super Classes	`dijit._Widget` `dijit.form._FormWidget` `dijit.form.Button` `dijit.form.DropDownButton`
File Location	dijit/form/Button.js Use `dojo.require("dijit.form.Button");`
Usage	This class creates a button combining the features of a `dijit.form.Button` and a `dijit.form.DropDownButton`. When the user clicks the down arrow icon on this widget, it acts as a `DropDownButton` and displays its child widget. When the user clicks the button outside the down arrow, this widget acts as a `Button` and runs its `onclick` event handler. This is useful when some default behavior can be tied to the button while the child widget asks for or applies some restrictions or further characteristics for the behavior. A classic example of this would be where the primary button does a "Save," but the child widget performs a "Save" or "Save As…"
Display Examples	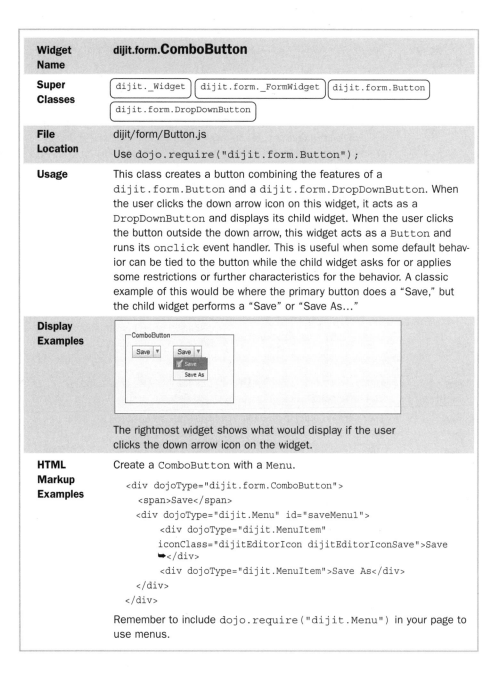 The rightmost widget shows what would display if the user clicks the down arrow icon on the widget.

HTML Markup Examples	Create a `ComboButton` with a `Menu`.
	
	`<div dojoType="dijit.form.ComboButton">`
	`  <span>Save</span>`
	`  <div dojoType="dijit.Menu" id="saveMenu1">`
	`    <div dojoType="dijit.MenuItem"`
	`    iconClass="dijitEditorIcon dijitEditorIconSave">Save`
	`↪</div>`
	`    <div dojoType="dijit.MenuItem">Save As</div>`
	`  </div>`
	`</div>`
	
	Remember to include `dojo.require("dijit.Menu")` in your page to use menus.

JavaScript Constructor Examples	Constructor for creating a new `ComboButton` with a label of "Click me":
	
	``js
	new dijit.form.ComboButton({label: "Save"},
	   dojo.byId("form1");
	``
	
	This code automatically adds the widget to an existing widget in the DOM whose id is "form1". If you don't specify a node for attaching the widget, it will not appear on the page.

Key Properties	There are no additional public properties for this widget, just those that have been inherited from its super classes.
Key Methods	There are no additional public methods for this widget, just those that have been inherited from its super classes.
Key Styles	<table><tr><th>Style Name</th><th>Description</th></tr><tr><td>`dijitButtonText`</td><td>Text for button label.</td></tr><tr><td>`dijitDownArrowButton`</td><td>Class for the down arrow icon.</td></tr></table>
Key Events	There are no additional public events for this widget, just those that have been inherited from its super classes.
Notes	None

Widget Name	**dijit.form.ToggleButton**
Super Classes	`dijit._Widget` `dijit.form._FormWidget` `dijit.form.Button`
File Location	dijit/form/Button.js Use `dojo.require("dijit.form.Button");`
Usage	This class creates a button that can be in two states (checked or not). Use this widget to provide users with a means of flipping some internal state. It looks like a regular `Button`. However, it has a built-in feature to automatically change the button CSS and icon CSS when it is toggled.
Display Examples	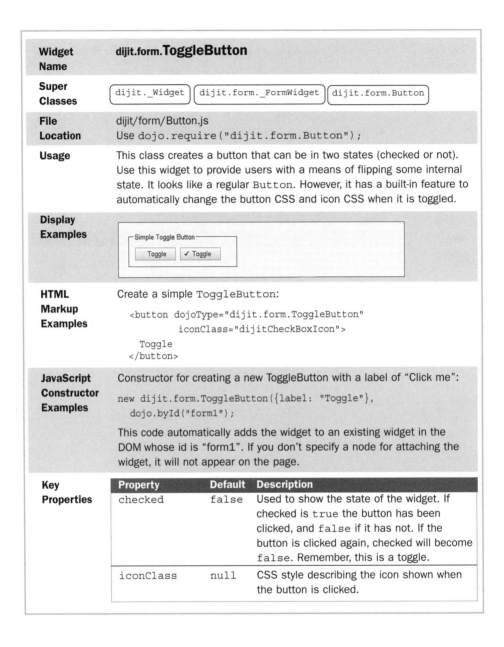

HTML Markup Examples	Create a simple `ToggleButton`:
	
	`<button dojoType="dijit.form.ToggleButton"`
	`        iconClass="dijitCheckBoxIcon">`
	`    Toggle`
	`</button>`

JavaScript Constructor Examples	Constructor for creating a new ToggleButton with a label of "Click me":
	
	`new dijit.form.ToggleButton({label: "Toggle"},`
	`  dojo.byId("form1");`
	
	This code automatically adds the widget to an existing widget in the DOM whose id is "form1". If you don't specify a node for attaching the widget, it will not appear on the page.

Key Properties	Property	Default	Description
	`checked`	`false`	Used to show the state of the widget. If checked is `true` the button has been clicked, and `false` if it has not. If the button is clicked again, checked will become `false`. Remember, this is a toggle.
	`iconClass`	`null`	CSS style describing the icon shown when the button is clicked.

Key Methods	Method	Description
	`setChecked(checked)`	This function sets the property `checked` to either `true` or `false` determined by the argument of the method.

Key Styles	Style Name	Description
	`dijitButtonText`	Style for the button label text.
	`dijitToggleButton`	Style for the button.

Key Events	Style Name	Description
	`dijitButtonText`	Style for the button label text.
	`dijitCheckBoxIcon`	Style for the check box icon (a check).

Notes	ToggleButton is a base class for checkboxes and radio buttons.

Widget Name	dijit.form.**CheckBox**
Super Classes	`dijit._Widget` `dijit.form._FormWidget` `dijit.form.Button` `dijit.form.ToggleButton`
File Location	dijit/form/CheckBox.js Use `dojo.require("dijit.form.CheckBox");`
Usage	This class creates a widget that can be in two states (checked or not). These widgets can be combined into a group. This is a replacement for the HTML `<input type="checkbox" name="c1"/>` tag. Although only a single widget is required, you would usually use multiple instances for each possible checkbox item. As with standard HTML, you can use the same value for the `name` attribute to link the individual checkboxes together into a group.
Display Examples	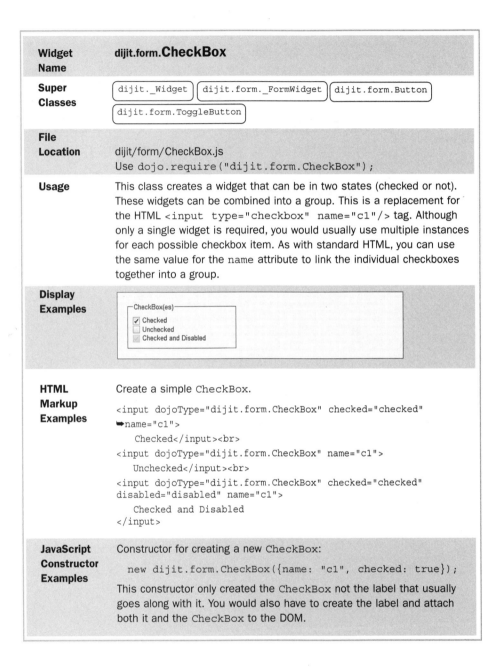
HTML Markup Examples	Create a simple `CheckBox`. `<input dojoType="dijit.form.CheckBox" checked="checked"` ➥`name="c1">` `    Checked</input> ` `<input dojoType="dijit.form.CheckBox" name="c1">` `    Unchecked</input> ` `<input dojoType="dijit.form.CheckBox" checked="checked"` `disabled="disabled" name="c1">` `    Checked and Disabled` `</input>`
JavaScript Constructor Examples	Constructor for creating a new `CheckBox`: `    new dijit.form.CheckBox({name: "c1", checked: true});` This constructor only created the `CheckBox` not the label that usually goes along with it. You would also have to create the label and attach both it and the `CheckBox` to the DOM.

Key Properties	Property	Default	Description
	`checked`	`false`	Used to hold the state of the widget. If checked is `true`, the button has been clicked and `false` if it has not. If the button is clicked again, checked will become `false`. Remember, this is a toggle.
	`name`	`null`	Assigns the `name` attribute in the <HTML> tag associated with this widget. This is especially important in this widget because it is also used to assign multiple instances of this widget to a single group.

Key Methods	Method	Description
	`setChecked( Boolean)`	Set the property `checked` to either `true` or `false` based on the argument of the method.

Key Styles	Style Name	Description
	`dijitButtonText`	Style for the button label text.
	`dijitCheckBoxIcon`	Style for the check box icon (a check).

Key Events	Style Name	Description
	`onClick`	Checking the box will cause this event handler to run. Although this method is really part of `dijit.form._FormWidget`, it is included here because it is the primary method you typically use for this widget.

Notes	Use an <input> tag rather than a <button> tag for `dijit.form.CheckBox`.

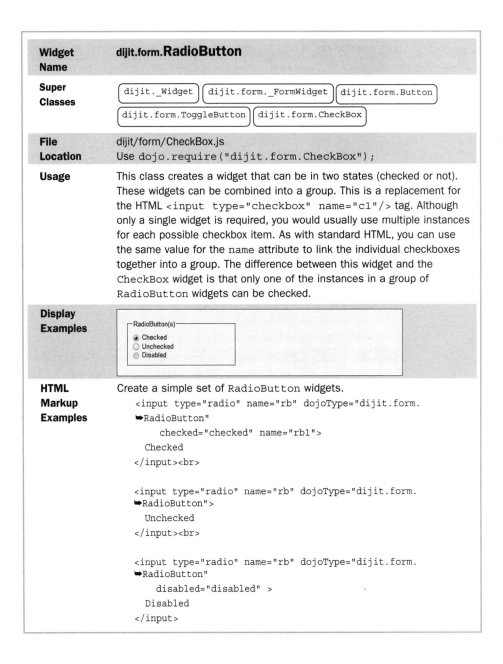

Widget Name	dijit.form.**RadioButton**
Super Classes	`dijit._Widget` `dijit.form._FormWidget` `dijit.form.Button` `dijit.form.ToggleButton` `dijit.form.CheckBox`
File Location	dijit/form/CheckBox.js Use `dojo.require("dijit.form.CheckBox");`
Usage	This class creates a widget that can be in two states (checked or not). These widgets can be combined into a group. This is a replacement for the HTML `<input type="checkbox" name="c1"/>` tag. Although only a single widget is required, you would usually use multiple instances for each possible checkbox item. As with standard HTML, you can use the same value for the `name` attribute to link the individual checkboxes together into a group. The difference between this widget and the `CheckBox` widget is that only one of the instances in a group of `RadioButton` widgets can be checked.

Display Examples	┌─RadioButton(s)──────────┐
	  ◉ Checked
	  ○ Unchecked
	  ◉ Disabled

HTML Markup Examples

Create a simple set of RadioButton widgets.

```
<input type="radio" name="rb" dojoType="dijit.form.
➥RadioButton"
    checked="checked" name="rb1">
  Checked
</input><br>

<input type="radio" name="rb" dojoType="dijit.form.
➥RadioButton">
  Unchecked
</input><br>

<input type="radio" name="rb" dojoType="dijit.form.
➥RadioButton"
    disabled="disabled" >
  Disabled
</input>
```

JavaScript Constructor Examples	Constructor for creating a new RadioButton:

`new dijit.form.Radiobutton({name: "c1", checked: true});`

This constructor only created a single `RadionButton` widget, not the label that usually goes along with it. You would also have to create the label and attach both it and the `RadioButton` to the DOM.

Key Properties

Property	Default	Description
checked	false	Used to hold the state of the widget. If checked is `true`, the button has been clicked and `false` if it has not. If the button is clicked again, checked will become `false`. Remember, this is a toggle.
name	null	Assigns the `name` attribute in the <HTML> tag associated with this widget. This is especially important in this widget because it is also used to assign multiple instances of this widget to a single group.

Key Methods

Method	Description
setChecked(Boolean)	Set the property `checked` to either `true` or `false` based on the argument of the method.

Key Styles

Style Name	Description
dijitButtonText	Text for button label.
dijitRadioIcon	Style for the radio button icon (a radio button).

Key Events

Style Name	Description
onClick	Clicking the radio button icon will cause this event handler to run. Although this method is really part of `dijit.form._FormWidget`, it is included here because it is the primary method you typically use for this widget.

Notes   None

Widget Name	dijit.form.**TextBox**
Super Classes	`dijit._Widget` `dijit.form._FormWidget`
File Location	dijit/form/TextBox.js Use `dojo.require("dijit.form.TextBox");`
Usage	Creates a generic textbox field. This widget can be used as a replacement for the `<input type="text">` tag. By using the widget instead of the HTML tag you can get the benefits of consistent styling and a number of additional useful methods. This widget by itself does not provide any validation. However, Dojo does provide a number of subclasses of this widget that do provide lots of validation features. Details for each of these subclasses are provided on their own page, but they're also summarized in the following table.

TextBox **Subclass**	Purpose
`ValidationTextBox`	Text box providing validation
`MappedTextBox`	Like a `ValidationTextBox` but also provides a method to serialize the data value
`RangeBoundTextBox`	Text field with range validation (minimum and maximum values)
`NumberTextBox`	Text field requiring a numeric data type
`CurrencyTextBox`	Text field with currency validation
`TimeTextBox`	Field that allows for entry of time values
`DateTextBox`	Field that provides a calendar for selecting a date

Display Examples	┌─ Simple TextBox ──────────────┐ │ ┌─────────────────────────┐ │ │ └─────────────────────────┘ │ └───────────────────────────────┘
	A label would usually be associated with this field but is not part of the widget itself.
HTML Markup Examples	Create a simple TextBox `<input type="text" name="f1" dojoType="dijit.form.TextBox"/>`

JavaScript Constructor Examples	Constructor for creating a new `TextBox`
	`new dijit.form.TextBox({}, dojo.byId("form1"));`
	This code automatically adds the widget to an existing widget in the DOM whose id is "form1". If you don't specify a node for attaching the widget, it will not appear on the page.

Key Properties	Property	Default	Description
	trim	false	If `true` will cause the widget to remove any whitespace characters such as spaces from the beginning and ending of the data.
	uppercase	false	If `true` will cause the widget to convert all characters in the data to their upper case values.
	lowercase	false	If `true` will cause the widget to convert all characters in the data to their lower case values.
	propercase	false	If `true` will cause the widget to convert the first character of each word in the data to upper case like a proper name.
	maxLength	null	Assigns the value of the `maxLength` HTML attribute for input tags, which limits the number of characters that the user can enter in the field (but doesn't affect the size of the field—use CSS for that).

Key Methods	Method	Description
	getDisplayedValue()	This function will return the value of the data being displayed to the user.
	getValue()	This function will return the internal data value for the widget.
	setValue(value)	This function will set the internal value of the data value for the widget.
	setDisplayedValue(value)	This function will set the value of the data being displayed to the user.
	format()	The internal data value for a widget may be different than the displayed value that the user sees. This function converts the internal value to the displayed value.

| parse() | This function takes data entered by the user and removes the formatting so that it can be stored as an internal property of the widget. |
| filter() | A "filter" is the generic term for the various transformations that can be performed on the data value for the widget such as "trim" and "proper-case". This function applies to filters to the displayed data value. |

Key Styles

Style Name	Description
dijitTextBox	Text for button label.

Key Events

Style Name	Description
OnChange	Entering data in the field and moving focus away from the field (i.e. pressing the tab key) causes this event handler to run. Although this method is really part of dijit.form._FormWidget, it is included here because it is the primary method you typically use for this widget.

Notes

Even though this class is used as a root class for other more useful validating textbox types, it can still be used by itself and often is when validation is not required.

The autocomplete property is set to off. This prevents the browser from displaying suggestions for this field based on previously entered values.

This widget allows the user to enter a single field. However, you can think of the data for the entry as being stored in two properties. The first property, displayedValue, contains the data as it is entered and seen by the user. The second property, value, contains the data as it is manipulated by the widget. The parse() method of the widget may transform the data in some way, and it is run whenever the displayedValue is changed. The format() method transforms the data in value back to the format required for display. The methods are intended to be the inverse of each other. The following diagram depicts this process visually.

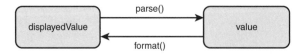

The default behavior for these methods is to perform no transformation so that the internal value is the same as the externally displayed displayedValue.

Widget Name	**dijit.form.ValidationTextBox**
Super Classes	`dijit._Widget` `dijit.form._FormWidget` `dijit.form.TextBox`
File Location	dijit/form/ValidationTextBox.js Use `dojo.require("dijit.form.ValidationTextBox");`
Usage	This widget can be used as a replacement for the `<input type="text">` tag, just like `TextBox`, with the additional benefit that validations can be automatically applied to the data when it is entered by the user. Validations can be defined by setting values for certain properties on the widget. Validation messages will appear as pop-ups next to the entered fields. Standard validation messages also exist but can be overridden. You can also define a helpful message that appears when the field is in focus and no data has been entered. This message can be defined in the `promptMessage` property of the widget.
Display Examples	 This widget requires that a value be entered. The prompt message appears when the widget is in focus and no value has been entered.

HTML Markup Examples	Create a simple `ValidationTextBox`
	
	<pre><code><input id="q01" type="text" name="age"
	    dojoType="dijit.form.ValidationTextBox"
	    promptMessage="Enter an age between 0 and 120"
	    required="true" /></code></pre>

JavaScript Constructor Examples	Constructor for creating a new `ValidationTextBox`
	
	<pre><code>new dijit.form.ValidationTextBox(
	  { promptMessage: "Enter an age between 0 and 120",
	    required: "true"},
	    dojo.byId("form1");</code></pre>
	
	This code automatically adds the widget to an existing widget in the DOM whose id is "form1". If you don't specify a node for attaching the widget, it will not appear on the page.

Key Properties	Property	Default	Description
	required	false	Set to true to specify that data must be entered.
	promptMessage	null	Message displayed as a tool tip when the field is in focus.
	invalidMessage	null	Message displayed when the data in the field is invalid.
	constraints	null	Object to be passed to the validator method that contains properties that are meaningful for certain kinds of validations. These will be discussed in the various ValidationTextBox subclasses.
	regExp	.*	A regular expression used to validate the entered data.
	regExpGen	null	Meant to be overridden by a custom method that should dynamically generate a regular expression. This property should be set instead of regExp because it will generate a value for regExp.

Key Methods	Method	Description
	validator()	This method performs the validations for the field using the constraints and regExp properties.
	isValid()	Runs the validator method to determine if the data is valid. Returns true for yes and false for no. This method can be overridden to provide even more sophisticated custom validations.
	getErrorMessage()	Returns an error message from the invalidMessage property.
	getPromptMessage()	Returns the prompt message.
	validate()	Shows missing or invalid messages if appropriate and highlights textbox fields.
	displayMessage(msg)	Displays message msg as a tool tip.

Key Styles	Style Name	Description
	dijitInputField	Style for data entry area.
	dijitTooltip	Style for tool tip used for prompt messages and error messages.

Key Events	Style Name	Description
	onChange	Entering data in the field and moving focus away from the field (i.e. pressing the tab key) causes this event handler to run. Although this method is really part of `dijit.form._FormWidget`, it is included here because it is the primary method you typically use for this widget.

Notes	The regular expression validation is extremely powerful. Regular expressions can be created for a huge variety of validations, although they can be somewhat difficult to work with at first. Regular expression syntax is beyond the scope of the book, but many good references exist.

Widget Name	dijit.form.**MappedTextBox**
Super Classes	`dijit._Widget` `dijit.form._FormWidget` `dijit.form.TextBox` `dijit.form.ValidationTextBox`
File Location	dijit/form/ValidationTextBox.js Use `dojo.require("dijit.form.ValidationTextBox");`
Usage	This widget is the same as `ValidationTextBox` with a few differences. Additional methods are provided to allow the entered data to have special serialization performed and saved in a hidden field. The typical purpose of this is to allow you to transform the value for the widget before it is submitted to the server. In other words, this widget actually maps to two form elements, one of which is a hidden field whose value is passed to the server. The other element is the field actually entered by the user. Although it is possible to create widgets from this class it usually isn't done. Instead, this is used as a base class for other validation widgets. You could think of this as an abstract class used to implement inheritance in the class hierarchy.
Display Examples	Not applicable.
HTML Markup Examples	Not applicable.
JavaScript Constructor Examples	Not applicable.
Key Properties	None
Key Methods	**Method** / **Description**

Method	Description
`serialize`	This function takes the value of the data that was entered by the user and converts it to another form that will be saved in a hidden field and set to the server. This conversion is called *serialization* here.
`toString`	String representation of the data value for the widget.

| Key Styles | None |

Key Events	Not applicable.
Notes	This widget is used as a base class for other validation wizards and would probably not be used directly.
	You might wonder what the purpose of the `serialize` method is given that Dojo form widgets get serialized automatically by the browser on form submission because they populate the value property of the DOM node. The `serialize` method in this widget can be overridden to provide specialized serialization, transforming the data before submission to the server. That is the difference.

Widget Name	dijit.form.**RangeBoundTextBox**		
Super Classes	`dijit._Widget` `dijit.form._FormWidget` `dijit.form.TextBox` `dijit.form.ValidationTextBox` `dijit.form.MappedTextBox`		
File Location	dijit/form/ValidationTextBox.js Use `dojo.require("dijit.form.ValidationTextBox");`		
Usage	This widget is a subclass of `MappedTextBox` that provides the ability to check for a minimum value, a maximum value, or both. Like `MappedTextBox` it tends to be used as an abstract class for inheritance to subclasses and not as a concrete class. In other words, you probably won't create widgets from this class directly. You may use it as a super class to define your own custom widgets. Its two subclasses are `NumberTextBox` and `TimeTextBox`.		
Display Examples	Not applicable.		
HTML Markup Examples	Not applicable.		
JavaScript Constructor Examples	Not applicable.		
Key Properties	**Property**	**Default**	**Description**
	rangeMessage	null	Contains message to be displayed when the data value is outside the range of allowed values as determined by the `rangeCheck` method.
	constraints	null	Object to be passed to the `validator` method that contains properties that are meaningful for certain subclasses. See the subclasses for details.
Key Methods	**Method**		**Description**
	rangeCheck(number, constraints)		This function uses properties in the `constraints` object to validate the data value `number`. By default, the function looks for a `min` and `max` property and compares them to the value of the widget. This function can be overridden by the user for more sophisticated validation.

Key Methods	Method	Description
	`isInRange()`	This function returns `true` if the value of the widget is in range and `false` otherwise. It runs the `rangeCheck` function.
	`compare(value1, value2)`	This function returns one of three values depending on the relative values of `value1` and `value2`. Returns 0 if `value1` and `value2` are equal. Returns a negative number if `value2` is greater than `value1`. Returns a positive number if `value1` is greater than `value2`.
Key Styles	None	
Key Events	None	
Notes	None	

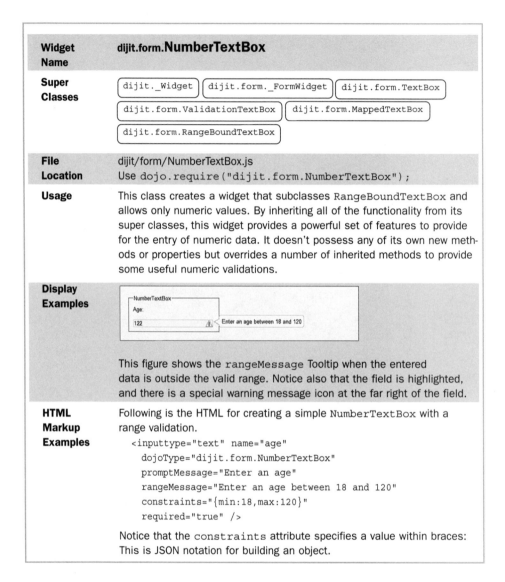

Widget Name	dijit.form.**NumberTextBox**
Super Classes	dijit._Widget dijit.form._FormWidget dijit.form.TextBox dijit.form.ValidationTextBox dijit.form.MappedTextBox dijit.form.RangeBoundTextBox
File Location	dijit/form/NumberTextBox.js Use dojo.require("dijit.form.NumberTextBox");
Usage	This class creates a widget that subclasses RangeBoundTextBox and allows only numeric values. By inheriting all of the functionality from its super classes, this widget provides a powerful set of features to provide for the entry of numeric data. It doesn't possess any of its own new methods or properties but overrides a number of inherited methods to provide some useful numeric validations.
Display Examples	NumberTextBox Age: 122 ⚠ Enter an age between 18 and 120 This figure shows the rangeMessage Tooltip when the entered data is outside the valid range. Notice also that the field is highlighted, and there is a special warning message icon at the far right of the field.

HTML Markup Examples	Following is the HTML for creating a simple NumberTextBox with a range validation.
	<pre><inputtype="text" name="age"
	  dojoType="dijit.form.NumberTextBox"
	  promptMessage="Enter an age"
	  rangeMessage="Enter an age between 18 and 120"
	  constraints="{min:18,max:120}"
	  required="true" /></pre>Notice that the constraints attribute specifies a value within braces: This is JSON notation for building an object.

JavaScript Constructor Examples	Create a `NumberTextBox` widget using JavaScript.

```
var obj = {
  name: "temperature",
  value: 98.6,
  constraints: {min:90,max:110,places:1},
  promptMessage: "Enter a value between 90 and 110",
  required: "true" ,
  invalidMessage: "Invalid temperature."
};

var f1 = new dijit.form.NumberTextBox(obj, "form1");
```

Notice that the `places` property has a value of 1 in the constraint attribute. This forces the user to type a one decimal digit in the value.

Key Properties	Property	Default	Description
	`constraints`	`null`	This is the object that contains properties used to validate the data for any widget that is a subclass of `ValidationTextBox`. This widget, `NumberTextBox`, allows the following properties: min—Minimum value of data max—Maximum value of data places—Number of decimal digits required All of the constraint properties are optional.

Key Methods	None
Key Styles	None
Key Events	None
Notes	None

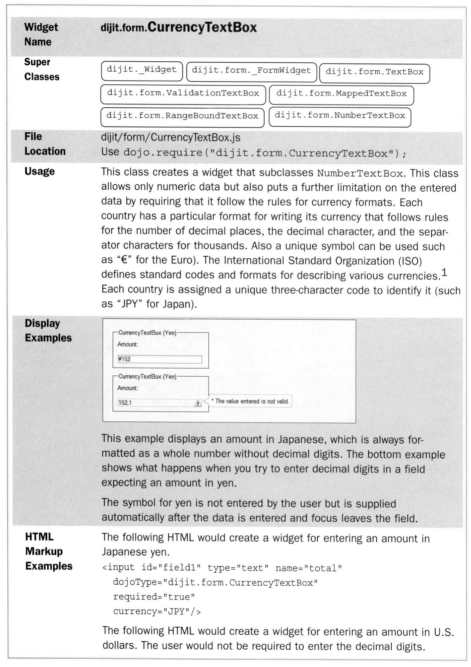

Widget Name	dijit.form.**CurrencyTextBox**
Super Classes	dijit._Widget dijit.form._FormWidget dijit.form.TextBox dijit.form.ValidationTextBox dijit.form.MappedTextBox dijit.form.RangeBoundTextBox dijit.form.NumberTextBox
File Location	dijit/form/CurrencyTextBox.js Use dojo.require("dijit.form.CurrencyTextBox");
Usage	This class creates a widget that subclasses NumberTextBox. This class allows only numeric data but also puts a further limitation on the entered data by requiring that it follow the rules for currency formats. Each country has a particular format for writing its currency that follows rules for the number of decimal places, the decimal character, and the separator characters for thousands. Also a unique symbol can be used such as "€" for the Euro). The International Standard Organization (ISO) defines standard codes and formats for describing various currencies.[1] Each country is assigned a unique three-character code to identify it (such as "JPY" for Japan).
Display Examples	This example displays an amount in Japanese, which is always formatted as a whole number without decimal digits. The bottom example shows what happens when you try to enter decimal digits in a field expecting an amount in yen. The symbol for yen is not entered by the user but is supplied automatically after the data is entered and focus leaves the field.

HTML Markup Examples	The following HTML would create a widget for entering an amount in Japanese yen.
	`<input id="field1" type="text" name="total"`
	`  dojoType="dijit.form.CurrencyTextBox"`
	`  required="true"`
	`  currency="JPY"/>`
	
	The following HTML would create a widget for entering an amount in U.S. dollars. The user would not be required to enter the decimal digits.

1. For a detailed explanation of currency codes, visit the following page on Wikipedia: http://en.wikipedia.og/siki/ISO_4217

```
<input id="field1" type="text" name="total"
  dojoType="dijit.form.CurrencyTextBox"
  required="true"
  currency="USD"
  constraints="{fractional:false}"/>
```

JavaScript Constructor Examples	Create a `NumberTextBox` widget using JavaScript.
	``var obj = {
	    name: "cost",
	    promptMessage="Enter the item cost."
	    constraints="{fractional: true}"
	    currency="USD"
	};```
	
	```var f1 = new dijit.form.CurrencyTextBox(obj);```
	This widget must still be added to the DOM so it displays on the page.

Key Properties

Property	Default	Description
`constraints`	`null`	This is the object that contains properties used to validate the entered data. This widget, `CurrencyTextBox`, allows the following properties: fractional—requires entry of decimal digits If "fractional" is `false` or not entered at all, the user is not required to enter decimal digits (although they may), and the decimal digits will be added automatically.
`currency`	`null`	Contains the currency code to be used for formatting and validating the entered amount (i.e., "USD" for United States dollars).

Key Methods	None
Key Styles	None
Key Events	None
Notes	None

Widget Name	dijit.form.**TimeTextBox**
Super Classes	dijit._Widget dijit.form._FormWidget dijit.form.TextBox dijit.form.ValidationTextBox dijit.form.MappedTextBox dijit.form.RangeBoundTextBox
File Location	dijit/form/TimeTextBox.js Use dojo.require("dijit.form.TimeTextBox");
Usage	This class creates a widget that allows the user to enter data representing time. It also performs validation on the data to ensure that it is a time value and that it is in an appropriate format. The widget can be configured so that various time formats can be selected. Another very useful feature of this widget is its ability to display a scrollable list of times from which the user can select a value. So there is no need to actually type the time. This feature is provided by a special pop-up widget created from the dijit._TimePicker class. There are many formatting options for displaying time and date data. Dojo uses the Unicode locale conventions, which are explained in more detail at the Unicode Consortium web site. The URL for additional information on date and time conventions is as follows: http://www.unicode.org/reports/tr35/#Date_Format_Patterns
Display Examples	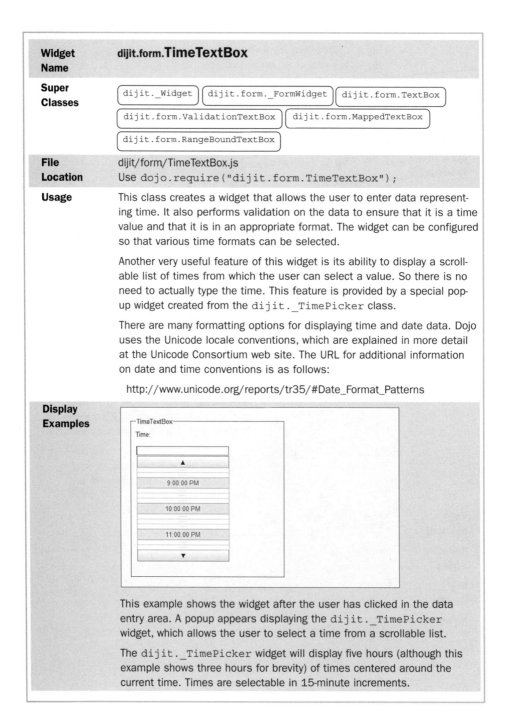 This example shows the widget after the user has clicked in the data entry area. A popup appears displaying the dijit._TimePicker widget, which allows the user to select a time from a scrollable list. The dijit._TimePicker widget will display five hours (although this example shows three hours for brevity) of times centered around the current time. Times are selectable in 15-minute increments.

HTML Markup Examples	Here is the HTML markup for creating a widget to display a time using the "medium" value for `formatLength`.

```
<input id="time1" type="text" name="time1"
       dojoType="dijit.form.TimeTextBox"
       constraints="{formatLength:'medium'}"
/>
``` |
| **JavaScript Constructor Examples** | Create a `TimeTextBox` widget using JavaScript.

```
var obj = {
    name: "time",
    promptMessage="Enter the time.",
    constraints="{formatLength: 'medium'}"
};

var f1 = new dijit.form.TimeTextBox(obj);
```

This widget must still be added to the DOM so it displays on the page. |

	Property	Default	Description
Key Properties	constraints	null	This is the object that contains properties used to validate the data for any widget that is a subclass of `ValidationTextBox`. This widget, `TimeTextBox`, allows the following properties: min—Minimum value of data max—Maximum value of data The format of the date value should be 'YYYY-MM-DD'. All of the constraint properties are optional.
	am	"AM"	Provide an override for the "am" string.
	pm	"PM"	Provide an override for the "pm" string.
	timePattern	"hh:mm"	Specify the string pattern for displaying time values. Following are some of the available markers: H...hours M...minutes S...seconds

Key Properties	Property	Default	Description
	formatLength	short	Specify the format to be used when displaying the time.

		Value	Resulting Format
		short	5:45 PM
		medium	5:45:31 PM
		long	5:45:31 PM Central Standard Time

	Property	Default	Description
	strict	false	When `true` exact matches are required for white space and abbreviations. When `false` requirements are looser.
Key Methods	None		
Key Styles	None		
Key Events	None		
Notes	None		

Widget Name	dijit.form.**DateTextBox**
Super Classes	dijit._Widget dijit.form._FormWidget dijit.form.TextBox dijit.form.ValidationTextBox dijit.form.MappedTextBox dijit.form.RangeBoundTextBox dijit.form.TimeTextBox
File Location	dijit/form/DateTextBox.js Use `dojo.require("dijit.form.DateTextBox");`
Usage	This class creates a widget that allows the user to enter data representing a date. It also performs validation on the data to ensure that it is a properly formatted date value. The widget can be configured so that various date formats can be specified. Another very useful feature of this widget is its ability to display a calendar from which the user can select a value. This feature is provided by a special pop-up widget created from the `dijit._Calendar` class. There are many formatting options for displaying time and date data. Dojo uses the Unicode locale conventions, which are explained in more detail at the Unicode Consortium web site. The URL for additional information on date and time conventions is as follows: http://www.unicode.org/reports/tr35/#Date_Format_Patterns
Display Examples	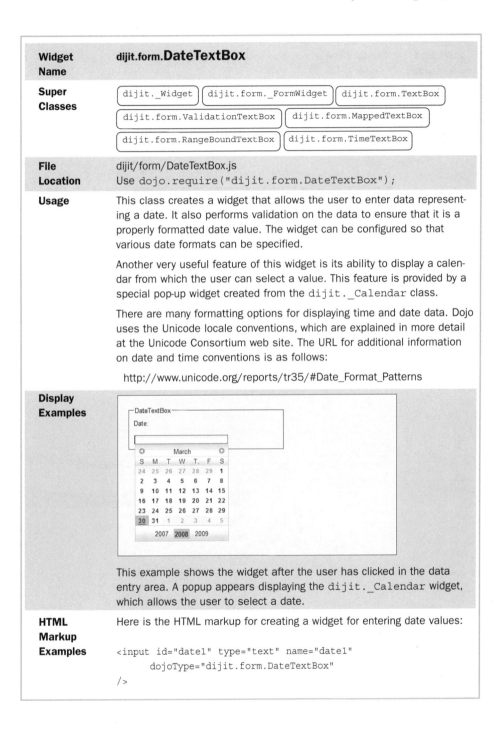 This example shows the widget after the user has clicked in the data entry area. A popup appears displaying the `dijit._Calendar` widget, which allows the user to select a date.

HTML Markup Examples	Here is the HTML markup for creating a widget for entering date values:
	
	 ```<input id="date1" type="text" name="date1"```
	 ``` dojoType="dijit.form.DateTextBox"```
	 ```/>```

JavaScript Constructor Examples	Create a `DateTextBox` widget using JavaScript.
	
	``js
	var obj = {
	  name: "date",
	  promptMessage="Enter the date."
	};
	
	var f1 = new dijit.form.DateTextBox(obj);
	``
	
	This widget must still be added to the DOM so it displays on the page.		

Key Properties	**Property**	**Default**	**Description**

	`constraints`	`null`	This is the object that contains properties used to validate the data for any widget that is a subclass of `ValidationTextBox`. This widget, `TimeTextBox`, allows the following properties:
			    min—Minimum value of data
			    max—Maximum value of data
			All of the constraint properties are optional.

	`am`	`"AM"`	Provide an override for the "am" string.
	`pm`	`"PM"`	Provide an override for the "pm" string.

	`datePattern`	`"m/d/yy"`	Specify the string pattern for displaying time values. Following are some of the available markers:
			    y—years
			    m—months
			    d—day

	`formatLength`	`short`	Specify the format to be used when displaying the date. | Value	Resulting Format
---	---
short	2/1/08
medium	Feb 1, 2008
long	February 1, 2008
full	Friday, February 1, 2008	
	`strict`	`false`	When `true` exact matches are required for white space and abbreviations. When `false` requirements are looser.

Key Methods	None
Key Styles	None
Key Events	None
Notes	None

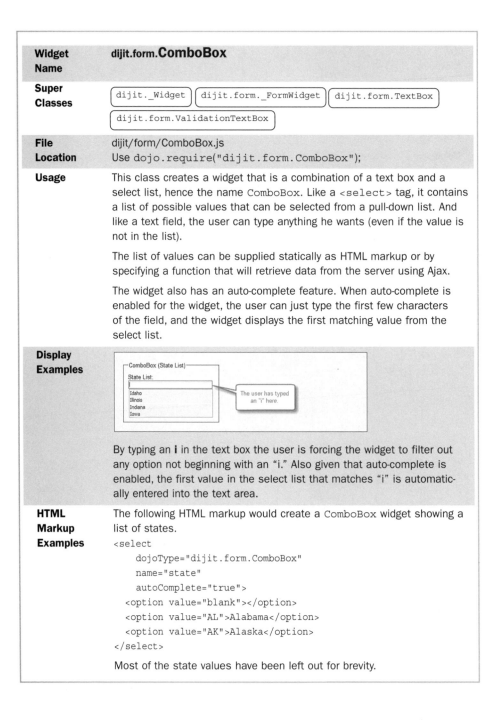

Widget Name	dijit.form.**ComboBox**
Super Classes	`dijit._Widget` `dijit.form._FormWidget` `dijit.form.TextBox` `dijit.form.ValidationTextBox`
File Location	dijit/form/ComboBox.js Use `dojo.require("dijit.form.ComboBox");`
Usage	This class creates a widget that is a combination of a text box and a select list, hence the name `ComboBox`. Like a `<select>` tag, it contains a list of possible values that can be selected from a pull-down list. And like a text field, the user can type anything he wants (even if the value is not in the list). The list of values can be supplied statically as HTML markup or by specifying a function that will retrieve data from the server using Ajax. The widget also has an auto-complete feature. When auto-complete is enabled for the widget, the user can just type the first few characters of the field, and the widget displays the first matching value from the select list.
Display Examples	By typing an **i** in the text box the user is forcing the widget to filter out any option not beginning with an "i." Also given that auto-complete is enabled, the first value in the select list that matches "i" is automatically entered into the text area.

HTML Markup Examples	The following HTML markup would create a `ComboBox` widget showing a list of states.
	<pre><select
	    dojoType="dijit.form.ComboBox"
	    name="state"
	    autoComplete="true">
	  <option value="blank"></option>
	  <option value="AL">Alabama</option>
	  <option value="AK">Alaska</option>
	</select></pre>Most of the state values have been left out for brevity.

JavaScript Constructor Examples	The following JavaScript code would create a `ComboBox` widget with auto-complete enabled. The data will be populated from a data store retrieved from the server when the widget is built.

```
var st = new dojo.data.ItemFileReadStore({url: 'states.json'});
cb = new dijit.form.ComboBox({
        name: "state",
        autoComplete: true,
        store: st,
}, dojo.byId("stateList"));
```

This version of the constructor also automatically adds the widget to the DOM as a child of the DOM element with an id of "stateList".

Key Properties

Property	Default	Description
item	null	This is the item that has been selected or entered on the widget.
pageSize	Infinity	This determines the number of items shown on the pull-down list.
store	null	This is a reference to the data store that provides the values for the pull-down list.
query	null	A data store may have more items than actually appear on the list. By specifying a query, the list will show only those items matching the query.
autocomplete	true	When `true` the widget will complete the data entered by the user by filling in the rest of the field based on first match in the list with whatever characters the user types in the text box.
searchDelay	100	This property introduces a delay between when the user types a key and when the search of the select list is started. The amount is in milliseconds. This is useful so that a number of keystrokes can be buffered, and the search is only started when the user pauses in their typing.
searchAttr	"name"	Determines the field from the data store that is used for matching.
ignoreCase	true	A value of `false` forces matching on case also. Otherwise, case is ignored.
hasDownArrow	true	A value of `true` specifies that the text box will have a down arrow icon. Otherwise, the text box has no down arrow icon.

Key Methods	None
Key Styles	None
Key Events	None
Notes	None

Widget Name	dijit.form.**FilteringSelect**
Super Classes	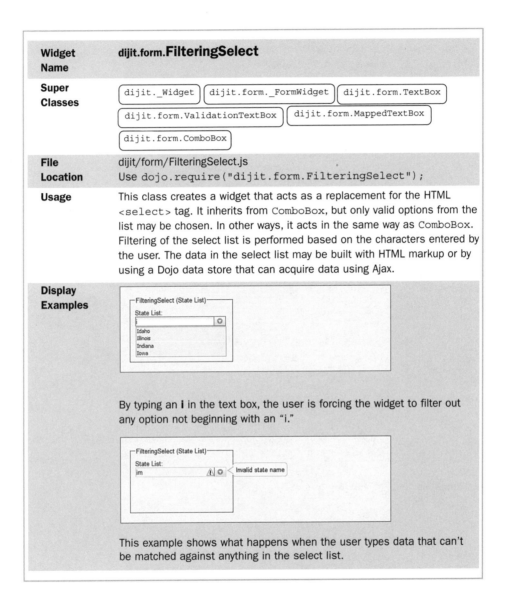
File Location	dijit/form/FilteringSelect.js Use `dojo.require("dijit.form.FilteringSelect");`
Usage	This class creates a widget that acts as a replacement for the HTML `<select>` tag. It inherits from `ComboBox`, but only valid options from the list may be chosen. In other ways, it acts in the same way as `ComboBox`. Filtering of the select list is performed based on the characters entered by the user. The data in the select list may be built with HTML markup or by using a Dojo data store that can acquire data using Ajax.
Display Examples	By typing an **i** in the text box, the user is forcing the widget to filter out any option not beginning with an "i." This example shows what happens when the user types data that can't be matched against anything in the select list.

HTML Markup Examples	The following HTML markup would create a `FilteringSelect` widget showing a list of states.
| | ```
<select
    dojoType="dijit.form.FilteringSelect"
    name="state"
    invalidMessage="Invalid state name"
    autoComplete="true">
  <option value="blank"></option>
  <option value="AL">Alabama</option>
  <option value="AK">Alaska</option>
</select>
``` |
| | Most of the state values have been left out for brevity. |
| **JavaScript Constructor Examples** | The following JavaScript code would create a `FilteringSelect` widget with auto-complete enabled. The data will be populated from a data store retrieved from the server when the widget is built. |
| | ```
var st = new dojo.data.ItemFileReadStore({url: 'states.json'});
cb = new dijit.form.FilteringSelect({
        name: "state",
        autoComplete: true,
        store: st,
}, dojo.byId("stateList"));
``` |
	This version of the constructor also automatically adds the widget to the DOM as a child of the DOM element with an id of "stateList".
Key Properties	Same as for `ComboBox`.
Key Methods	Same as for `ComboBox`.
Key Styles	Same as for `ComboBox`.
Key Events	Same as for `ComboBox`.
Notes	When the user types invalid text, the last correct entry is saved so that only valid data is ever sent to the server.

Widget Name	dijit.form.**Form**
Super Classes	`dijit._Widget`
File Location	dijit/form/Form.js Use `dojo.require("dijit.form.Form");`
Usage	This widget corresponds to the HTML `<form>` tag. It turns the standard `<form>` into a Dojo widget that allows you to use Dojo to manipulate it and connect events. The other advantage is that you can populate the values for the form elements using a JSON object or convert the values of elements in the form into a JSON object. So it makes working with the form elements as a group much easier.
Display Examples	There is not an HTML template associated with this widget, so there is specific visual display.

HTML Markup Examples	`<form action="submit.jsp" dojoType="dijit.form.Form"`
	`    id="form1" method="POST">`
	`        Name: <input type="text" name="name" />`
	`</form>`

JavaScript Constructor Examples	Create a new `Form` widget.
	
	`new dijit.form.Form(`
	`    {method: "POST", id: "form1", action: "submit.jsp" });`
	
	Additionally, you would need to add every child element (form widgets) that you want in your form to this widget. Given the amount of code you would need to write to create all the form elements, it is likely that you would create this widget with HTML markup rather than with JavaScript.

Key Properties	Property	Default	Description
	`action`	`null`	Standard `<form>` property `action` for specifying the server resource to be requested when the form is submitted.
	`method`	`null`	Standard `<form>` property `method` for specifying the HTTP message type (GET or POST).
	`name`	`null`	Standard `<form>` property `name` for specifying the name property of the form DOM element.
	`target`	`null`	Standard `<form>` property `target` for the destination for the response from the server when the form is submitted.

Key Methods	Method	Description
	execute	Function to be run when user hits the submit button.
	submit	Programmatically submit form.
	setValues	Fill in form values from a JSON structure. The properties in the JSON structure should correspond to existing elements in the form (matched on the name property in the HTML).
	getValues()	Returns a JSON string containing properties created from the form element names and values. Both Dojo widget form elements and standard HTML form elements will be included in the JSON string.
	isValid()	Run the isValid method for every widget in the form. Returns true only if every widget is valid otherwise returns false.
Key Styles		No corresponding HTML template exists for this widget so there are no Dojo styles.
Key Events		The primary event for this widget is the submission of the form either through user input by clicking the Submit button or programmatically by running the submit method for this widget. In both cases, the developer can provide custom behavior for form submission by overriding the submit method.
Notes		This widget is very useful when you wish to submit the form using Ajax rather than having the browser submit it automatically.

Summary

HTML forms allow the web page to capture data from the user.

Standard HTML form elements (text boxes, check buttons, select lists, and so on) provide very limited functionality.

Dojo provides form widgets that are more feature rich replacements for the standard HTML elements.

Dojo also provides form widgets that don't correspond to any existing HTML form elements.

All form widgets extend `dijit.form._FormWidget` and reside in the `dijit.form` package.

The basic job of a Dojo form widget is to capture some single value from the user by presenting them with the appropriate widget that corresponds to their usage of the data. For example, a field representing a date should be presented with a calendar as the visual representation.

This chapter provides a short write-up for most of the Dojo form widgets containing basic usage information.

Now that we've studied the various form widgets, we can move on to the next major category of widgets: layout widgets. We use the same approach to analyze them.

8

Dojo Layout Widgets

The world is but a canvas to the imagination.

—Henry David Thoreau

The blank web page is the empty canvas on which you paint your application. Your brush is HTML markup, and your paint is the various widgets available to you. But layout without structure is chaos. We need a way to organize the visual elements of our site into a form that has meaning. The various layout widgets provided by Dojo give us that structure by providing organized containers into which we pour our content. In this chapter, we explore the various layout widgets provided in Dijit and try to understand the proper use of each.

8.1 Understanding Page Layout

For many years, the standard technique for laying out a web page was to create a table with rows and cells that would contain the content. Each page element or widget could be placed in a single table cell, and by adjusting the height and width of the cells, the designer could create exactly the look that she desired. As the Cascading Style Sheet (CSS) specification evolved, it became possible to define layout with CSS properties, and the use of tables became much less common. But as Ajax techniques became more popular, and more sophisticated user interfaces became the norm for web sites, it was more and more necessary to find ways to make working with groups of page elements easier. One technique was to group elements into `<DIV>` tags. The `<DIV>` could be treated as a single page element and moved, hidden, or styled in a single step. In effect, the `<DIV>` tag could act as a container that could hold other elements including complete widgets. Instead, we'll use a special Dojo widget, which will act as a container for other widgets.

The community of user interface developers has already developed a set of patterns for containers in desktop applications. For instance, one of the most useful patterns involves allowing child widgets to be placed in a container and automatically positioned to the top, bottom, left, or right sides of the container. This is known as the BorderLayout container in the Java AWT toolkit, and similar counterparts exist in many other GUI environments. In addition to this layout container, a number of other types of containers were also common in desktop applications.

Dojo provides layout container widgets that implement many of the patterns common in desktop user interfaces. In this chapter we explore those widgets. Let's start by examining the common features shared by the various layout containers. As we examine each of the Dojo container widgets, keep in mind that they contain children, which may themselves be other container widgets. The most typical child widget is a ContentPane, which can contain any arbitrary content—which is why we look at that one first.

8.1.1 The dijit.layout._LayoutWidget Class

The first thing to keep in mind when discussing the properties and methods of LayoutWidget is that it is a subclass of dijit._Widget, so any widget created from this class also inherits all the properties and methods of dijit._Widget. See Chapter 6, "Introduction to Dojo Widgets," to review those properties and methods.

Additionally, dijit.form._LayoutWidget has its own properties and methods and also inherits methods and properties from dijit._Container and dijit._Contained. These are the properties and methods we are going to review now.

8.1.1.1 Properties in dijit.layout._LayoutWidget

Much of the functionality derived from the layout widgets actually resides in the widgets that they contain. Layout widgets are the gift boxes that contain the widgets that we wish to use. Like a box, one of the most important aspects of a layout container is simply how large it is. We'll see that reflected in the properties that allow us to define the size and placement of a layout container.

The reason that size is such an important consideration for containers is that the size of the container constrains the size of the child widgets that are displayed within the container. Usually, HTML works in the opposite way. In other words, most DOM elements expand to the size of the DOM elements that they contain. But a Dojo container generally will occupy a fixed portion of the page regardless of how large its children are.

The primary properties for a layout widget define its height and width and its position. However, these are style properties not properties of the widget object itself. So you should define them the way you would define other CSS properties, using stylesheets, named styles or by adding them as a style property of the widget tag itself as shown:

```
style="width=95%; height=200px; left=50px; top=75px"
```

Other properties are inherited from dijit._Widget. Remember that inheritance allows the object to contain all of the properties and methods of its superclass. For a refresher on the dijit._Widget class, review Chapter 6.

8.1.1.2 Methods in `dijit.layout._LayoutWidget`

Table 8.1 describes the key methods for `dijit.layout._LayoutWidget`. As discussed before, these are not necessarily all the methods, just the ones that are most likely to be useful to a developer.

Except for resize, the methods involve selecting children widgets of the container.

Table 8.1   **Methods in** `dijit.layout._LayoutWidget`

Method	Description
`resize(args)`	This method will change the size of the layout container and then redisplay it by running the `layout()` method. It takes an argument that contains properties describing the new size and placement. Notice that the property names in the arg object are shorter than their corresponding CSS style names.
	The `args` object should have the following properties:
	w—width of the layout container in pixels
	h—height of the layout container in pixels
	l—left position of the layout container in pixels
	t—top position of the layout container in pixels
`getPreviousSibling`	Return the child widget before the current widget without setting focus to that widget.
`getNextSibling`	Return the child widget after the current child widget without setting focus to that widget.
`addChild(widget)`	Add a child widget to the container.
`removeChild(widget)`	Remove the child widget specified in the argument as widget from the container.
`getChildren`	Return a collection of children of the container.
`hasChildren`	Return `true` if the container has children.
`focusNext`	Change the focus to the child widget that is just after the widget currently having focus.
`focusPrev`	Change the focus to the child widget that is just before the widget currently having focus.
`focusChild(widget)`	Set the focus to the child widget specified in the parameter widget.

8.2 Explanation of Dojo Layout Widgets

Now that we've reviewed the properties and methods that are a part of all layout container widgets, let's review the specific container widgets available to us in Dojo. We use the same format for explaining each widget that was described in Chapter 7, "Dojo Form Widgets."

Widget Name	dijit.layout.**ContentPane**
Super Classes	dijit._Widget
File Location	dijit/form/ContentPane.js Use `dojo.require("dijit.layout.ContentPane");`
Usage	This class creates a simple container for content. The content can be any HTML elements or Dojo widgets. It acts like a `<DIV>`, which can be used to group child elements so they can be moved and hidden as a single entity, but it has some advantages. Like a `<DIV>` it can size itself to the content. However, if you specify the size of the `ContentPane` but its children would display beyond its boundaries, this widget will produce scroll bars so that the content can be viewed. Any HTML body elements can be put in the content pane along with Dojo widgets. `ContentPane` widgets can be used by themselves but they are typically children of other layout containers such as `LayoutContainer`. The really powerful feature of this widget is that content can be loaded dynamically from the server using either a property when the widget is created or running a method after the widget is created. See the Key Properties and Key Methods sections for more detail.
Display Examples	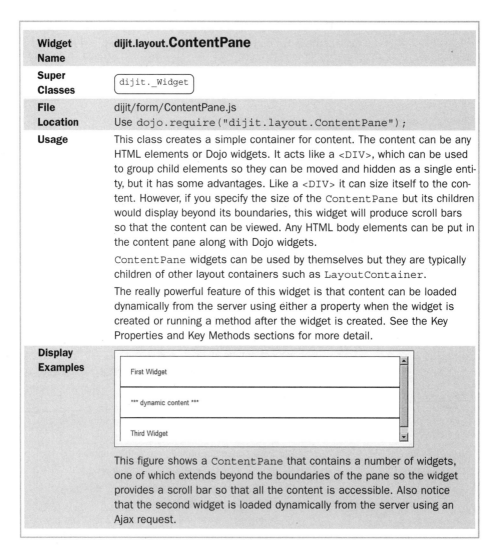 This figure shows a `ContentPane` that contains a number of widgets, one of which extends beyond the boundaries of the pane so the widget provides a scroll bar so that all the content is accessible. Also notice that the second widget is loaded dynamically from the server using an Ajax request.

HTML Markup Examples	Create a new `ContainerPane` with three child elements, which are themselves also `ContainerPane` widgets. Notice that the second widget has content that is dynamically loaded from the server.

```
<div dojoType="dijit.layout.ContentPane"
    style="width: 100%; height: 150px;">
    <div id="c1" dojoType="dijit.layout.ContentPane">
      First Widget
    </div>
    <div id="c2" dojoType="dijit.layout.ContentPane"
      href="dynamic.html">
    </div>
    <div id="c3" dojoType="dijit.layout.ContentPane">
      Third Widget
    </div>
</div>
```

JavaScript Constructor Examples	The following code will create a content pane and attach it to an existing DOM element.

```
cp = new dijit.layout.ContentPane( {}, dojo.byId("d1"));
cp.setContent('<b>Miscellaneous Content</b>');
```

Note that the `setContent` method can be used to create child elements inside the pane instead of creating new children using their constructors. This is like using the innerHTML method on a regular DOM element.

Key Properties	Property	Default	Description
	`href`	`null`	Reference to server resource containing dynamic content. The content will be requested when the `ContentPane` is shown.
	`preload`	`false`	Determines when the dynamic content specified by `href` is actually fetched from the server. If `preload` is true, the content is fetched when the `ContentPane` is created; otherwise, the content is not fetched until the `ContentPane` is shown.
	`refreshOnShow`	`false`	If this property is true, content will be fetched again every time the widget is shown.

Property	Default	Description
loadingMessage	"Loading..."	Message shown when dynamic content is being fetched.
errorMessage	"Sorry, an error occurred"	Message shown if an error occurs while fetching dynamic content.
isLoaded	false	When true, the dynamic content has been loaded.

Key Methods	Method	Description
	setContent(HTML)	To change the innerHTML use .setContent('new content')
	setHref(URL)	To do an Ajax update use .setHref('url')
	cancel()	Running this method will cancel any outstanding fetches for content.
	refresh()	Runs the last content fetch again.

Key Styles	Style Name	Description
	dijitContentPaneLoading	Style for content loading message.
	dijitContentPaneError	Style for content fetch error message.

Key Events	Style Name	Description
	onLoad	This event is called after new content is fetched and has been completely loaded.
	onUnload	This event is called before a new fetch of content is started and before the existing content is removed.
	onDownloadStart	This event is called before the fetch of dynamic content is started.
	onContentError	This event is called if there is an error creating the content.
	onDownloadError	This event is called if there is an error fetching dynamic content.
	onDownloadEnd	This event is called after new dynamic content is fetched.

Notes	None

Widget Name	**dijit.layout.LayoutContainer**
Super Classes	`dijit._Widget` `dijit.layout._LayoutWidget`
File Location	dijit/form/LayoutContainer.js Use `dojo.require("dijit.layout.LayoutContainer");`
Usage	This class will create a widget that provides compartments for holding content. The compartments can be formatted using alignment properties. This is most like the traditional use of the `<table>` tag to perform layout. `LayoutContainer` is an example of a container widget that displays multiple children at one time.
Display Examples	 In the figure, each of the content blocks is a `ContentPane` containing a small amount of text describing its position within the layout.

HTML Markup Examples	Create a LayoutContainer widget with all five positions in it containing content.
	
	`<div dojoType="dijit.layout.LayoutContainer"`
	`    style=" height: 150px;">`
	`    <div id="c1" dojoType="dijit.layout.ContentPane"`
	`        layoutAlign="left">`
	`        Left Content`
	`    </div>`
	`    <div id="c2" dojoType="dijit.layout.ContentPane"`
	`        layoutAlign="right">`
	`        Left Content`
	`</div>`
	`    <div id="c3" dojoType="dijit.layout.ContentPane"`
	`        layoutAlign="top">`
	`        Top Content`
	`</div>`
	`    <div id="c4" dojoType="dijit.layout.ContentPane"`
	`        layoutAlign="bottom">`
	`        Bottom Content`

```
            </div>
              <div id="c5" dojoType="dijit.layout.ContentPane"
                  layoutAlign="client">
                  Client Content
            </div>
            </div>
```

JavaScript Constructor Examples	The following code will create a new `LayoutContainer` widget and add some content to it.

```
layout = new dijit.layout.LayoutContainer( {}, dojo.byId("d1"));

menu = new dijit.Menu();
menuItem1 = new dijit.MenuItem({label: "Item 1"});

menu.addChild(menuItem1);

layout.addChild(menu);
```

Note: Although we're adding a menu in this example, we could be adding any arbitrary content.

Key Properties	None
Key Methods	None
Key Styles	None
Key Events	None
Notes	None

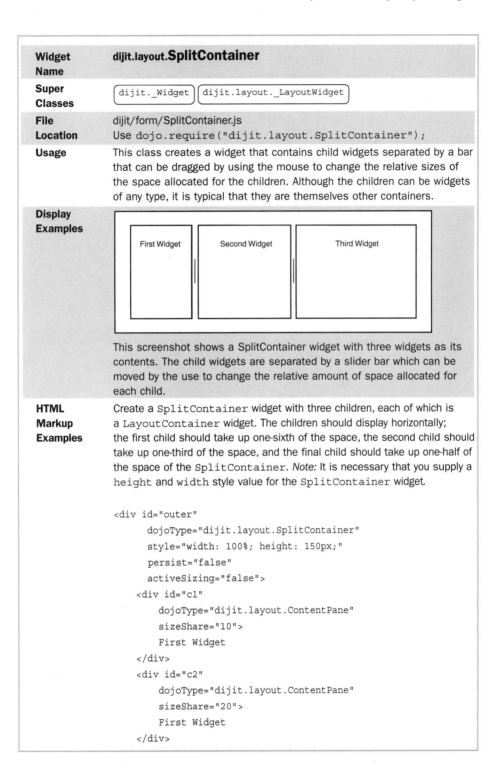

Widget Name	dijit.layout.**SplitContainer**
Super Classes	`dijit._Widget` `dijit.layout._LayoutWidget`
File Location	dijit/form/SplitContainer.js Use `dojo.require("dijit.layout.SplitContainer");`
Usage	This class creates a widget that contains child widgets separated by a bar that can be dragged by using the mouse to change the relative sizes of the space allocated for the children. Although the children can be widgets of any type, it is typical that they are themselves other containers.
Display Examples	This screenshot shows a SplitContainer widget with three widgets as its contents. The child widgets are separated by a slider bar which can be moved by the use to change the relative amount of space allocated for each child.
HTML Markup Examples	Create a `SplitContainer` widget with three children, each of which is a `LayoutContainer` widget. The children should display horizontally; the first child should take up one-sixth of the space, the second child should take up one-third of the space, and the final child should take up one-half of the space of the `SplitContainer`. *Note:* It is necessary that you supply a `height` and `width` style value for the `SplitContainer` widget.

Display Examples contents:

First Widget   Second Widget   Third Widget

```
<div id="outer"
    dojoType="dijit.layout.SplitContainer"
    style="width: 100%; height: 150px;"
    persist="false"
    activeSizing="false">
    <div id="c1"
        dojoType="dijit.layout.ContentPane"
        sizeShare="10">
        First Widget
    </div>
    <div id="c2"
        dojoType="dijit.layout.ContentPane"
        sizeShare="20">
        First Widget
    </div>
```

```
        <div id="c3"
            dojoType="dijit.layout.ContentPane"
            sizeShare="30">
            First Widget
        </div>
    </div>
```

JavaScript Constructor Examples	The following code will create a new `SplitContainer` widget containing two `ContentPane` widgets.

```
container = new dijit.layout.SplitContainer( {} );

content1 = new dijit.layout.ContentPane({} );
container.addChild(content1);
content2 = new dijit.layout.ContentPane({} );
container.addChild(content2);
```

Note: We would still need to add content to each of the `ContentPane` widgets.

Key Properties	Property	Default	Description
	`activeSizing`	false	Determines whether the children compartments change size as the slider is dragged. If true the compartments change size; if false the compartments don't change size until the slider is released.
	`sizerWidth`	7	The width in pixels of the slide border between compartments.
	`orientation`	"horizontal"	The children must be arranged in one direction, either "horizontal," which is the default, or "vertical."
	`persist`	true	After the split bar is moved (or multiple split bars considering one bar exists between each child), the position of the bar can be saved as a cookie so that the user will see the widget configured the same way when he comes back to the page.
	`sizeMin`	10	*Note:* This property is actually a property of the child widget, not the `SplitContainer` widget itself. This property sets the minimum size for either the widget or height of the space allocated to the child widget.

	sizeShare	10	*Note:* This property is actually a property of the child widget, not the `SplitContainer` widget itself.
			This property determines the amount of space (either horizontally or vertically) that will be dedicated to the child widget. The `sizeShare` properties for all of the children widgets are added together to produce a total weight, and the percentage size of each widget is based on its `sizeShare` relative to the total.

Key Methods	Method	Description
	addChild	Adds an additional widget to the `SplitContainer`. The child will be added to the end, and a new split bar will be displayed between the last widget and the new one.
	removeChild	Removes a child widget from the `SplitContainer` and closes up the space between the prior and next child widget.

Key Styles	None
Key Events	None
Notes	It is necessary that you supply a size and width value for the `SplitContainer` widget.

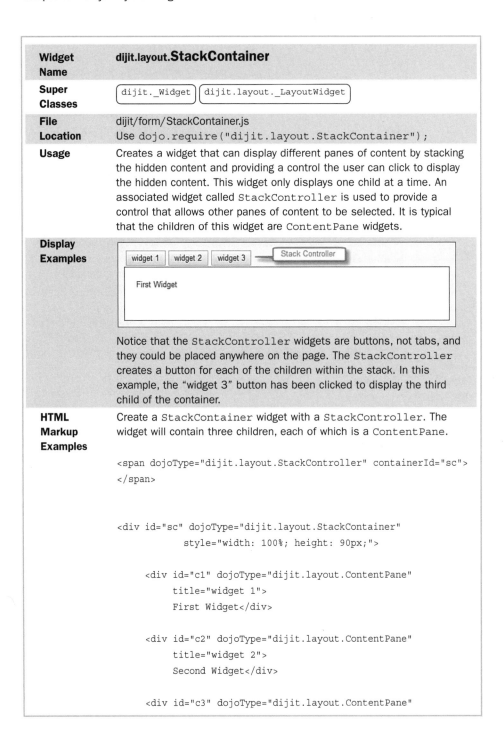

Widget Name	dijit.layout.**StackContainer**
Super Classes	dijit._Widget dijit.layout._LayoutWidget
File Location	dijit/form/StackContainer.js Use `dojo.require("dijit.layout.StackContainer");`
Usage	Creates a widget that can display different panes of content by stacking the hidden content and providing a control the user can click to display the hidden content. This widget only displays one child at a time. An associated widget called `StackController` is used to provide a control that allows other panes of content to be selected. It is typical that the children of this widget are `ContentPane` widgets.
Display Examples	Notice that the `StackController` widgets are buttons, not tabs, and they could be placed anywhere on the page. The `StackController` creates a button for each of the children within the stack. In this example, the "widget 3" button has been clicked to display the third child of the container.

HTML Markup Examples	Create a `StackContainer` widget with a `StackController`. The widget will contain three children, each of which is a `ContentPane`.
	
	`<span dojoType="dijit.layout.StackController" containerId="sc">`
	`</span>`
	
	`<div id="sc" dojoType="dijit.layout.StackContainer"`
	`         style="width: 100%; height: 90px;">`
	
	`     <div id="c1" dojoType="dijit.layout.ContentPane"`
	`         title="widget 1">`
	`         First Widget</div>`
	
	`     <div id="c2" dojoType="dijit.layout.ContentPane"`
	`         title="widget 2">`
	`         Second Widget</div>`
	
	`     <div id="c3" dojoType="dijit.layout.ContentPane"`

```
                    title="widget 3">
                    Third Widget</div>

            </div>

    </div>
```

Notice that the `StackController` must refer to the `StackContainer` that it acts as a controller for. This is accomplished with the `containerId` property.

JavaScript Constructor Examples	The following code will create a new `StackContainer` widget containing two `ContentPane` widgets.
	
	```container = new dijit.layout.StackContainer({});```
	
	```content1 = new dijit.layout.ContentPane({});```
	```container.addChild(content1);```
	```content2 = new dijit.layout.ContentPane({});```
	```container.addChild(content2);```
	
	Note: We would still need to add content to each of the `ContentPane` widgets and attach the container to the DOM.

Key Properties	None
Key Methods	None
Key Styles	None
Key Events	None
Notes	None

Widget Name	dijit.layout.**AccordionContainer**
Super Classes	`dijit._Widget` `dijit.layout._LayoutWidget` `dijit.layout.StackContainer`
File Location	dijit/form/AccordionContainer.js Use `dojo.require("dijit.layout.AccordionContainer");`
Usage	Creates a widget that can display different panes of content by stacking the hidden content and providing a control the user can click to display the hidden content. Most layout containers can contain children of any content type. However, this widget must have children of type `AccordionPane`. The reason for this is that each child must have a title bar with a label and a control. `AccordionPane` acts as a wrapper around `ContentPane` and adds the additional features for title and control. This widget contains children of type `AccordionPane`, which can contain any content including other layout widgets. When the widget is first built, one pane is visible, and the other panes are stacked beneath it with only their controls showing. When the control icon is clicked, the first pane will close, and the clicked pane will slide open producing an effect like an accordion being played (hence the name).
Display Examples	 Notice that the Pane Control Icon is different depending on whether the pane is open or closed. Only one pane may be open at a time. The user can click anywhere on the pane control to open it (not just on the icon).

HTML Markup Examples	Create a new `AccordionContainer` widget with three children, each of type `AccordionPane`.
	
	`<div id="sc" dojoType="dijit.layout.AccordionContainer"`
	`        duration="25">`
	
	`    <div id="c1" dojoType="dijit.layout.AccordionPane"`
	`        title="Pane 1">`
	`      <p style="padding:20px">First Widget</p></div>`

```
<div id="c1" dojoType="dijit.layout.AccordionPane"
     title="Pane 2">
    <p style="padding:20px">Second Widget</p></div>


   <div id="c1" dojoType="dijit.layout.AccordionPane"
title="Pane 3">
<p style="padding:20px">Third Widget</p></div>


</div>
```

JavaScript Constructor Examples	The following code will create a new `AccordionContainer` widget containing two `AccordionPane` widgets.
	
	 ```container = new dijit.layout.AccordionContainer({});```
	
	 ```content1 = new dijit.layout.AccordionPane({});```
	 ```container.addChild(content1);```
	 ```content2 = new dijit.layout.AccordionPane({});```
	 ```container.addChild(content2);```
	
	 Note: We would still need to add content to each of the `AccordionPane` widgets and attach the container to the DOM.

Key Properties	Property	Default	Description
	`duration`	250	Number of milliseconds from the moment that the pane control is clicked on a `AccordianPane` until the pane is completely open. The pane slides open during this interval.

Key Methods	Method	Description
	`selectChild (widget)`	Display the child widget `widget` and make it active.
	`closeChild (widget)`	Close the child widget `widget`.
	`back()`	Close the current open child widget and open the prior child widget and make it active.
	`forward()`	Close the current open child widget and open the next child widget and make it active.

Key Styles	None
Key Events	None
Notes	None

Widget Name	dijit.layout.**TabContainer**
Super Classes	`dijit._Widget` `dijit.layout._LayoutWidget` `dijit.layout.StackContainer`
File Location	dijit/form/TabContainer.js Use `dojo.require("dijit.layout.TabContainer");`
Usage	This class creates a widget that acts as a container for `ContentPane` widgets. A `TabController` is automatically created to allow each child `ContentPane` to be selected. This widget works very much like a `StackContainer` except the controller is built automatically and doesn't require a separate tag. Also the controller displays as tabs instead of buttons. Remember, the content for the tabs is also dynamic and can be retrieved from the server using an Ajax request when the tab is selected and the `ContentPane` is displayed. This is determined by setting the `href` property on the `ContentPane`.
Display Examples	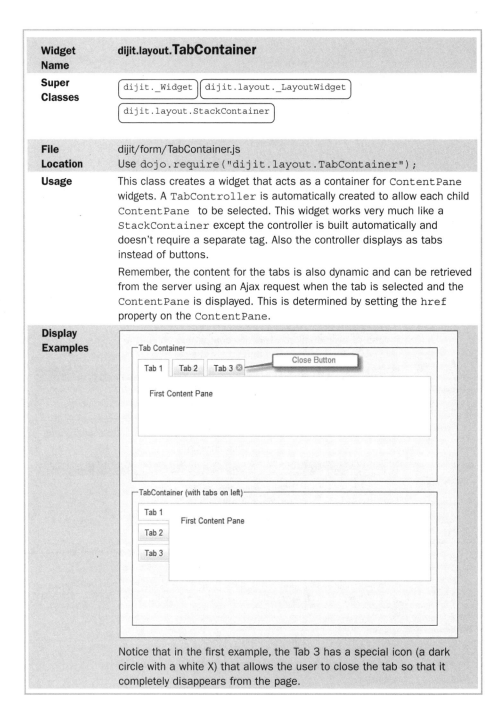 Notice that in the first example, the Tab 3 has a special icon (a dark circle with a white X) that allows the user to close the tab so that it completely disappears from the page.

HTML Markup Examples	Create a `TabContainer` with the tabs on top containing three `ContentPane` widgets.
	
	``html
	<div id="sc1"
	     dojoType="dijit.layout.TabContainer"
	     style="width: 100%; height: 10em;">
	  <div dojoType="dijit.layout.ContentPane" title="Tab 1">
	     First Content Pane
	  </div>
	
	  <div dojoType="dijit.layout.ContentPane" title="Tab 2">
	     Second Content Pane
	  </div>
	  <div dojoType="dijit.layout.ContentPane" title="Tab 3">
	     Third Content Pane
	  </div>
	</div>
	``

JavaScript Constructor Examples	The following code will create a new `TabContainer` widget containing two `ContentPane` widgets.
	
	``javascript
	container = new dijit.layout.TabContainer({});
	
	content1 = new dijit.layout.ContentPane({});
	container.addChild(content1);
	content2 = new dijit.layout.ContentPane({});
	container.addChild(content2);
	``
	
	Note: We would still need to add content to each of the `ContentPane` widgets and attach the container to the DOM.

Property	Default	Description
		Key Properties
`tabPosition`	`"top"`	This property determines the position of the tags relative to the content area. top bottom left-h right-h
`closable`	`false`	*Note:* This property is on the child `ContentPane` widget and determines if the tab associated with the widget has a close icon on it. By clicking the icon, the tab (and its contents) will be removed from the `TabContainer`.

Key	Method	Description
Methods	`selectChild(widget)`	Display the child widget `widget` and make it active.
	`closeChild(widget)`	Close the child widget `widget`.
	`back()`	Close the current open child widget and open the prior child widget and make it active.
	`forward()`	Close the current open child widget and open the next child widget and make it active.
Key Styles	None	
Key Events	None	
Notes	None	

Summary

The widgets in the layout package provide containers for other content, usually multiple instances of content we refer to as a "pane."

The `ContentPane` acts as generic holder for other content, which can be fetched from the server using an Ajax request.

The `LayoutContainer` allows multiple panes of content to be automatically arranged to the left, right, top, bottom, and center of the container.

The `StackContainer` allows multiple panes of content to be stacked so that only one pane of content is visible at a time. This container also can provide a control to allow the user to select the pane he or she would like to see.

The `SplitContainer` allows multiple panes of content to be displayed at the same time and separated by a bar that can be moved by the user to change the relative amount of space allocated to each content pane.

The `AccordionContainer` allows multiple panes of content to be stacked so that only one pane is visible at a time. Each pane is provided with a control that allows it to be selected. All the controls are visible even though only one content pane is visible.

The `TabContainer` allows multiple panes of content to be stacked so that only one pane is visible. This widget provides a set of tabs, one for each content pane, that allows the user to select the content pane he wants to see.

Now we can turn our attention to some of the special widgets that don't fall into the categories we've already reviewed. These are some of the most powerful and interesting widgets that Dojo provides. So fasten your seatbelt and get ready!

9

Other Specialized
Dojo Widgets

Form follows function—that has been misunderstood. Form and function should be one...

—Frank Floyd Wright

The problem with the standard widgets available in the HTML toolkit (such as text boxes, radio buttons, and so on) isn't that they are ineffective themselves: It's that there just aren't enough of them. There are certain functions for which the standard widgets are a perfect fit. And in those functions they find their proper homes. The purpose of a widget is to represent some piece of data or process to the user. The degree to which the widget corresponds to the user's model of that data or process determines it success. When widget form and function correspond, the user interface can seem to become almost transparent, and users no longer perceive themselves as working through widgets but as working with their content directly. This chapter describes a number of Dojo widgets that each perform a specialized function to which they are perfectly matched.

9.1 What Are Specialized Widgets?

The widgets described in this chapter each have some unique function. They are not necessarily the most advanced or complicated of the Dojo widgets, but because of their uniqueness they have been grouped together. There is no other unifying theme to tie them together as there was with the form widgets described in Chapter 7, "Dojo Form Widgets," or the layout widgets described in Chapter 8, "Dojo Layout Widgets."

However, we're not entering terra incognita here. Although the specific function of the widgets might be unique, they way we construct them and use them will be quite familiar. All the widgets in this chapter are descendents of `digit._Widget` and inherit all the operations of that mother of all widgets.

This chapter takes the same approach to describing these widgets as have the previous two chapters: Each widget will be described using the same standard layout as introduced in Chapter 7—except with the first widget covered in this chapter; it has a little more detail to be included.

9.2 Menu Widget

Like the animals in *Animal Farm*, all widgets are equal, but some are more equal than others. That is, some widgets will probably be used much more often than others. For this reason and because of involvement of multiple component widgets, some extra time is spent describing the `Menu` widget.

One of the most often used features on a web page is navigation. Menus are used for executing commands and providing links to other web sites and documents, and they appear on almost every web page on the Net, so you would expect Dojo to have numerous options for creating menus. And you would be right.

The Dojo `Menu` widget is really a collection of widgets working together. The base class for building menus is `dijit.Menu`. A `Menu` widget can have `MenuItem` widgets as children in addition to two other widgets, `dijit.MenuSeparator` and `dijit.PopupMenuItem`. Figure 9.1 shows the relationship of the components to each other.

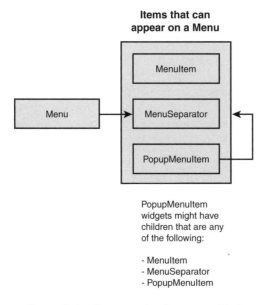

Figure 9.1   Components of a `Menu` widget

9.2.1 `dijit.Menu`

The `dijit.Menu` widget is the container for menu elements. It is typically displayed either by linking it to a button on a `Toolbar` widget or by associating it with some other element that can be right-clicked to display the menu. Also by using a mouseover event, the menu could be displayed when the user rolls over some other widget on the page. This is a typical technique employed on some sites.

9.2.2 `dijit.MenuItem`

The `dijit.MenuItem` widget represents a command or link available on a menu. By activating the item, the user selects some function to be performed. Menu items can have a text label, an icon, or both. Tables 9.1 and 9.2 that follow describe the properties and method of this widget.

Table 9.1 **Properties for** `dijit.MenuItem`

Property	Default	Description
label	" "	The text containing the displayed label for the item.
iconClass	" "	If the menu item should also have an icon displayed with it, this property contains the value for the CSS class describing the icon.
disabled	false	This property shows whether the item has been deactivated or not. Disabled items still display, but clicking them does not trigger their onClick() method.

Table 9.2 **Methods for** `dijit.MenuItem`

Method	Description
onClick()	This is the key event for this widget. It determines the functionality that the menu item provides. The handler associated with this event will be executed when the user selects this item by clicking it.
setDisabled()	This method will disable a menu item. The item will still display on the menu but will appear in lighter text to indicate that it is not active. Also the onClick() event will not be triggered if the user should click the item.

9.2.3 `dijit.MenuSeparator`

The `dijit.MenuSeparator` widget is used to organize the display of menu items. It creates a gray horizontal line in the list of menu items that separates groups of related menu items. It can't receive focus and isn't clickable. It does provide a class, `dijitMenuSeparatorTop`, which can be used to style the link, perhaps changing the color or making it larger for example. See Figure 9.2 for an example of a menu with two separators.

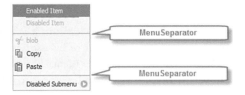

Figure 9.2   Example of `dijit.MenuSeparator` widget

9.2.4 `dijit.PopupMenuItem`

The `dijit.PopupMenuItem` widget allows nested menus to be added to a menu. This widget can then act as a container for other menu elements including `MenuItem` widgets, `MenuSeparator` widgets, and even additional `PopupMenuItem` widgets, which provide the ability to have as many levels of nested menus as desired.

The standard technique for specifying a popup menu is to include a `<SPAN>` child element as the label for the popup and then to include a tag representing the widget to be shown when the popup is activated. In the case of submenus, the popup widget would be a `digit.Menu` as shown in the following code sample.

```
<div dojoType="dijit.PopupMenuItem">
    <span>Submenu Label</span>
    <div dojoType="dijit.Menu" id="submenu1" style="display: none;">
        <div dojoType="dijit.MenuItem" onClick="sub1Action()">
            Submenu Item One Label</div>
        <div dojoType="dijit.MenuItem" onClick="sub2Action()">
            Submenu Item Two Label</div>
    </div>
</div>
```

The general discussion of the `dijit.Menu` widget is now complete, so let's continue with the standard presentation of the specialized widgets covered in this chapter.

Widget Name	dijit.**Menu**
Super Classes	```dijit._Widget```
File Location	dijit/Menu.js Use `dojo.require("dijit.Menu");`
Usage	This class creates a widget containing a list of items that can be selected to trigger some function.
Display Examples	 This figure shows a Menu widget containing MenuItem widgets, MenuSeparator widgets, and a PopupMenuItem widget containing a menu of its own. The widget was activated by right-clicking its parent `<div>`.
HTML Markup Examples	Create a new Menu widget containing a list of menu items with separators to group related items. Also include a pop-up menu with a submenu containing a couple of items.

```
<div dojoType="dijit.Menu" id="menu1"
   contextMenuForWindow="true">
   <div dojoType="dijit.MenuItem" >Enabled Item</div>
   <div dojoType="dijit.MenuItem" disabled="true">
      Disabled Item</div>
   <div dojoType="dijit.MenuSeparator"></div>
   <div dojoType="dijit.MenuItem"
      iconClass="dijitEditorIcon dijitEditorIconCut"
      onClick="action1()" label="Cut" disabled="true">
      Cut</div>
   <div dojoType="dijit.MenuItem"
      iconClass="dijitEditorIcon dijitEditorIconCopy"
      onClick="action2()">
      Copy</div>
   <div dojoType="dijit.MenuSeparator"></div>
   <div dojoType="dijit.PopupMenuItem">
      <span>Submenu Label</span>
      <div dojoType="dijit.Menu" id="submenu1">
            <div dojoType="dijit.MenuItem"
```

```
                            onClick="subAction1">Submenu Item One</div>
            <div dojoType="dijit.MenuItem"
                onClick="subAction2()">Submenu Item Two</div>
            </div>
        </div>
```

Notice that some of the items are disabled using the attribute `disabled="true"`.

Also notice the `style="display: none;"` attribute on the first `Menu` widget. This hides the menu of the initial view of the page. The user can make the menu appear by right-clicking anywhere on the page because of the `contextMenuForWindow="true"` attribute.

JavaScript Constructor Examples	The following code will create a `Menu` widget with two items. ```\nmenu1 = new dijit.Menu(\n {targetNodeIds:["nodeId"], id:"menu1"});\n\n\nmenu1.addChild(new dijit.MenuItem(\n {label:"Menu Item 1", onClick:menuAction1}));\n\n\nmenu1.addChild(new dijit.MenuItem(\n {label:"Menu Item 2", onClick:menuAction2}));\n``` Notice that the `"nodeId"` is the id for the DOM element that the menu will be attached to. This menu will be a context menu requiring the user to right-click the parent DOM node. The functions `menuAction1` and `menuAction2` will be called when the user clicks each of the respective menu items.

Key Properties	Property	Default	Description
	contextMenuForWindow	false	When this property is `true`, the user may click anywhere on the page to open the menu. When the property is `false`, the user may only click the node(s) that this menu is assigned to.
	targetNodeIds	[]	DOM nodes the `Menu` widget should be assigned to.
	parentMenu	null	Reference to the `Menu` widget that this widget is part of.

Key Methods	Method	Description
	addChild(Widget)	This function adds a child element to the widget. Use this when manipulating the widget programmatically.

Key Styles	Style Name	Description
	dijitMenuTable	Class for styling table containing menu items.

Key Events	Style Name	Description
	onExecute()	Function to be called when a menu item has been executed.
	onCancel()	Function to be called when a user cancels a menu item.
	onClose()	Function to be called when the menu is closed.
	onOpen()	Function to be called when the menu is opened.

Notes	To close the menu, use the <esc> key.

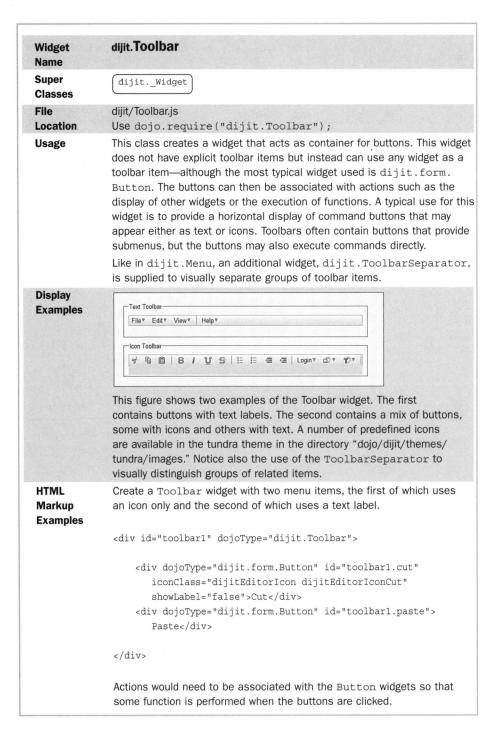

Widget Name	dijit.**Toolbar**
Super Classes	dijit._Widget
File Location	dijit/Toolbar.js Use `dojo.require("dijit.Toolbar");`
Usage	This class creates a widget that acts as container for buttons. This widget does not have explicit toolbar items but instead can use any widget as a toolbar item—although the most typical widget used is `dijit.form.Button`. The buttons can then be associated with actions such as the display of other widgets or the execution of functions. A typical use for this widget is to provide a horizontal display of command buttons that may appear either as text or icons. Toolbars often contain buttons that provide submenus, but the buttons may also execute commands directly. Like in `dijit.Menu`, an additional widget, `dijit.ToolbarSeparator`, is supplied to visually separate groups of toolbar items.
Display Examples	*[Toolbar display examples shown]* This figure shows two examples of the Toolbar widget. The first contains buttons with text labels. The second contains a mix of buttons, some with icons and others with text. A number of predefined icons are available in the tundra theme in the directory "dojo/dijit/themes/tundra/images." Notice also the use of the `ToolbarSeparator` to visually distinguish groups of related items.

HTML Markup Examples	Create a `Toolbar` widget with two menu items, the first of which uses an icon only and the second of which uses a text label.
	
	`<div id="toolbar1" dojoType="dijit.Toolbar">`
	
	`    <div dojoType="dijit.form.Button" id="toolbar1.cut"`
	`        iconClass="dijitEditorIcon dijitEditorIconCut"`
	`        showLabel="false">Cut</div>`
	`    <div dojoType="dijit.form.Button" id="toolbar1.paste">`
	`        Paste</div>`
	
	`</div>`
	
	Actions would need to be associated with the `Button` widgets so that some function is performed when the buttons are clicked.

JavaScript Constructor Examples	The following code will create a toolbar with two items.

```
menu1 = new dijit.Toolbar({}, dojo.byId("d1"));

menu1.addChild(new dijit.form.Button(
{label:"Item1", onClick:menuAction1}));

menu1.addChild(new dijit.form.Button(
{label:"Item2", onClick:menuAction2}));
```

Key Properties	None	
Key Methods	**Method**	**Description**
	addChild(Widget)	Function to programmatically add widgets to the toolbar.
Key Styles	None	
Key Events	None	
Notes	None	

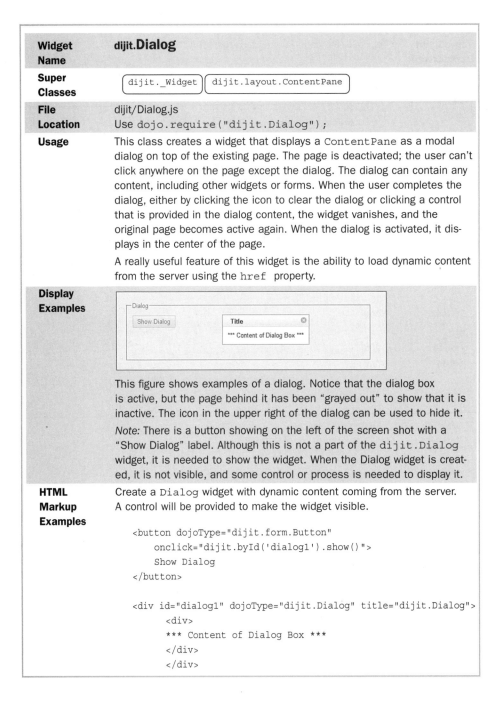

Widget Name	dijit.**Dialog**
Super Classes	`dijit._Widget` `dijit.layout.ContentPane`
File Location	dijit/Dialog.js Use `dojo.require("dijit.Dialog");`
Usage	This class creates a widget that displays a `ContentPane` as a modal dialog on top of the existing page. The page is deactivated; the user can't click anywhere on the page except the dialog. The dialog can contain any content, including other widgets or forms. When the user completes the dialog, either by clicking the icon to clear the dialog or clicking a control that is provided in the dialog content, the widget vanishes, and the original page becomes active again. When the dialog is activated, it displays in the center of the page. A really useful feature of this widget is the ability to load dynamic content from the server using the `href` property.
Display Examples	This figure shows examples of a dialog. Notice that the dialog box is active, but the page behind it has been "grayed out" to show that it is inactive. The icon in the upper right of the dialog can be used to hide it. *Note:* There is a button showing on the left of the screen shot with a "Show Dialog" label. Although this is not a part of the dijit.Dialog widget, it is needed to show the widget. When the Dialog widget is created, it is not visible, and some control or process is needed to display it.

HTML Markup Examples	Create a `Dialog` widget with dynamic content coming from the server. A control will be provided to make the widget visible.
	
	<pre><code><button dojoType="dijit.form.Button"
	    onclick="dijit.byId('dialog1').show()">
	    Show Dialog
	</button>
	
	<div id="dialog1" dojoType="dijit.Dialog" title="dijit.Dialog">
	        <div>
	        *** Content of Dialog Box ***
	        </div>
	        </div></code></pre>

The following example also creates a `Dialog` widget, but in this case, the content is dynamically loaded from the server.

```
<button dojoType="dijit.form.Button"
    onclick="dijit.byId('dialog2').show()">
    Show Dialog
</button>

<div id="dialog2"
    dojoType="dijit.Dialog"
    href="content.html"
    title="Dynamic Content">
</div>
```

JavaScript Constructor Examples	The following code will create a `Dialog` with dynamic content retrieved from the server resource "content.jsp."

```
new dijit.Dialog({
    title: "Dialog",
    href: "content.jsp" });
```

The `Dialog` must be connected to the DOM and activated using its `show()` method.

Key Properties	Property	Default	Description
	open	false	Is the dialog visible or not?
	duration	400	Number of milliseconds from when the dialog window is started to when it fully appears. It fades in over this period of time.
	href	null	The URL for the server resource that will provide the content for the dialog.
	title	null	Text for the title bar of the `Dialog` widget.

Key Methods	Method	Description
	show()	Make the widget visible.
	hide()	Hide the widget.

Key Styles	Style Name	Description
	dijitDialogPaneContent	Style of the `ContentPane` containing the widget's content.

Key Events	Style Name	Description
	onLoad	Executes when the content is loaded into the widget.

Notes	None

Widget Name	dijit.**TooltipDialog**
Super Classes	`dijit._Widget` `dijit.layout.ContentPane`
File Location	dijit/Dialog.js Use `dojo.require("dijit.Dialog");`
Usage	This class creates a widget that displays a dialog that has the same appearance as a Tooltip. This dialog slightly differs from a `dijit.Dialog` in two primary ways. First, the dialog is not a model; the user can click on the page behind the dialog, which causes the dialog to be hidden. Secondly, the dialog contains a marker pointing to the widget that it is associated with. Regular `dijit.Dialog` widgets display in the center of the page, but a `TooltipDialog` will appear next to the widget it is associated with. This widget is used to capture additional information for a Toolbar command by providing a form. When used this way, the widget will be hidden when the form is submitted.
Display Examples	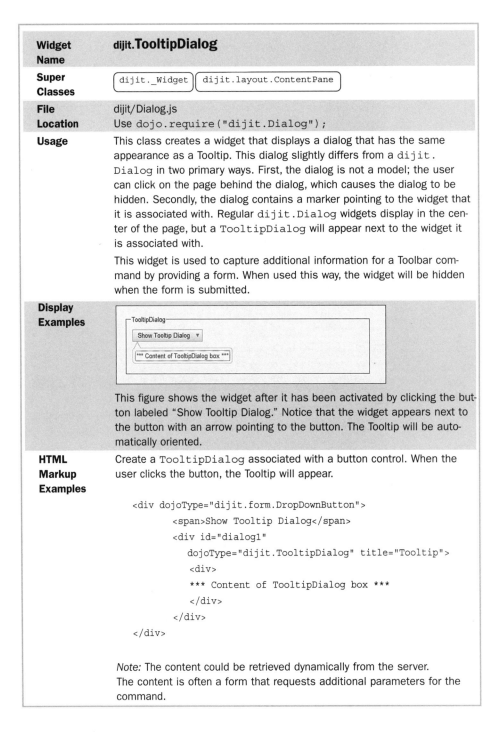 This figure shows the widget after it has been activated by clicking the button labeled "Show Tooltip Dialog." Notice that the widget appears next to the button with an arrow pointing to the button. The Tooltip will be automatically oriented.

HTML Markup Examples	Create a `TooltipDialog` associated with a button control. When the user clicks the button, the Tooltip will appear.
	
	`<div dojoType="dijit.form.DropDownButton">`
	`    <span>Show Tooltip Dialog</span>`
	`    <div id="dialog1"`
	`        dojoType="dijit.TooltipDialog" title="Tooltip">`
	`        <div>`
	`        *** Content of TooltipDialog box ***`
	`        </div>`
	`    </div>`
	`</div>`
	
	Note: The content could be retrieved dynamically from the server. The content is often a form that requests additional parameters for the command.

JavaScript Constructor Examples	This widget would normally be created through HTML markup.
Key Properties	None
Key Methods	None
Key Styles	None
Key Events	None
Notes	None

Widget Name	dijit.**Tooltip**
Super Classes	dijit._Widget
File Location	dijit/Tooltip.js Use `dojo.require("dijit.Tooltip");`
Usage	This class creates a widget that displays a pop-up message next to a field. The message appears automatically when the field receives focus and will disappear when focus is gone. The widget displays on top of any underlying page elements. This widget is similar to a `TooltipDialog` except that this widget is best used for a brief helpful display of text or HTML, while the `TooltipDialog` can be used to be more interactive, displaying a form for additional data entry or even displaying other widgets. This widget acts as a more powerful replacement for the `title` attribute available in HTML.
Display Examples	 This figure shows the `Tooltip` widget appearing as the field receives focus.
HTML Markup Examples	Create a `Tooltip` widget and associate it with an existing field. ```\n<span dojoType="dijit.Tooltip" connectId="field1">\n*** Tooltip content ***\n</span>\n``` The preceding code assumes the existence of a form field with an id of "field1".
JavaScript Constructor Examples	The following code will create a Tooltip. ```\nnew dijit.Tooltip({\n connectId:["id3"],\n label:" *** content ***"});\n```

Key Properties	Property	Default	Description
	`label`	`""`	Text of the label on the Tooltip.
	`showDelay`	`400`	Number of milliseconds from when the associated widget received focus until the Tooltip is displayed.
	`connectId`	`[]`	Array of widgets that the Tooltip is associated with.

Key Methods	None

Key Styles	Style Name	Description
	`dijitTooltipContents`	CSS style of content of `Tooltip`.

Key Events	None

Notes	None

Widget Name	dijit.**ProgressBar**
Super Classes	`dijit._Widget`
File Location	dijit/ProgressBar.js Use `dojo.require("dijit.ProgressBar");`
Usage	This class creates a widget that displays the completion state a process using a horizontal bar. This widget only displays the status unlike the Slider, which can be used as a control to change the status measurement. Also this widget can be displayed only horizontally. The progress is updated programmatically by this widget's `update()` function.
Display Examples	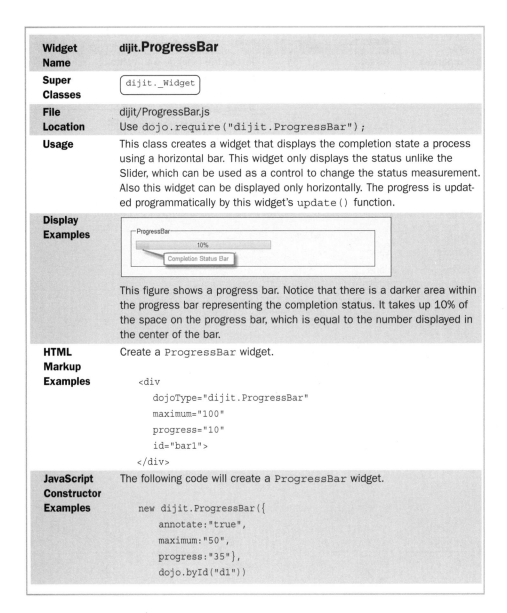 This figure shows a progress bar. Notice that there is a darker area within the progress bar representing the completion status. It takes up 10% of the space on the progress bar, which is equal to the number displayed in the center of the bar.
HTML Markup Examples	Create a `ProgressBar` widget. ```<div\n dojoType="dijit.ProgressBar"\n maximum="100"\n progress="10"\n id="bar1">\n</div>```
JavaScript Constructor Examples	The following code will create a `ProgressBar` widget. ```new dijit.ProgressBar({\n annotate:"true",\n maximum:"50",\n progress:"35"},\n dojo.byId("d1"))```

Key Properties	Property	Default	Description
	`progress`	`"0"`	This property contains the value of the progress. It can be specified as a percentage using "nn%" or as an absolute number, which will be converted into a percentage of the value specified in the `maximum` property.
	`maximum`	`100`	This property contains the upper limit of the value used to calculate the percentage of progress.
	`places`	`0`	This property specifies the number of decimal places to show in the progress value.
	`indeterminate`	`false`	When this property is `true`, the progress value is unknown and is not shown.

Key Methods	Method	Description
	`update()`	Function for updating the progress status of the widget.

Key Styles	None

Key Events	None

Notes	None

Widget Name	**dijit.ColorPalette**		
Super Classes	`dijit._Widget`		
File Location	dijit/ColorPalette.js Use `dojo.require("dijit.ColorPalette");`		
Usage	This class creates a widget that displays a grid containing a selection of colors, one of which may be selected by the user. There are two built-in palettes available, the 7 x 10 and the 3 x 4. The specific colors are also built into the palette. After the user selects a color, the value of the widget is set to the RGB value of the selected color.		
Display Examples	 This figure shows the 7 × 10 version of the widget.		

HTML Markup Examples	Create a `ColorPalette` widget.
	
	`<div dojoType="dijit.ColorPalette"`
	`        palette="3x4" />`		

JavaScript Constructor Examples	The following code will create a `ColorPalette`. `new dijit.ColorPalette({palette:"7x10"}, dojo.byId("d1"))`		
Key Properties	**Property**	**Default**	**Description**
	`palette`	`"7 x 10"`	The 7 x 10 or 3 x 4 values are only valid ones defined by default.
	`value`	`null`	RGB value of the selected color.
Key Methods	None		
Key Styles	None		
Key Events	**Style Name**	**Description**	
	`onChange()`	Function called when a color is selected.	
Notes	None		

Widget Name	dijit.**Tree**
Super Classes	`dijit._Widget` `dijit._TreeNode`
File Location	dijit/Tree.js Use `dojo.require("dijit.Tree");`
Usage	This class creates a widget that displays a collapsible and expandable outline structure. Nodes in the tree can be clicked to trigger some action. Also when nodes are expanded, their content can be dynamically loaded from the server. It is possible to build trees programmatically or through HTML, but the simplest technique is to use a Dojo data store, which can be directly associated with the widget and populates the widget automatically. It is also possible to enable a drag and drop mode so that tree items can be moved from one parent item to another.
Display Examples	 This figure shows fully expanded `Tree` widget with a number of levels. Although this example shows text for each tree node, it is also possible to add an icon.

HTML Markup Examples	Create a `Tree` widget from a Dojo data store.
	
	`<div dojoType="dojo.data.ItemFileReadStore"`
	`    jsId="treeStore"`
	`    url="tree.json"></div>`
	
	`<div dojoType="dijit.Tree"`
	`    store="treeStore"`
	`    query="{type:'category'}"`
	`    label="Rocks">`

Note: Following is an example of the original JSON content of the data store corresponding to the Display Example.

```
{ label: 'name',
  identifier: 'name',
    items: [
       { name:'Igneous', type:'category'},
       { name:'Metamorphic',
         type: 'category',
         children: [
            { name:'Slate', type:'subtype' },
            { name:'Gneiss', type:'subtype' },
            { name:'Quartzite', type:'subtype' }
         ]
       },
       { name:'Sedimentary', type: 'category'}
    ]
}
```

JavaScript Constructor Examples	The programmatic construction of this widget is beyond the scope of this book. See the Dojo documentation on the web site for more details.

Key Properties

Property	Default	Description
store	null	The Dojo data store associated with this widget.
query	null	The data store associated with this object should contain objects with a `category` property. The `query` property should specify a value containing the value of `category`, which should be considered first-level items in the tree.

The following table describes properties for tree nodes themselves which are of class `dijit._TreeNode`, which is an internal Dojo function.

Property	Default	Description
label	" "	Contains text for label of tree node. *Note:* This property belongs to each tree node.
isExpandable	true	Can the node be expanded?
isExpanded	false	Has the node been expanded?

Key Methods	None

Key Styles	Style Name	Description
	dijitTreeLabel	CSS class for item text on a tree node.

Key Events	Event Name	Description
	onClick(item, node)	This function is called when the user clicks a tree item.

Notes	Tree is a collection of _TreeNodes with the Tree itself being a sub class of tree node.

Widget Name	dijit.form.**Slider**
Super Classes	dijit._Widget dijit.form.HorizontalSlider dijit.form.VerticalSlider
File Location	dijit/form/Slider.js Use dojo.require("dijit.form.Slider");
Usage	This class creates a horizontal or vertical bar with a slider that can be moved by the user to select a specific value. The slider bar can have hash marks on either side that are labeled.
Display Examples	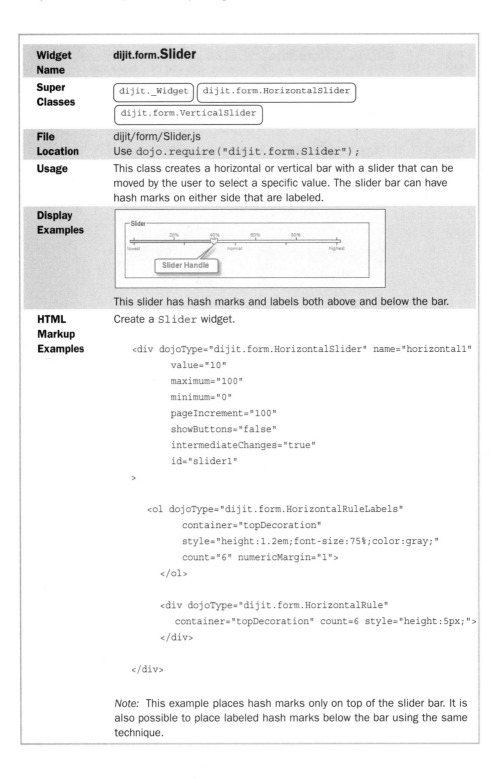 This slider has hash marks and labels both above and below the bar.
HTML Markup Examples	Create a Slider widget. ```<div dojoType="dijit.form.HorizontalSlider" name="horizontal1"\n value="10"\n maximum="100"\n minimum="0"\n pageIncrement="100"\n showButtons="false"\n intermediateChanges="true"\n id="slider1"\n >\n\n <ol dojoType="dijit.form.HorizontalRuleLabels"\n container="topDecoration"\n style="height:1.2em;font-size:75%;color:gray;"\n count="6" numericMargin="1">\n </ol>\n\n <div dojoType="dijit.form.HorizontalRule"\n container="topDecoration" count=6 style="height:5px;">\n </div>\n\n </div>``` *Note:* This example places hash marks only on top of the slider bar. It is also possible to place labeled hash marks below the bar using the same technique.

JavaScript Constructor Examples	Because of the number of components of this widget, it is more typical to create it using HTML than to create it programmatically.

Key Properties

Property	Default	Description
showButtons	true	Display controls at each end of the bar for incrementing and decrementing the slider value. Specifying `false` for this property causes the controls not to display.
minimum	0	The lowest value that the slider can be set to, even though the slider bar may appear to be lower.
maximum	100	The highest value that the slider can be set to, even though the slider bar may appear to be higher.
discreteValues	Infinity	Possible number of settings between the lowest and highest values.
pageIncrement	2	The amount of slider increments or decrements when the `<Page Up>` or `<Page Down>` keys are used.
clickSelect	true	Determines if clicking the progress bar will move the slider handle.
value	0	Initial value setting for the slider.

The following table contains properties for either the `HorizontalRule` or the `VerticalRule`. These are the hash marks that appear to either side of the slider bar.

Property	Default	Description
container	""	Specifies which set of hash marks this rule should describe. Possible values are topDecoration bottomDecoration leftDecoration rightDecoration
count	3	Number of hash marks.
ruleStyle	""	CSS style for hash marks.

The following table contains properties for either the `HorizontalRuleLabels` or the `VerticalRuleLabels`. These are the labels that appear on the hash marks on either side of the slider bar.

Property	Default	Description
container	" "	Specifies which set of hash mark labels this rule should describe. Possible values are topDecoration bottomDecoration leftDecoration rightDecoration
labels	[]	Array of labels for hash marks.
labelStyle	" "	CSS style for the hash mark labels.

Key Methods	Method	Description
	increment()	Increase the slider value by one position. The slider handle will also move.
	decrement()	Decrease the slider value by one position. The slider handle will also move.
	setValue(value)	Change the slider value. The slider handle will also move to the corresponding position.

Key Styles	None
Key Events	None
Notes	None

Widget Name	dijit.form.**NumberSpinner**		
Super Classes	`dijit._Widget` `dijit.form.NumberTextBoxMixin` `dijit.form._Spinner`		
File Location	dijit/form/NumberSpinner.js Use `dojo.require("dijit.form.NumberSpinner");`		
Usage	This class creates a text box for numbers that contains a control that allows the user to change the value by clicking the control. The control consists of an up arrow and down arrow icon. Clicking the up arrow increases the value, and clicking the down arrow decreases the value. This is superior to a regular `NumberTextBox` because it is easier for the user to make small changes to the value. Also when the controls are held down, the speed of the change in the value increases.		
Display Examples	NumberSpinner 900 The user can increment or decrement the value by clicking the up or down arrow icons.		

HTML Markup Examples	Create a `NumberSpinner` widget.
	
	`<input`
	    `dojoType="dijit.form.NumberSpinner"`
	    `value="900"`
	    `constraints="{max:1550,places:0}"`
	    `name="integerspinner1"`
	    `id="integerspinner1">`
	
	Note: This widget is inherits the `constraints` property.		

JavaScript Constructor Examples	The following code will create a Tooltip.		
Key Properties	**Property**	**Default**	**Description**
	`smallDelta`	1	Amount by which the value of the number will increase or decrease when incremented or decremented.
	`largeDelta`	10	Amount by which the value of the number will increase or decrease when the `<Page Up>` or `<Page Down>` keys are used.

Key Methods	None
Key Styles	None
Key Events	None
Notes	This widget is a subclass dijit.form.NumberTextBox, so it inherits all the validation properties of that type. For simplicity, most of those properties have not been shown in this example.

Widget Name	dijit.**InlineEditBox**
Super Classes	`dijit._Widget`
File Location	dijit/InlineEditBox.js Use `dojo.require("dijit.InlineEditBox");`
Usage	This class creates a widget that allows displayed text to be converted into a text box so that it can be edited by the user.
Display Examples	 This screen shot shows the widget in operation. The first line, "My hobby is running," appears as normal displayed text. The second line shows the text as highlighted when the mouse passes over it. The third line shows the text box that appears when the editable text is clicked.

HTML Markup Examples	Create a `InlineEditBox` widget.
	
	 ``
	<span
	    dojoType="dijit.InlineEditBox"
	    editor="dijit.form.TextBox"
	    width="100px" title="hobby"
	    style="border-bottom: 1px dashed blue;"
	>
	    running
	</span>
	``
	
	 Note: In this widget, the editable text is underlined with a blue dashed line to indicate that it is editable.

JavaScript Constructor Examples	This widget is normally created using HTML.

Key Properties	Property	Default	Description
	`editing`	`false`	Specifies whether the widget is currently in edit mode, `false` if no.
	`autoSave`	`true`	When set to `true`, the changes are automatically saved when the edit box is closed, not just when the save icon is clicked.
	`buttonSave`	`" "`	Text containing label for Save button.
	`buttonCancel`	`" "`	Text containing label for Cancel button.
	`renderAsHtml`	`false`	Property is `true` if the selected editor uses HTML rather than just plain text.
	`value`	`" "`	Value of the text string.
	`editor`	`dijit.form.TextBox`	Widget that will be used as the editor for the text.

Key Methods	Method	Description
	`cancel()`	This function cancels the edit session and reverts to the original value of the text.

Key Styles	None	

Key Events	Style Name	Description
	`onChange()`	This function is called when the user changes the value of the editable text.

Notes	Use a style attribute to emphasize the editable word.

Widget Name	**dijit.form.Textarea**
Super Classes	dijit.form._FormWidget
File Location	dijit/form/Textarea.js Use dojo.require("dijit.form.TextArea");
Usage	This class creates a widget that replaces the standard HTML `<textarea>` tag, which allows multi-line input. One of its primary advantages is that it automatically resizes itself when the amount of text changes rather than displaying scroll bars as the standard `<textarea>` tag does.
Display Examples	 This figure shows the widget with some lines of content. If the content extended beyond the boundaries of the widget, the size of the widget would change automatically.

HTML Markup Examples	Create a `Textarea` widget.
	
	`<textarea dojoType="dijit.form.Textarea" name="textArea1">`
	`    This is the content of the text area.`
	`</textarea>`

JavaScript Constructor Examples	This widget is normally created with HTML.
Key Properties	None
Key Methods	None
Key Styles	None
Key Events	None
Notes	Use the `<textarea>` tag for this widget. The standard attributes for specifying the size of the text area in HTML are "cols" and "rows" corresponding to the number of columns and rows. Do not use these attributes when using `dijit.form.Textarea`. Instead, specify the size of the widget using the style properties "width" and "height."

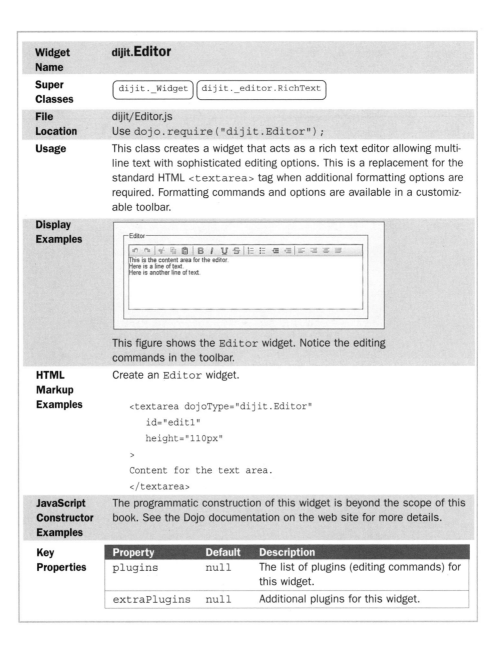

Widget Name	dijit.**Editor**
Super Classes	`dijit._Widget` `dijit._editor.RichText`
File Location	dijit/Editor.js Use `dojo.require("dijit.Editor");`
Usage	This class creates a widget that acts as a rich text editor allowing multi-line text with sophisticated editing options. This is a replacement for the standard HTML `<textarea>` tag when additional formatting options are required. Formatting commands and options are available in a customizable toolbar.
Display Examples	This figure shows the `Editor` widget. Notice the editing commands in the toolbar.

HTML Markup Examples	Create an `Editor` widget.
	
	`<textarea dojoType="dijit.Editor"`
	`    id="edit1"`
	`    height="110px"`
	`>`
	`Content for the text area.`
	`</textarea>`

JavaScript Constructor Examples	The programmatic construction of this widget is beyond the scope of this book. See the Dojo documentation on the web site for more details.

Key Properties

Property	Default	Description
plugins	null	The list of plugins (editing commands) for this widget.
extraPlugins	null	Additional plugins for this widget.

Key Methods	None
Key Styles	None
Key Events	None
Notes	None

Summary

A number of specialized widgets exist in Dojo that provide unique functionality far beyond the default widgets in HTML.

This chapter covers some of those specialized widgets but not all of them.

New widgets are being developed for Dojo constantly.

We've now concluded our exploration of the Dojo widgets. We continue in the next section of the book by exploring some of the nonvisual elements of Dojo, the features that augment JavaScript programming. These are the hidden features of Dojo that don't impact the visual display of the page directly but make JavaScript programming much easier.

III

Dojo in Detail

10

What Is Dojo?

There is nothing more difficult to take in hand, more perilous to conduct or more uncertain in its success than to take the lead in the introduction of a new order of things.

—Niccolo Machiavelli (1469–1527)

It has been said that we can't understand where we're going without knowing where we came from. Why does Dojo exist? What should it be used for? Who should use it? These are the questions that this chapter will address. We'll introduce Dojo, describe a bit of its history and give a view of it from 20,000 feet. The technical details will be left for a later chapter and for now we'll focus on the big picture.

10.1 History of JavaScript and AJAX

Because you picked up this book, I'm guessing that you probably already know a little about Dojo. You probably know that it is a tool for working with JavaScript. So before we delve into the specific history of Dojo, we should say just a little about JavaScript.

JavaScript is the programming language built into a browser. It has been available in almost all browsers since 1995. By utilizing JavaScript in a web page you can make your pages come alive by interacting much more directly with the user. For example, JavaScript can be used to validate user input, display interesting visual effects, perform calculations, and respond to user events. In an effort to describe these wonderful features a new term was even coined—*dynamic HTML* (DHTML). JavaScript can turn HTML from a dry, dead, static markup language into a dynamic interactive visual environment for the user.

If you're having trouble remembering all the wonderful interactive web sites available in the 90s, it's because the nirvana promised by DHTML never quite materialized. It turned out that DHTML had a number of problems. Different versions of the browsers supported different versions of JavaScript. The object used to represent the web page internally (what we would now call the DOM) also differed from browser to browser, making it difficult to write JavaScript that could work in any browser. So some developers avoided using JavaScript at all. Other developers used it but in isolated ways, never taking full advantage of the language. After the browser wars of the 90s subsided, when Microsoft and Netscape stopped constantly releasing new versions of their browsers to introduce some new feature, a *Pax Microsoft* settled over the land. The early 2000s were characterized by relative calm in the browser market place, the good news being that the browser feature set became more settled and consistent, the bad news being that the pace of new feature introduction slowed enormously.

By the beginning of 2005 some standard patterns for using DHTML had evolved. Developers would use it to ensure certain kinds of client-side validation. For example, JavaScript was often used to ensure that the user had entered a required field before a form was submitted to the server. It was also used to develop stand-alone GUI widgets such as calendar widgets to be used for selecting dates rather then entering them as plain text.

Page designers often knew very little about how the DHTML JavaScript worked. They would often add DHTML to their pages by cutting and pasting from other sites when they found a feature they liked or by downloading DHTML snippets from a number of web sites dedicated to providing useful DHTML code. Pages might contain multiple widgets obtained from different sources that provided some stand-alone feature but weren't integrated with each other. Developers didn't think of JavaScript as a cohesive full-blown programming model but as more of a primitive scripting language that could be used to add some neat features here and there in the page.

That all changed in early 2005. Google released a couple of extremely interesting applications, Google Mail and Google Maps. Both applications behaved much more like traditional desktop applications with rich user interfaces than like the clunky HTML applications common at the time. Google Maps especially caused a paradigm shift in how developers thought about the limitations of user interface by implementing a sophisticated drag-and-drop capability in the maps. Up until that time, the most popular mapping sites, Yahoo and MapQuest, allowed a user to move around a map by clicking a direction icon, which would request an entire new page from the server so that the user moved from right-to-left or up-and-down in a herky-jerky fashion. Google Map users could smoothly scroll in any direction, using their mouse without a page being refreshed.

The new paradigm couldn't be complete until it was given a name. And that is exactly what Jesse James Garrett, a San Francisco-based user interface designer, did when he published a paper on the new techniques and christened them as "AJAX." He described a set of technologies that could be used to request data from the server while a page was displaying the browser without refreshing the page. The data from the server would then be used to update the display using DHTML. Google had demonstrated what wondrous pages could now be created, and Jesse had given it a name. The web development community was shaken out of its collective slumber and began work on Web 2.0. AJAX became *Ajax*—what once was a description for some specific technology components (*Asynchronous JavaScript And XML*) became a more general description of web pages that adopted user interface techniques that had only been seen before in non-browser applications.

Note that the actual techniques used to implement Ajax had been around for a number of years and had even been used in a number of web sites. The coinage of the term "Ajax" helped to popularize the techniques.

The use of JavaScript within web pages exploded, which resulted in a few painful repercussions. Developers realized that JavaScript was a full-blown programming language, not just a toy for script kiddies. It was a mature object-oriented language that required the developer to understand object-oriented programming techniques. Unfortunately, developers also realized that many of the tools and libraries that had been developed in other programming environments had not yet been developed for JavaScript. In addition, there were still a number of inconsistencies between popular browser versions in how JavaScript, the Event Model, and the DOM worked. And that set the stage for the emergence of the Dojo DHTML toolkit.

10.2 History of Dojo

The increasing importance of JavaScript did not go unnoticed. More and more developers were spending time working with JavaScript and dealing with its many complexities, idiosyncrasies, and outright bugs. Some of the lead developers in the community were strategizing on how to address these problems. One particular group of developers decided the solution might lie in creating their own DHTML library. And in September 2004 the first version of Dojo was released. Although the product was a community effort, Alex Russell and Dylan Schiemann were among the lead developers. In early 2005, the Dojo foundation was established by Alex and Dylan to manage the ownership of the product.

Dojo has attracted a large community of both users and developers. As of early 2007, Dojo had gone through four releases and had been downloaded hundreds of thousands of times.

You can find more detailed information on the history of Dojo at the web site: http://www.dojotoolkit.org.

10.3 Purpose of Dojo

The primary purpose in developing Dojo was to address the inadequacies inherent in JavaScript programming, in other words, to make JavaScript programming easier.

Following are some of the specific goals that the developers wanted to achieve:

- Hiding some of the complexities of writing JavaScript that is compatible across different browsers

- Maintaining a small footprint
- Maintaining excellent performance
- Achieving high quality by supporting modern web standards such as Internationalization and Accessibility
- Being a robust, all-in-one toolkit
- Providing useful widgets
- Providing techniques for creating custom widgets

Although some of these goals are at cross purposes (for example, it is hard both to have a small footprint and still be robust) Dojo has achieved a harmonious balance.

10.4 Description of Dojo

To quote the web site, "Dojo is an open source, DHTML toolkit written in JavaScript." Let's break this down a bit to understand what it means. We'll start with the last part of the statement first.

- **Dojo is written in JavaScript.** Dojo is *all* JavaScript and *only* JavaScript. There is no plug-in necessary to run Dojo. It runs in the web page just as any JavaScript you might write yourself. To the browser, the Dojo JavaScript is indistinguishable from any other JavaScript on the page, whether written by the developer or part of some other JavaScript framework that might be included. It must be included on each web page that uses it. There are some advantages to this approach. For example, Dojo is compatible with any browser that can run modern versions of JavaScript. However, there are disadvantages also. Dojo can only do what is possible in native JavaScript. Some other frameworks that require plugins are able to extend the capabilities of the browser.

- **Dojo is a DHTML toolkit.** The traditional focus of DHTML was to allow easy manipulation of a web page to create GUI widgets and visual effects. This included working with the DOM, the event model, and CSS. That is certainly still the focus for Dojo. We'll see many useful functions and object types that can be used to create amazing visual effects for your users.

- **Dojo is open source.** When you download Dojo, you get the entire source. You can see every line of JavaScript written for Dojo. There is nothing hidden. That means that the browser also sees the entire source, so a sophisticated user of your page has access to the original JavaScript source, including not just Dojo, but any additional JavaScript that you write. Unfortunately, this is an inherent problem with the Web. It is very difficult to hide anything from the browser.

  Also because Dojo provides the source code, you can do almost anything you want with the toolkit, including changing it. Be warned, however, that this might make upgrading more difficult later. Also certain legal restrictions may apply when using Dojo. We'll discuss those a little later in the section on licenses.

In the next chapter, we begin to drill down into the Dojo source code, but for now, let's describe it at a high level. Dojo consists of a set of files that contain JavaScript code. By including one or more of the files in your web page, you can write JavaScript code that uses Dojo. This allows you to write much less code than you would normally have to. Most of the Dojo code contains either functions that your custom code can call or constructors that allow your custom code to create objects such as GUI widgets. Dojo functions and constructors don't contain any magic. If you don't believe me, you can check it out yourself—all the source code is there for you to see. It's all just JavaScript that you could've written yourself, but because of all the hard work of the Dojo community, you don't have to.

Dojo functions and constructors run within the browser. Dojo does not provide any components to run on the server. This makes the Dojo server agnostic. In other words, it doesn't care what the server is as long as that server knows how to process HTTP requests. So web sites can be developed that use Dojo in the browser while the server may use Java J2EE, PHP, or Ruby on Rails, among others. Because of this, when creating an application using Dojo, you will also usually need to develop components on the server side, which respond to Ajax requests from the browser. More on this later, but for now, just remember that Dojo provides components only for the browser.

10.5 What Problems Does Dojo Solve?

As we've said, Dojo was developed to address some of the problems with JavaScript development. But what, specifically, were those problems? Following is a list of the major issues that Dojo was created to solve:

- Different browsers support different versions of JavaScript. Without Dojo, you would need to write code for each of the different browsers that your application would run in.

- HTML supports only a small set of standard GUI widgets (text, check boxes, radio buttons, and so on). More sophisticated widgets are needed. For example, choosing a date from a calendar widget is much easier than just typing in a date and hoping that the format is correct. Not only does HTML lack many widgets, but it doesn't provide a method for building new widgets.

- The Document Object Model (DOM) behaves differently in different browser versions.

- Event handling is done differently in different versions of the browser.

- The set of classes in native JavaScript is small compared to what was needed.

The last point is especially interesting and can be further explained by an example. The Java programming language (that's "Java," not to be confused with "JavaScript") contains a little less than 50 different object types in its core package. However, there are an additional 5,000 object types defined in the class libraries that come with the standard

Java development kit. JavaScript also contains somewhat less than 50 standard objects and object types, but it lacks any standard class libraries to augment that number. We're not saying that JavaScript needs another 5,000 data types, but surely it needs more than 50, and Dojo supplies many of those. Later we talk specifically about what those missing classes are.

10.6 Who Should Use Dojo?

Dojo can be used by anyone who develops Web pages. But there are three groups for whom Dojo is an almost perfect fit. The first group is developers who are already writing complex JavaScript. They are already encountering all the problems that Dojo was meant to solve. By adopting Dojo, they can increase their productivity and reduce their level of frustration. And the good news for this group is that they can adopt Dojo as quickly or as slowly as they wish. Dojo won't step on any of their existing code because of its use of a separate namespace. So they can began adding Dojo to existing pages for new features and to slowly convert their old code as they have time. This is a really important advantage for Dojo, and makes it easy to get started. You can bite off as much or as little as you want.

The second group of developers who should be using Dojo are page designers. The stereotypical page designer has skills in graphic design, page layout, and the use of the HTML tag language. The skill that they don't usually possess and often aren't interested in acquiring is the ability to write programs. They don't want to write JavaScript. However, they would still love to get access to some of the beautiful widgets available on the Dojo toolkit. Luckily for them, Dojo widgets can be added to a webpage simply through HTML markup with little or no coding.

The third group of developers who should be using Dojo are server-side developers. These are the developers responsible for creating the backend part of the web site, the programs that run on the web server itself. Although we might not think of them as typically being involved in page design, there is a role for them. Server side developers usually receive HTML files provided by the page designer and add the extensions that allow the page to communicate with the backend functionality that the site requires. These developers might be PHP developers, Ruby on Rails developers, Java developers, or developers experienced in any of a host of backend technologies available today. They usually know enough HTML to get by but not much JavaScript. Now with the introduction of Ajax and the focus on creating more dynamic web pages, they're being asked to become JavaScript programmers. Given their current responsibilities they can't really be expected to become JavaScript experts overnight and to understand all the possible pitfalls of JavaScript programming that we've already discussed. This is where Dojo is the perfect fit for them. By using the Dojo functions and constructors, these developers can avoid having to learn all the ins and outs of JavaScript and benefit from the years of experience already built in to Dojo.

10.7 Licensing

I'm not a lawyer, nor do I play one on TV. So I'm not really one who should be giving legal advice. But here goes anyway. Dojo is an open source project, and the common perception of open source projects is that they can be used in any way that you wish. Developers often think of open source projects as products that they don't have to license like they do typical vendor software. However, that perception is wrong. Open source projects are made available under varying licenses that convey rights and responsibilities. By using Dojo, you're accepting one of those licenses, and there are some restrictions.

Dojo is made available under two licenses. This is known as *dual licensing*. You're not, however, constrained by both licenses, only the license you pick. So whichever one provides the terms that you are looking for can be used. And there's no requirement for notifying Dojo which license you pick. You don't have to pay any money, sign any contracts, or deal with any paperwork of any kind.

The first license, known as the *Academic Free License*, allows you to use the code in both non-profit and commercial applications. Changes that you make to Dojo do not have to be submitted back to the Dojo community. And there is no requirement that you make your source code that uses Dojo available to anyone. The intent of the license is to encourage the adoption of Dojo without adding any unreasonable restraints.

The second license is the modified BSD license. It contains many of the same covenants as the first license. It allows you to use Dojo, modify it, or package it within your commercial application without having to submit your changes to Dojo or make your source code public.

In many ways the purpose of Dojo licensing is not to restrict you as a developer but simply to protect Dojo. You can't sue Dojo for bugs that it may have or that you introduce. And you can't claim that you now own Dojo and start suing anybody else who uses it.

Disclaimer and fine print: As I've already said, I am not a lawyer. This licensing discussion is merely my opinion and represents my understanding. You or your organization will have to determine which license is appropriate and what restrictions really apply to you.

10.8 Competitors and Alternatives

Internet applications with sophisticated graphical widgets are also know as *Rich Internet Applications* (RIAs). Dojo is an important toolkit for creating RIAs but is not the only solution. Let's briefly talk about some of the products that address the same needs as Dojo.

First is a product that is most like Dojo—an open source DHTML toolkit that provides no server-side components:

- **Prototype and script.aculo.us.** Prototype is a very popular JavaScript toolkit for web development. It is open source like Dojo and consists of a single JavaScript file containing functions and constructors. However, most of the functionality of Prototype is unrelated to the user interface. That is why it is typical for Prototype to be used in combination with another JavaScript library called script.aculo.us. Together, they begin to achieve some of the breadth present in the Dojo toolkit. However, a number of issues, such as the absence of a separate namespace for Prototype functions make it less desirable for enterprise development.

> **Note**
> Two other very popular toolkits are Yahoo User Interface (YUI) and jQuery.

Next is a product that allows users to develop RIAs but is based on a client-side plugin:

- **Adobe Integrated Runtime (AIR).** This approach requires a runtime plugin to be installed on the browser, which is done the first time an Adobe Air application is run. This product can use its own programming language called ActiveScript, which is very similar to JavaScript. Although an excellent programming environment, Adobe is a commercial vendor, and AIR can make use of proprietary components on the client (the runtime) and on the server, an approach that many open source developers disagree with.

Finally, let's review a product that can also be used to develop RIAs but takes a completely different technical approach:

- **Google Web Toolkit (GWT).** This product provides a library of Java classes that can be used to construct RIAs. The developer writes custom Java classes using the GWT library and then uses a GWT program to create JavaScript from the Java code. Yes, you read that correctly. GWT treats the browser as a virtual machine for JavaScript. As a developer you won't work with the JavaScript directly, only indirectly as Java. This probably strikes you as a fairly unusual approach, and you may wonder if it can actually succeed. Well, if any organization can make it succeed, Google probably can, given their enormous capabilities and resources. It reminds me of the old joke, "Where does an 800 pound gorilla sleep? Anywhere it wants to!"

This is a very small and unscientific sampling of the alternatives to Dojo. There are many more—at last count over 100. You can read about them at the excellent site maintained by Michael Mahemoff at http://ajaxpatterns.org.

10.9 The Future of Dojo

While Dojo has existed in some form since 2004, it went through a major change at the end of 2007 when the 1.0 version of Dojo was released. This was the first version of the product that the Dojo team felt reached the level of quality necessary to be designated as the 1.0 version. It is of a consistent high quality, very lightweight, and provides the important functionality required of a DHTML toolkit.

Dojo has already had a large impact on the web development community, both as a toolkit used for many applications and as a thought leader that has pushed the frontier of web development. But what about its future? As Yogi Berra said, "I never make predictions, especially about the future." We should also be careful in making forward-looking statements. But I think it is safe to say that with the 1.0 release, the rate of adoption of Dojo should increase. Because of the robustness and completeness of the Dojo feature set, we should see further inroads for Dojo into large enterprise shops. And because of Dojo's ease of use and small footprint, small to mid-size organizations will also continue to be drawn to it. And because of the large and sophisticated developer community, I think we can expect Dojo to evolve and push the boundaries of web development for the foreseeable future.

Note

As of the final edits of this book, Dojo 1.1.0 was available for download but new versions are being released frequently. Check the website for the latest news.

Summary

Dojo is an open source toolkit for developing web applications using JavaScript.

Dojo was created to make JavaScript development easier and to solve many of the problems inherent in JavaScript development.

It consists of files containing JavaScript that can be included in a web page.

Developers write custom code using the Dojo functions and constructors to build their own functionality.

Dojo does not provide any server-side components. It can be used with any server that supports HTTP.

The license for Dojo is intended to not be restrictive so that Dojo can be widely adopted.

There are alternatives to Dojo from both open source and commercial organizations.

More information is available at the Dojo web site at http://www.DojoToolkit.org. The next chapter continues to introduce the Dojo Toolkit, but we change focus from a general discussion to a more technical discussion. And we start to look at the code. Like many developers, I don't really start to understand a new programming environment until I see the code. So on to the code!

Technical Description of Dojo

The devil is in the details.

—Anonymous

This chapter dives into the technical details of the Dojo framework. We review the files and directories you get when you download Dojo and peak inside to see what treasures lie there. If you're like me, when reading a technical book, your eyes quickly pass over the prose and focus on the code samples—a new programming paradigm just doesn't make sense until I see the code. We review some of the basic features of Dojo and describe others at a high level for subsequent explanation in further chapters. When you're through with this chapter, you'll know what's inside the pretty gift box that is Dojo!

Just a reminder: When you're reading this chapter you might get that "déjà vu all over again" feeling. After all, you've already been introduced to some of these same topics in the tutorial in Chapters 1 through 5. For example, you've probably already downloaded Dojo for the tutorial. The intent of the chapters in Part III is to dive down deeper than we could in the tutorial. Think of these chapters as flying over the same terrain but at a lower altitude so that more of the details are clearer!

11.1 What You Get in the Dojo Download

Before we can examine Dojo, we have to go get it. The most direct technique for downloading Dojo is to go to the Dojo web site and look for the download link on the front page. The link provides us the current stable release for Dojo. The front page also contains a link to the download page, which allows you to get older versions or even versions that are newer but might not quite be ready for general release yet. Unless you really need some cutting edge feature in a beta release, your best bet is just to get the current stable release.

The Dojo site is at www.dojotoolkit.org. Here is a current image of the page with the download icon visible on the right of the screen shot. The callout points to the download button.

Figure 11.1   Screenshot of Dojo home page

You will then be directed to the download page, which will show a huge button labeled "Download Now." Click the download button and follow the instructions to save the file on your computer. The file ends in the extension ".gz," which means it is an archive file and you need to unzip it. Most unzip utilities that work with ".zip" files will also be able to extract ".gz" files as well.

It will create a directory structure where the top-level directory name corresponds to the version number of the product. Inside that directory will be four subdirectories. Here's an image of the directory structure for version 1.1 of Dojo. Your actual version number may be different, of course.

Figure 11.2   Screenshot of Dojo directory structure

Although it isn't necessary yet, you may wish to follow along with this text by browsing through the Dojo files on your own computer. At this point, you may put your Dojo files anywhere and choose your own tools to browse them. As I write this chapter, I'm using Eclipse to view the directories and read the files.

11.2 Organization of Dojo Source Code

We've now downloaded Dojo, but exactly what is it that we've gotten? Dojo is just a bunch of files organized in a hierarchy of directories and subdirectories. Wow! That's helpful. But what kind of files do we have, and what is the scheme used to organize them? Simply put, most of the files contain JavaScript functions, and they are organized by module (a group of related functions). Along with the JavaScript files (over 300 of them) are a handful of files containing such things as license text and other stuff. Let's drill down level by level into Dojo and explore what we have.

11.2.1 First-level Directories

The main directory in my downloaded code is called "dojo_1.0" and consists of four subdirectories. These represent the four major categories of Dojo features. Let's describe each subdirectory.

dojo

Here are all of the functions and constructors in Dojo except for the widgets. Some developers are using Dojo only to get access to the many visually stunning and highly functional GUI widgets that it provides, so they may be surprised that there is an entire hidden underworld in Dojo consisting of many functions to make JavaScript coding easier but that don't require GUI widgets at all. This directory is where all that under-the-hood plumbing code resides.

dijit

Here are the Dojo widgets. Why didn't the creators of Dojo just combine this with the "dojo" directory? Actually, that is how early versions of Dojo were packaged. But by separating out the widgets from the rest of the Dojo code, it made Dojo more organized. And even more importantly, it makes it easier for developers to use just the parts of Dojo they need.

dojox

These are the extended features of Dojo that, for one reason or another, are not considered ready to be included in "dojo" or "dijit" yet. The reasons for exclusion. The functions may not be robust enough. They may not be fully internationalized yet, or maybe they won't be used by enough developers to justify taking up space in the main "dojo" directory. Then why include them at all? Well, for those developers who do need them, the functionality is very powerful and useful. Over time, functions in "dojox" may migrate into "dojo" or "digit."

util

These are files needed to perform unit testing on the Dojo functions during development. You can also use these features to run unit testing for code that you develop. Nothing in this directory is needed for an application that is in production.

11.2.2 Digging Deeper into the Dojo Directory

Now let's drill down into the second level of directories and files, starting with "dojo." Here's an image of the directory for my version of Dojo.

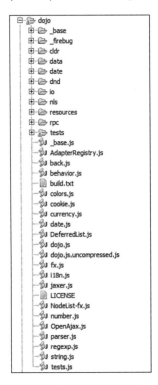

Figure 11.3   Screenshot of dojo-release-1.1.0/dojo Subdirectory

As you can see, this directory is pretty full. At first it may seem like a confusing mix, but we'll "peel the onion" one layer at a time so that we can really understand what it contains. Let's view the directory from 20,000 feet: There are various subdirectories and then some JavaScript files along with one text file called "build.txt."

Let's start with the most important file first: "dojo.js." Why is it the most important? Because it is the first file that you include in your web pages to make Dojo functions available to your own JavaScript code. But in another way, this specific file isn't important at all. And may not even be used when you first start to use Dojo. Confusing? Yes. A bit of an enigma inside a conundrum, as the old saying goes.

Why do I say that this file isn't important at all? Because every function inside this file really comes from somewhere else. The files in `dojo.js` are originally contained in separate files found in the "dojo-release-1.0/dojo/_base" subdirectory. Related functions are grouped together in a single file. You can think of these individual files as modules, which is the term Dojo uses. The modules in the "base" directory are ones that the designers of Dojo felt should always be available. So the "dojo.js" file is just used as a convenience to combine all the modules in the "base" directory into a single file that is easy to include in your pages. And that is why the file isn't really important—because all the functions in "dojo.js" also appear in other files.

And the second puzzle: Why might you not even use this file at all? This seems especially strange given that the file contains the functions that you supposedly always need. The reason you don't need `dojo.js` is that there is a companion file called `dojo.js.uncompressed.js` that contains all the same functions. The difference is that `dojo.js` contains a compressed version of the JavaScript with all the comments and extra spacing removed, while `dojo.js.uncompressed.js` contains comments and spacing so that it is easily readable by a developer (and is more useful when using a line-by-line debugger—more on that later). So when you first start using Dojo, you'll want to use the version that contains comments and white space: `"dojo.js.uncompressed.js."`

To write code that uses the Dojo functions, you need to include it in each of your web pages. Following is the code you would use to add Dojo to your page.

```
<script type="text/javascript"
        src="dojo-1.0/dojo/dojo.js.uncompressed.js"
        djConfig="isDebug: true, debugAtAllCosts: true"></script>
```

This code assumes that you have unzipped Dojo to the root of your web application and that the page is running from that location. Although not required, the `<script>` tag also contains an attribute called `djConfig`, which turns on some additional debugging messages when something goes wrong. This is a good idea to use when you first start using Dojo. After you publish the page to production, turn off debugging and use the compressed version of the code as shown here:

```
<script type="text/javascript"
        src="dojo-1.0/dojo/dojo.js "</script>
```

Let's review what we've learned so far. The file `dojo.js` is just a compressed version of the file `dojo.js.uncompressed.js`, which is itself a file containing functions defined in other Dojo files. These are functions the designers felt would be the most often used features. They even came up with a name to describe this set of functions. They call them Dojo "base." If you want to see the original home for these functions, look in the "_base" directory under the "dojo" directory.

11.3 Dojo Modules and Features

Dojo is organized into modules that contain groups of related functions. A module consists of a JavaScript file with the functions defined within it. The file also contains some special Dojo functions that register the module with Dojo. Every Dojo module used by a page must be registered when that page runs. So you'll see the following code repeated many times within the Dojo source code (although the specific module being registered will be different).

```
if(!dojo._hasResource["dojo._base.Color"])
dojo._hasResource["dojo._base.Color"] = true;
dojo.provide("dojo._base.Color");
```

The preceding code construct appears at the top of every module file and tells Dojo that a module has been loaded. In this case the loaded module is `dojo._base.Color`. This would correspond to a JavaScript file called `Color.js` in the directory `_base` under the `dojo` subdirectory. A module may have one or many functions within it. Functions do not require registration individually. Sometimes the module name and the name of the function are the same, but this is not required. The full name of a function is derived from the module name plus the function name. For example, the function `fromISOString` in the module `dojo.date.stamp` would be called in your code as shown in the following example:

```
var date = dojo.date.stamp.fromISOString()
```

11.3.1 Naming Conventions and Name Space

It is probably useful to talk about a few naming conventions at this point. Dojo functions are named with a multi-part convention. The first part of the name is always `dojo`. This designates that the function is part of Dojo and not a custom function created by you or a function from another class library. The advantage of using a separate name space for Dojo is that it is always clear when reading your code which functions are yours and which functions belong to Dojo. Furthermore, functions you write will not conflict with those from Dojo.

The next part of the name is the module and is preceded by a dot. For example, `_base` designates that this function is part of the base module. The module name may be followed by another dot and a sub-module name to further group functions. Otherwise the third part will be the function or constructor name. A constructor name would be capitalized. A lowercase name tells us it is a method or non-constructor function. Function names follow the "Camel Case" convention, which is a technique for creating names from multi-word descriptions where the words are concatenated together without spaces or special characters, and the leading letter of each word is lowercase (except for constructors where the first letter would be capitalized). For example, a method that calculates shipping charges might be called `calcShipCharge`, using the Camel Case naming convention. Sometimes, for frequently used functions, a short-cut name is assigned to the function that omits the module.

Remember, Dojo functions are named with the following conventions:

- The first part is always `dojo`.
- The second part is the module name.
- The third part is the function, constructor, or sub-module name.

- If the third part of the name is a sub-module, then the fourth part will be the function or constructor name.

A final note on names: When a leading underscore character is used in a function name, such as with `dojo.parser._nameAnonFunc`, the underscore marks the function as being one that a developer using Dojo would not use directly. The function would be used internally within the Dojo code. In essence, the underscore makes the function private.

11.3.2 Dojo Base Module

Now that we've introduced `dojo.js` and talked about the "base" features in it without detailing them, let's see what kinds of functions are actually included. James Burke provided an excellent summary of the Dojo base functions in the Dojo forum.[1] And although his description is nearly perfect, I'm going to provide my own summary of it also. As we review the modules included in Dojo "base," I'll just provide a summary description. Many of these functions will be reviewed in more detail in later chapters.

The term *API* is used frequently throughout this book. The term is an acronym for Application Program Interface and usually refers to the set of public functions available for a library and the exact parameters required to call those functions. Obviously, the exact Dojo API is extremely important in using Dojo. For many functions, detail on the API is included, but you should be aware that sometimes the API changes or alternate variations in the API for a particular function are available. An extremely important and useful resource to use for understanding the API and identifying variations and changes is the API documentation available on the Dojo site.[2]

You'll notice that in the function names for the functions in base that the second part of the name, the module, is missing. This is done as a convenience so that the function names are shorter in your code and yet still long enough to be meaningful.

Let's start with one of the simplest modules first and then advance to the more complex ones.

11.3.2.1 The `dojo.lang` Module

This module consists of a number of general functions used in many different contexts. The module name stands for "language" and is similar in purpose to the "java.lang" package that may be familiar to Java programmers. Think of them as foundational functions that can be used by other Dojo functions (and available to you in your custom JavaScript, of course).

---

1. Following is the link to James Burke's summary of the base module features in dojo.js, http://dojotoolkit.org/2007/08/22/dissecting-0-9s-dojo-js.
2. Following is the link to the online Dojo API documentation. Be aware that this link may be changed in the future, and you may need to search the site to find it (http://dojotoolkit.org/api).

Table 11.1   **List of** `dojo.lang` **Functions**

Function	Description
`dojo.isString()`	Determines if an object is a String.
`dojo.isArray()`	Determines if an object is an Array.
`dojo.isFunction()`	Determines if an object is a Function.
`dojo.isObject()`	Determines if a reference is to an Object.
`dojo.isArrayLike()`	Determines if a reference is to something that behaves like an Array.
`dojo.isAlien()`	Determines if a reference is to a Function that does not properly identify itself as a Function.
`dojo.mixin()`	Adds all the properties and methods from one object to another object.
`dojo.extend()`	Adds all the properties and methods from one object to the prototype of another object.
`dojo.hitch()`	Assigns a specific scope to a function so that the function always executes with that scope.
`dojo.partial()`	Assigns no scope to a function to force the scope to default to the execution context when the function runs.
`dojo.clone()`	Makes a copy of an object with all its children.
`dojo.trim()`	Trims whitespace from the beginning and end of a string.

11.3.2.2 The `dojo.declare` Module

This module consists of a single function, `dojo.declare`, which is used to create constructors used to build new objects. This is an extremely useful function but sometimes difficult to understand if you are new to Object Oriented Programming (OOP). That is why an entire chapter has been devoted to its use. For an in-depth discussion of OOP and the `dojo.declare` function, see Chapter 12, "Objects and Classes."

11.3.2.3 The `dojo.connect` Module

This module consists of functions that associate event handlers with events. Event handlers are simply functions that are called automatically when an event is triggered. The browser itself monitors the actions of the user to detect events. Almost anything the user does with the keyboard or mouse triggers an event that some event handler can be associated with. For instance, when the user places the cursor over a DOM element, an `onmouseover` event is triggered for that element. An event will only call the event handler if it has been associated with the event—otherwise nothing happens. For more on event handlers see Chapter 14, "Events and Event Handling."

The following table describes functions in the `dojo.connect` module. As a convenience to allow shorter function names, it is not necessary to specify the module name.

Table 11.2   **List of** `dojo.connect` **Functions**

Function	Description
`dojo.connect()`	Creates an association so that a certain function will be called whenever another function is called.
`dojo.disconnect()`	Removes the association between two functions.
`dojo.subscribe()`	Attaches a listener to a named topic.
`dojo.unsubscribe()`	Removes a listener from a named topic.
`dojo.publish()`	Invokes all listener methods subscribed to a topic.
`dojo.connectPublisher()`	Ensures that every time some function is called, a message is published on the topic.

11.3.2.4 The `dojo.Deferred` Module

This module consists of a single function, `dojo.Deferred`, which is used to provide communication between threads. "Threads!?" you might say. "But I thought that browsers don't support threading." And you would be right—except for the `XMLHttpRequest` object, which does run in its own separate thread. This function provides a generic technique for thread notification. And though we don't quite have one yet, we're just starting to hear about the beginnings of a threading model within JavaScript. So this function will have some special use now and possibly more use in the future as the threading model evolves. We cover this topic more thoroughly in Chapter 17, "Testing and Debugging."

11.3.2.5 The `dojo.json` Module

This module contains functions for working with JavaScript Object Notation (JSON), a text-based protocol for representing objects. It is quite popular in the JavaScript community as a replacement for XML. Table 11.3 summarizes the JSON functions, but we also cover them in more detail in Chapter 13, "Strings and JSON."

Table 11.3   **List of** `dojo.json` **Functions**

Function	Description
`dojo.fromJson()`	Creates an object from a JSON string.
`dojo.toJson()`	Creates a JSON string from an object.

11.3.2.6 The `dojo.array` Module

This module consists of functions that make it easier to work with array objects and other objects that have array-like features. Among other things, the functions provide the capability to easily iterate (loop) through all the elements in an array or iterate just through certain elements.

Table 11.4   **List of** `dojo.array` **Functions**

Function	Description
`dojo.indexOf()`	Returns the first position of a value within an array.
`dojo.lastIndexOf()`	Returns the last position of a value within an array.
`dojo.forEach()`	Provides an array iterator. Assigns a function to be called for each value in an array. The array value will be passed as an argument to the function.
`dojo.every()`	Assigns a function to be called for each value in an array. The array value will be passed as an argument to the function. The function should return a true or false. If all the function calls return true, then `every()` will also return true, otherwise this function will return false.
`dojo.some()`	Assign a function to be called for each value in an array. The array value will be passed as an argument to the function. The function should return a true or false. If any of the function calls return true, then `some()` will also return true; otherwise, this function will return false.
`dojo.map()`	Applies a function to each element of an array and creates an array with the results.
`dojo.filter()`	Returns a new array with those items that match a condition implemented by a callback function.

11.3.2.7 The `dojo.Color` Module

This module consists of functions that allow a developer to represent colors (used internally by Dojo to perform color transitions).

Table 11.5   **List of** `dojo.Color` **Functions**

Function	Description
`dojo.Color()`	Constructor for an object representing a single color. Allows a color to be represented as a type rather than as a specific RGB or Hex value.
`dojo.blendColors()`	Calculates a new color value between two given color values.

Table 11.5   **Continued**

Function	Description
`dojo.colorFromRgb()`	Returns a CSS style color value given a color value specified as an RGB color value.
`dojo.colorFromHex()`	Returns a `dojo.Color` object given a color value specified as a hex string starting with a # prefix.
`dojo.colorFromArray()`	Returns a `dojo.Color` object given an array of RGB color values.
`dojo.colorFromString()`	Returns a `dojo.Color` object given a string containing array values, RGB values, or Hex values representing a color.

11.3.2.8 The `dojo.event` Module

The way that events are handled differs between browsers. The functions in this module provide a consistent behavior for events and event handlers. Events and event handling are covered in much more detail in Chapter 14.

Table 11.6   **List of `dojo.event` Functions**

Function	Description
`dojo.fixEvent()`	Normalizes properties on the event object including event bubbling methods, keystroke normalization, and x/y positions.
`dojo.stopEvent()`	Prevents propagation and terminates the default action of the passed event.
`dojo.keys`	Object containing decimal values for various special keyboard keys. These are constants that can be used to make JavaScript code more readable (i.e., event code can refer to BACKSPACE rather than the decimal value 8). By convention, JavaScript constants are capitalized.

11.3.2.9 The `dojo._base.html` Module

This module consists of functions that can manipulate HTML and DOM objects. To understand how these functions work, you need to understand something called the "box model," which describes the components of a DOM element. For illustrative purposes, Figure 11.4 provides a reproduced a diagram showing the box model from the W3C specification.[3]

3. CSS basic box model, Edited by Bert Bos, August 2007, http://www.w3.org/TR/css3-box/ (Working Draft).

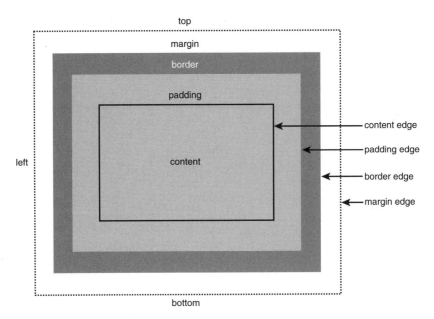

Figure 11.4   CSS box model

Some of the functions in this module allow a developer to access or set "box model" properties for a DOM element.

Table 11.7   **List of** `dojo._base` **Functions**

Function	Description
`dojo.byId()`	Returns a DOM node given a string representing the `id` of the node. Similar to the `$` function in many other class libraries. Basically, shorthand for `document. getElementById(id)`.
`dojo.isDescendant()`	Given two DOM nodes, returns true if one node is a descendant of the other.
`dojo.setSelectable()`	By default, browsers allow a user to select any visible portion of a DOM element. This function can disable that feature or turn it back on for an individual element.
`dojo.place()`	Insert a new DOM element relative to an existing one using one of the following controls: before, after, first, or last. First and last refer to placement in reference to siblings of the node to be inserted.
`dojo.boxModel`	The box model describes the components of a DOM node and is documented in the DOM specification. This property specifies which version of the box model is to be used. The default is "content-box." Some Dojo functions depend on which box model is to be used. The diagram below depicts the standard "content-box" model for DOM nodes.

Table 11.7   **Continued**

Function	Description
dojo.style()	Gets or sets the style property of a DOM node. The style property is specified in DOM accessor format (borderWidth, not border-width).
dojo.marginBox()	In the box model, the four edges around a DOM element's margin are known as its "margin box." This function allows you to get or set that value.
dojo.contentBox()	In the box model, the four edges around the content of a DOM element comprise its "content box." This function allows to you get or set that value.
dojo.coords()	Returns the coordinates for an object. The coordinates include the "margin box" and the absolute positioning data in the form: { l: 50, t: 200, w: 300: h: 150, x: 100, y: 300 }
dojo.hasClass()	For a DOM node, returns true if the node contains the specified class.
dojo.addClass()	Adds a class to a DOM node.
dojo.removeClass()	Removes a class from a DOM node.
dojo.toggleClass()	Adds a class to a DOM node if it is not present and removes the class if it is present.

11.3.2.10 The dojo._base.NodeList **Module**

This module consists of functions for working with a list of DOM elements. A NodeList is a subclass of Array and extends Array to include a plethora of additional handy functions that perform useful manipulations on DOM elements such as chaining, common iteration operations, animation, and node manipulation. Many of the methods in NodeList are versions of methods from the array and html modules, given that a NodeList is really just an array of DOM elements.

The NodeList functions operate a little differently than most other Dojo functions. Most Dojo functions take the object that they operate upon as an argument. Nodelist functions work on the object they are part of. To use these functions you must first create a new NodeList (or get one back from a function) and then run the functions as methods on that object. For example, if you wanted to perform some function on a DOM element with an id of tree, you would use the following code:

```
el = new dojo.NodeList(dojo.byId("tree"));
el.forEach(function() { // some code; });
```

Notice how the forEach method is run on el. The el object is not passed as a parameter to forEach. Also the given NodeList only contains a single element even if the DOM element tree has multiple children.

As a convenience, shortcut functions on `NodeList` provide features that are available on DOM elements directly. By having the functions also appear on a `NodeList`, your code can be smaller and more readable.

Some of the `NodeList` functions are rather complex, and the brief description next may seem inadequate. That is why a number of these functions get a more complete treatment later. For example, the animation functions (`fadeIn`, `fadeout`, and `animateProperty`) are described in more detail in Chapter 16, "Working with the DOM."

Table 11.8   List of Functions Available on a `NodeList` Object

Function	Description
`NodeList()`	A constructor for building a new object of type NodeList that contains a list of DOM elements. The standard constructor takes an element id and creates a `NodeList` containing that element.
`indexOf()`	Returns the numeric index of the first occurrence of a DOM element in the `NodeList`.
`lastIndexOf()`	Returns the numeric index of the last occurrence of a DOM element in the `NodeList`.
`every()`	Assign a function to be called for each element in the `NodeList`. The element will be passed as an argument to the function. The function should return a `true` or `false`. If all the function calls return `true`, then `every()` will also return `true`; otherwise, this function will return `false`.
`some()`	Assign a function to be called for each element in the `NodeList`. The element will be passed as an argument to the function. The function should return a `true` or `false`. If any of the function calls return `true`, then `some()` will also return `true`; otherwise, this function will return `false`.
`forEach()`	Runs a function on each element of a `NodeList`. This function returns the `NodeList` itself to support method chaining.
`map()`	Applies a function to each element of `NodeList` and creates a new `NodeList` with the results.
`coords()`	Returns the coordinates for each element in the `NodeList`. The coordinates include the "margin box" and the absolute positioning data. The function returns an `Array` *not* a `NodeList`.
`style()`	Gets or sets the style property of the first element of the `NodeList`. The style property is specified in DOM accessor format (`borderWidth` not `border-width`). When a style value is not passed to this function, the current style value is returned as a string.
`styles()`	Gets or sets the style property of the all the elements in the `NodeList`. When a style value is not passed to this function, the current style value for each element is returned as an array of strings.

Table 11.8   **Continued**

Function	Description
addClass()	Adds a class to each DOM node in NodeList.
removeClass()	Removes a specified class from each DOM node in NodeList.
place()	This function does quite a bit of heavy lifting. It takes as a parameter a DOM node or CSS3 selector that is used to find a DOM element in the document. Then it inserts the entire NodeList into the document relative to the found element. It inserts the NodeList relative to the found element based on a position parameter also passed to this function. Valid values for position are last, end, first, start, before, or after. The default is end.
connect()	This method attaches event handlers to every node in a NodeList.
orphan()	Removes nodes from document and returns them as a NodeList without parents. In other words, this function "orphans" DOM elements based on a filter passed into the function. All elements passing the filter are orphaned. When a NodeList is first created, the nodes in it exist both in the NodeList and in the document object (so they are on the page). By orphaning some of the nodes, they are removed from the page but still saved in a new NodeList.
adopt()	Places all elements in a specified query or NodeList at a position relative to the first element in this list. Returns a NodeList of the adopted elements.
query()	Uses a query string to select elements from the NodeList. For each selected element, all its children are added as elements to a new NodeList, which is returned by this function. The elements from the original list that were selected in the query are not returned. The Dojo documentation refers to this as "flattening" the NodeList.
filter()	The function provides a version of the filter function available on Array objects. It can be called with either a simple query or with a callback function that is executed against each element in the NodeList.
addContent()	This function takes either a string of HTML or a DOM element and adds it to each element in the NodeList at a specified position relative to each element. Valid values for position are last, end, first, start, before, or after. The default is end.
	This function does not add additional elements to the NodeList. Instead, it adds the elements to document, which changes the displayed page.
fadeIn()	This function will perform the fade in animation on all the elements in a NodeList, which will cause the elements to gradually transition to opaque.
	This function returns an array of objects of type dojo._Animation, which means they must be "played" to run the animation. For example, to fade in all the elements in a NodeList, use fadeIn().play() on the NodeList object.

Table 11.8   **Continued**

Function	Description
fadeOut()	This function will perform the fade out animation on all the elements in a NodeList, which will cause the displayed elements to gradually transition to transparent.
	This function returns an array of objects of type dojo._Animation, which means they must be "played" to run the animation. For example, to fade in all the elements in a NodeList use fadeOut().play() on the NodeList object.
animateProperty()	Returns an animation that will transition the properties of node. This function takes an animation property and transitions it from a beginning value to an ending value. There are a number of animation properties such as color and position that will be explained in more detail in Chapter 16.
	This function returns an array of objects of type dojo._Animation, which means they must be "played" to run the animation. Run the play() function on the returned object.
onmouseover() onclick() onmouseout() onmousemove() onblur() onmousedown() onmouseup() onmousemove() onkeydown() onkeyup() onkeypress()	Each of these methods is available on NodeList. They take an event handler parameter that is assigned to each of the elements in the NodeList. These functions are available on DOM elements directly but also having them on NodeList makes the code shorter and simpler.

11.3.2.11 The dojo._base.query **Module**

This module essentially consists of a single function, dojo.query. This may seem a little unbalanced, especially compared to all the functions in a module like dojo._base.NodeList. But what you'll soon see is that this single function is really quite a monster and extremely powerful.

The Document Object Model (DOM) contains the representation of the web page and for most pages contains a large number of individual elements, sometimes in the thousands. Cascading Style Sheets (CSS) introduced a technique for separating the style of an element from the tag itself but introduced a problem: How could a CSS style be easily applied to one or more page elements when so many elements existed? This problem was solved with a pattern matching language called "CSS selectors," which provided a syntax for identifying HTML elements based on one of their characteristics such as tag type, class, or some attribute value.

Many AJAX techniques also require manipulating elements, so it is very useful to be able to find the few elements you need from the many elements that exist in a typical DOM. The same solution already developed for applying CSS styles can also be used to find DOM elements for AJAX. And that is exactly what `dojo.query` gives us—a technique for using the CSS selector pattern matching language to find DOM elements. You specify the selector string, and the function will return an array of elements meeting that criterion. The array is returned as a `NodeList`, which is an object type that we've already reviewed and has lots of useful methods.

Following is an example of some code that will search the DOM for all HTML `<div>` tag elements that have a class of `codeSample`. The code returns an object of type `NodeList` containing zero or more elements.

```
nl = dojo.query("div.codeSample")
```

We'll explore this function, along with the syntax for CSS selector strings, in Chapter 16.

11.3.2.12 The `dojo._base.xhr` Module

This module consists of functions for working with the XMLHttpRequest (XHR) object, the heart of AJAX. Descriptions here will be brief because we spend more time on these functions in Chapter 15, "Ajax Remoting." The XHR object is used to send a request to the server without doing a page refresh. Different types of HTTP requests may be sent, such as GET and POST. This module provides wrappers that will be used to create the various types of requests. By providing these wrapper functions, Dojo allows your code to be simpler and easier to read than if you used the XHR object directly. It is usually necessary to send some data along with the request. This module also contains a number of useful functions for manipulating data and transferring it from one common format to another.

Table 11.9   **List of** `dojo._base.xhr` **Functions**

Function	Description

`dojo.xhrGet()`
`dojo.xhrPost()`
`dojo.xhrDelete()`
	These functions provide a wrapper around the underlying XHR request objects. Data is passed into the request using the `content` object. Each property in the object will be converted to a name/value pair.

`dojo.rawXhrPost()` `dojo.rawXhrPut()`	These functions provide a wrapper around the underlying XHR request objects. They are termed "raw" because the data to be placed in the body of the request is passed directly into the function using the `postData` property of the argument object.

Table 11.9   **Continued**

Function	Description
dojo.formToObject() dojo.objectToQuery() dojo.formToQuery() dojo.formToJson() dojo.queryToObject()	These are various functions that convert between common data formats. See Chapter 15 for more detail.

11.3.2.13 The dojo._base.fx **Module**

This module consists of a number of functions that can be used to provide basic visual effects on DOM elements. As you can see in Table 11.9, there seems to be a rather limited number of effects, just fadeIn, fadeout, and animateProperty. Although it may not at first seem like much, it turns out that one of the functions, animateProperty, is actually extremely powerful because it lets you work with *any* CSS property.

Some of these functions may remind you of similar functions associated with NodeList, and they should considering they are exactly the same! The difference is that these functions work by being passed a DOM element as the first parameter instead of operating against an array of DOM elements as they do in NodeList.

The signature for these methods is deceivingly simple. They all take a single object as their argument. That object, however, can be quite complex. It should always contain a property called node, which is the id of the element on which to perform the animation. Other properties control the animation itself. We explore these further in Chapter 16.

Table 11.10   **List of** dojo._base.fx **Functions**

Function	Description
dojo.fadeIn()	This function performs the fade in animation on the element specified as the node property in the argument object, which causes the element to gradually transition to opaque. This function returns an object of type dojo._Animation, which means it must be "played" to run the animation.
dojo.fadeOut()	This function performs the fade out animation on the element specified as the node property in the argument object, which causes the element to gradually transition to opaque. This function returns an object of type dojo._Animation, which means it must be "played" to run the animation.

Table 11.10   **Continued**

Function	Description
`dojo.animateProperty()`	Returns an animation that will transition the properties of the specified DOM node. This function takes an animation property and transitions it from a beginning value to an ending value. There are a number of animation properties such as color and position that will be explained in more detail in Chapter 16. This function returns an object of type `dojo._Animation`, which means it must be "played" to run the animation. Run the `play()` function on the returned object.

This ends the discussion of the "base" features. One final note: The technical reason that these are called "base" functions is that the original code for the features (before they are aggregated in `dojo.js`) is contained in the "_base" directory under "dojo," hence the name "base." Let's consider some additional features next. They're termed the "core" functions because they are still important and useful, just not part of "base."

11.3.3 Dojo Core Modules

As you can see from the prior discussion, Dojo has lots of features in its "base" modules. But what else is available? The next set of modules gives us additional functionality, but they are considered to be not quite as essential as "base" features—so they are not included in the base Dojo file and must be requested explicitly by your page. You must include these modules in your page by using the `dojo.require` function and naming the module containing the functions you wish to include.

For example, the following code shows how to use the "core" function `dojo.string.pad` for padding a string containing the text "52" with four leading zeroes.

```
dojo.require("dojo.string");

empID = dojo.string.pad("52", 4, '0');
```

Notice that before you could use `dojo.string.pad`, you needed to include the functions in the `string` module by using `dojo.require`. All the other `string` functions will be available as well. This is similar to the `import` statement in Java, with the exception that `require` causes Dojo to actually include the JavaScript for the `string` module in your page while `import` just makes the class available at compile time without actually including it in the byte code.

11.3.3.1 Dojo Modules

The way that files and directories are organized for "core" features is a little more complex than for "base" features. The organization of related JavaScript functions into files and subdirectories is termed "packaging," and a single group of related functions is called a "module."

Dojo features in the base module are included in the single "dojo.js" (or "dojo.js.uncompressed.js") files, while "core" features are organized in one of two different ways. A "core" module may consist of a single JavaScript file within the "dojo" directory. Or it may consist of a subdirectory under the "dojo" directory. Why two approaches? The primary purpose is two provide the developer with a fine-grained technique for including features within a single page. For example, the `dojo.date` module contains functions related to dates. However, you'll notice that these functions are included in two different JavaScript files ("locale.js" and "stamp.js") contained in a subdirectory called "date" under the main "dojo" directory. The functions in "locale.js" provide various internationalization processes on date strings. The functions in "stamp.js" allow conversion between various common date types. The Dojo architects are anticipating that developers may often need one or the other of these features sets, but not usually both.

A developer can include the functions for internationalization with the following code:

```
dojo.require("dojo.date.locale");
```

This would make the functions in "dojo/date/locale.js" available to the page but not the functions defined in "dojo/date/stamp.js." To include those you would need to provide an additional `dojo.require` statement in your code.

Note: There is a shortcut that provides a technique for including all the files within a module. You can use the * wildcard. The code that follows would make all the functions defined in both of the date files available to your page:

```
dojo.require("dojo.date.*");
```

Be careful when using this approach. While it will certainly work, the reason that Dojo organized the functions into two separate files is so that you don't have to include both of them. By including both in your page, the page may take longer to load and execute. So only include both files if you really need to use the functions in them.

You may notice that there is an additional file containing date functions, "dojo/date.js," which you may use. It contains functions such as `getDaysInMonth()`, which returns the number of days in the same month as a specified `Date` object. To include these functions, use the following code:

```
dojo.require("dojo.date");
```

Notice that this code does not use the wildcard because it is getting a single specific file "dojo/date.js."

Another subtlety in using Dojo modules is that some functions require functions defined in other modules. Those modules also need to be included in your page for the code to work properly. The `dojo.date.locale` functions are examples of this. To work, they also need the following modules to be included:

- `dojo.date`
- `dojo.cldr.supplemental`
- `dojo.regexp`
- `dojo.string`
- `dojo.i18n`

At this point, you may be breaking out into a cold sweat. How can you possibly be expected to know all the dependencies between various Dojo modules? The good news as that you don't have to. Dojo modules contain this information. Near the top of the file "dojo/date/locale.js" you can find the following lines of code that cause Dojo to load all the dependent modules:

```
dojo.require("dojo.date");
dojo.require("dojo.cldr.supplemental");
dojo.require("dojo.regexp");
dojo.require("dojo.string");
dojo.require("dojo.i18n");
```

We've now exhausted the various approaches to including date-related Dojo functions in your page. The date module uses all the various approaches to packaging available in Dojo and is a good module to study to understand the techniques. However, most of the modules are simpler. So after you understand how the date module works, the others will be more obvious.

The Dojo packaging system is very powerful and allows us to achieve the best of all possible worlds (at least in the context of loading JavaScript files!).

- We can load only the functions we want, keeping our pages small and minimizing the amount of included JavaScript code.
- We can use functions with dependencies on other modules without knowing what the dependencies are.
- We can keep the number of `require` statements small by using the wildcard features of module loading.

As a final comment, much thought and effort have gone into the creation of the Dojo packaging system. It addresses the problems of making complex JavaScript code available to a web page. You will face the same problems in organizing the JavaScript code that you write yourself. And the good news is that you can use the Dojo packaging system on your own code!

11.3.3.2 Dojo Core Features

There are a number of Dojo "core" modules, some of which are so important and useful that they require their own chapters to describe them. So for now, we examine them at a summary level, merely describing their purpose without delineating the functions they contain.

Table 11.11 summarizes the purpose of the primary "core" modules in Dojo. (*Note:* If you're checking for completeness, there are a few modules I've skipped because you are unlikely to use them such as `AdapterRegistry`).

Table 11.11   **Dojo Modules**

Module name (used in the `require` statement)	Description of Module
`dojo.back`	Functions for working with the browser "back" button and maintains a history of URLs.
`dojo.behavior`	Functions for associating other functions (behaviors) with DOM elements.
`dojo.cookie`	Functions for reading and writing browser cookies.
`dojo.currency`	Functions for working with numbers that represent currency.
`dojo.data`	Functions for accessing persistence data sources.
`dojo.date`	Functions for working with `Date` objects.
`dojo.date.locale`	Functions for internationalizing dates.
`dojo.date.stamp`	Functions for converting between common types of date formats.
`dojo.dnd`	Functions for implementing "Drag and Drop" capabilities on DOM elements.
`dojo.fx`	Functions for adding visual effects to DOM elements.
`dojo.i18n`	Functions for performing internationalization.
`dojo.io`	Functions for using `<iframe>` and for generating `<script>` tags dynamically.
`dojo.number`	Functions to manipulate and format numbers.
`dojo.parser`	Functions for reading HTML (or the elements created from HTML) and producing additional objects.
`dojo.regexp`	Functions for using Regular Expressions.
`dojo.string`	Functions for manipulating string objects.

This concludes are introductory discussion of the Dojo "base" and "core" features. As you can see, Dojo covers a broad range of functionality. Subsequent chapters allow us to explore these features in more detail and review more examples of actual usage.

Summary

Dojo "base" functions are contained in "dojo.js" and are always available to the page when using Dojo by using the `<script>` tag to include the "dojo.js" file.

Dojo "core" features must be explicitly requested by the page using the `dojo.require()` function.

The Dojo packaging system allows a web developer to specify which Dojo functions (and related JavaScript files) are included on a page.

The Dojo packaging system is available to developers to package their own JavaScript code.

The next chapter provides an overview of using Object Oriented Programming (OOP) techniques when working with Dojo. This is important because the Dojo features are exposed to developers as objects. So if you not familiar with OOP, as Bette Davis once famously said, "Get ready for a bumpy ride." Only kidding, OOP concepts aren't really that difficult, and after you understand them, you'll be able to program in a new and useful way.

12

Objects and Classes

Crude classifications and false generalizations are the curse of organized life.

—George Bernard Shaw (1856–1950)

Organizing the artifacts of your application into appropriate classes is one of the key goals of Object Oriented (OO) Analysis and Design. JavaScript is a fully Object Oriented language, and to achieve its full power we need to take full advantage of its OO features. However, we'll see that Dojo provides some additional ways to work with the OO feature set of JavaScript that you'll find really helpful when defining new classes and creating new objects. This chapter explores Objects, the OO features of JavaScript, and the OO enhancements provided by Dojo.

12.1 Objects Explained

JavaScript is an object oriented language. An application written in JavaScript exists at run-time as a clamorous conversation of objects interacting with each other through their method calls. Another way to say this is that in JavaScript "EIAO" (Everything Is An Object). This view of an application is different than the procedural approach in which you can think of a program simply as a sequence of instructions (a procedure) to be executed in sequential order with the occasional detour provided by conditional or looping statements. You may not have thought of JavaScript as a fully mature object oriented programming environment but, if you haven't, now is the time to start.

But what is an object? The classical definition in object oriented design describes an object as a separate entity within an application that implements some behavior and contains some internal representation of its state. A more concrete way to think about objects in JavaScript is to describe them as a sequence of run-time memory containing data and functions that can be referenced and manipulated as a single entity. There are many objects built into JavaScript such as the "document" object, which encapsulates the browser's internal representation of the current web page (the Document Object Model or DOM) and contains many methods to allow the DOM to be manipulated in some way. But the real power in using objects in JavaScript is to create your own custom objects to represent the various important entities in your application.

12.1.1 Creating Objects

So the first lesson in using objects is to see how you can create objects of your own. There are many ways of creating objects. The simplest way is to create an object using the new keyword.

Although it is the simplest, it is also the least functional. An object is a collection of properties, and in JavaScript these properties can be either pointers to other objects such as arrays and functions or simple properties like strings and numbers. One of the key pillars of an object oriented programming language is its ability to represent an abstraction. For instance, a customer application does not consist of little tiny customers running around inside our computer, but instead it consists of objects representing those customers interacting with each other and with other components in the system.

12.1.2 Encapsulation

Another key pillar of object orientation is encapsulation. This is the ability to wall off an object, separating the inside of the object from the outside world. The inside of an object is known as its implementation. Access to the outside world is provided through methods that are called by other objects. For example, an employee object might contain a method called getAge that returns the age of the employees. But how does the object implement this function? Does it do it by keeping track of the age of the employee as an integer and updating this age annually on the employee's birthday? Or does the object keep track of the employee's date of birth and then calculate the employees age each time that the object is asked to getAge? The answer is that "we don't know and we don't care." As long as the getAge method always returns the correct age of the employee, the implementation is not relevant. Over the life of the object, the implementation could even change to use a better algorithm or improve performance. To the outside world, as long as the external interface to the object does not change, any part of the application using the object is unaffected by internal changes in the object's implementation. And that is the value of encapsulation—to allow the object to present a public face to the world while managing its own private concerns.

Let's explore how the public face of the object is created. The developer of the object defines properties and methods that will be available in the object. Some properties are simple data types such as strings or numbers. Other properties are more complex and may be pointers to other objects. The methods consist of both the internal functions that the object needs to perform its implementation and the external functions that are available to the outside world so that the object can be used. A simple customer object might have properties such as customerID, "customerName, customerType, and customerStatus. Although it would be possible to change the status of the customer simply by changing the property, we may choose to implement this by hiding the actual property that describes status and use a public method such as updateStatus to allow us to change the way the status is internally represented within the object.

The OO principal of *encapsulation* defines the technique of hiding some properties and methods from the outside world while exposing others. In many languages this is accomplished through the use of a "public" and "private" keyword, which designates members within the object as being hidden or visible. JavaScript does not implement public and private directly but does provide a technique for hygiene properties and methods within an object. In other words, it is possible to have functions defined within an object that are only callable by other functions within the object and not by external calls to the object. Douglas Crockford provides an excellent description of how to do this on his web site:

```
http://www.crockford.com/javascript/private.html
```

Because JavaScript objects are mutable (modifiable), new properties and methods can be added to the object at any time simply by referencing a member and giving it a value. Our first technique for creating objects is to create a new object using the new keyword and then to assign various properties using the dot notation.

```
o1 = new Object();
o1.counter = 0;
o1.incrementCounter = function() {this.counter++;}
```

The code here creates a new object containing a single property called counter, which has a starting value of numeric 0. The object also contains a function called incrementCounter, which adds 1 to the current value of counter.

The problem with this approach is that each time we create a new instance of an object type, all the properties and methods must be explicitly assigned. If there are any default values, they must be set. All of the members must be defined, and there is no way to use existing definitions for these properties and methods. This is a fairly unsatisfactory approach for most object oriented developers. Given the size and complexity of most applications today, it is very useful to be able to have a standard template for what a new instance of an object should look like. This provides for an important level of reuse necessary to ensure our productivity.

12.1.3 Object Templates

There are two primary techniques for providing object templates. The first technique is to define the template explicitly as its own entity. A blueprint for how to build the object is created in its own separate file as a class definition. This option is utilized by the Java programming language by allowing developers to create class definitions in their own ".java" files. These template blueprints are very much like the blueprint for a house. When you desire to build a new house, you create the house from an existing blueprint. There's no limit to how houses you may create from the same blueprint, just as there is no limit to how many objects may be created from the class definition.

Note

Just about every object oriented programming language follows an approach similar to that used by Java. JavaScript is one of the few exceptions.

In Java, after the new object is created from its class definition, the properties and methods defined in that object cannot change. No properties can be added or taken away, and no new methods can be defined or removed. The values of the properties can be changed, of course, but not the existence of the properties. In Java, class definition files are compiled and included with the application at runtime, and they can be used over and over again to create as many instances of an object as the application programmer desires.

JavaScript is not constrained by limitation imposed in Java. JavaScript does not use the class definition technique. JavaScript uses an entirely different approach known as a *prototype*. Rather than creating a new house from an existing blueprint, an existing house is copied to build a new one. JavaScript objects are built from existing JavaScript objects. You can think of a prototype as acting as the model for the new object.

While the analogy to building objects in Java is like building houses from blueprints, a better analogy for JavaScript is the creation of new objects by copying existing objects. If you copy a 20-page document, your new document will also be 20 pages long, and it will in turn contain all the text and the typos of the original document. To use the prototype technique for creating new objects, it is necessary to have an existing object containing the properties and methods that you want the new object to possess.

Although the prototype process is the technique that JavaScript uses to build new objects, it doesn't implement it as directly as you might expect. For instance, there is no "clone" or "build from" function or keyword in JavaScript that allows you to directly build a new object from an existing object. Rather the technique is a little more circuitous. To define a prototype to be used as a model for creating new objects, an additional object called the constructor must also be defined. The constructor is a function used to build and initialize new instances of an object for a given data type. The constructor function is called when the new keyword is used in JavaScript. The constructor function can contain assignments for the properties and methods of the new object.

There are still a few problems with this approach. By defining the functions within the constructor, we are repeating code for the functions in every instance of an object that is created from the constructor. Because functions can be rather large and because there is duplication of the exact same function code in each object, this approach provides us with objects that are much larger than necessary. And if we desire to remove a function from each instance of the object or to change the function, it would be necessary to find all the existing objects of that datatype and to explicitly manipulate each one to either remove or change the function. We would also be missing out on one of our key pillars of object oriented programming: inheritance. Inheritance is the ability for an object of one type to inherit properties and methods from an object of their type.

12.1.4 JavaScript Prototypes

Fortunately both of these problems can be solved by using JavaScript prototypes. To understand prototypes, we first have to discuss constructors. A constructor is an object of type function that will be executed when we want to create a new instance of an object. Following is an example of a constructor called `DataItem`, which can be used to create an unlimited number of new objects of type `DataItem`.

```
function DataItem() {this.counter = 0;};  // Constructor function

d1 = new DataItem();  // Create a new object of type DataItem

d1.counter++;  // this increments the counter
```

In the given code, the object `d1` contains the following properties and methods: `{counter: 0}`.

The secret to using constructor functions is to make sure that the data type following the new keyword is the same as the name of the constructor function. By convention, it is typical to capitalize constructor function names to differentiate them from other functions.

All constructor functions have a property called `prototype`. This property points to the object to be used as a model for the new object to be built from the constructor. By default this prototype object is a simple object that looks very much like the `Object` data type. It has a small number of properties and methods. These are the same properties and methods that appear in the `Object` object (no that isn't a typo; there is an object of type `Object`, which all other objects inherit from!). The prototype property of the constructor function is automatically initialized with a pointer to this empty prototype object. But it is simple to override the default prototype object with one of our own. By using the `function.prototype` reference, we can assign it to an existing object, which will then act as the model for the new object we want to build.

But even using this technique, the prototype is not used to create the new object. It is used to contain properties that will be referenced through the new object. For example, a customer constructor has a reference to a customer prototype that can be used to create as many new instances of customer type objects as desired. We could define all the properties and methods that all customers should have in the customer prototype. You might think that a new instance of customer would have these properties and methods copied into it, but you would be wrong. What actually happens is that a new object is created, and that object has a property that points to its constructor. When a property or method of customer is referenced in the newly created instance, the JavaScript runtime environment takes over. It first looks for the property in the object instance, and if it is there it will use it. But if it is not there, the JavaScript runner works its way up through the prototype chain until it finds the property or gets to the end of the chain.

For example, if the program needs to reference the `customerType` property in a new customer object, we would use the dot notation `c.customerType` to reference the property. The JavaScript runner would first look for the property in the `customer` object, but it would not find it. Then it would use the object's constructor property to find the constructor function for `customer`. Then using the constructor functions property called `prototype`, the JavaScript runner would find the prototype object and see if it had the type property. In our example, `customerType` would be a property of the customer prototype object.

Sadly, one solution seems to create a new set of problems for us. Different instances of objects of `Customer` type would have the same constructor function, and that single constructor function would point to a single prototype object. If one instance of an object changed a property in the customer prototype, then all the instances of the customer objects would get that new property. This might not be what we really want to happen. Instead we may want each instance of the object to get its own values of the properties. This can be accomplished by assigning the properties directly in the constructor function using the `this` keyword to prefix the properties as in `this.customerType` as the following example demonstrates.

```
function Customer() {  // Constructor function
    this.customerType = "RETAIL";
}
```

You'll notice that we still want to keep the function definitions within the prototype because they can be shared between different instances of the `Customer` objects. One last twist—the prototype objects also have a property called `prototype` that can be used to point to another object that will behave as the first prototype object does. It will be used by the JavaScript runner to continue to look for properties and methods not defined in the object itself or in the object's prototype. This is known as *prototype chaining*.

12.2 Using Dojo to Work with Objects

We've now reviewed various ways of creating and using objects in JavaScript. But, after all, this is a Dojo book and not simply a JavaScript book. What role does Dojo play, if any, in helping us to use objects? There is a certain amount of complexity in using objects in JavaScript. Your goal may be a simple one: creating a template from which new objects of a particular type may be built. But JavaScript provides many features for doing this from the use of prototypes to constructors to private members. Though JavaScript provides a number of ways to create and use objects, all of them are problematic and inconvenient at best. The developers of Dojo, working to create a JavaScript toolkit, faced the same problems all JavaScript developers do. Luckily, the Dojo developers created something better: an idiom and supporting code for defining classes.

Dojo provides value by giving us a standard idiom for defining classes (the templates from which objects are built). An *idiom* is a specific syntactic structure for a language. Dojo provides us with this specific structure in the form of a function call with various parameters to allow the definition of a class. We will achieve our goal of creating an object class definition in a single standard Dojo function call. And, drum roll please, that function is `dojo.declare`!

12.2.1 Dojo Function: `dojo.declare`

The `dojo.declare` function is used to create a constructor that can be used to create object with the `new` keyword. It can also automatically create a prototype with properties and methods. A prototype chain can also be created automatically. This is a very powerful function and is used extensively throughout the Dojo library code. It is also one of the most common functions that you will use in your own application code. So spending some time learning how to use this function properly is certainly time well spent.

Let's examine a number of typical scenarios that may appear in your application code when you wish to create a new class definition. First let's look at the simplest possible usage for `dojo.declare`. We'll create a constructor for a new type of object that doesn't even provide any properties, methods, or superclasses for the object.

```
dojo.declare("DataItem");

d1 = new DataItem();
```

In the preceding code the object `d1` contains the following properties and methods:

```
{
    "preamble": null,
    "_initializer": null,
    "declaredClass": "DataItem"
}
```

Calling `dojo.declare` creates a constructor function that you can use as you would any normal constructor function. The example shows a constructor named `DataItem`, which has been created by Dojo. The following code shows the plain JavaScript technique for creating constructors as a comparison to the Dojo technique.

```
function DataItem() {};

d1 = new DataItem();
```

In this code the object `d1` contains the following properties and methods: { }.

The object created using Dojo isn't exactly the same as the object created through the regular constructor. It contains a few extra properties (`preamble` and `_initializer`, which we can ignore for now). It also contains a property called `declaredClass`, which contains the name of the class we are trying to create. Although this name is the same as the name of the constructor, we shouldn't think of it that way. Think of it as the name of the class definition.

12.3 Defining a Class

Now let's look at a more complex class definition that contains some properties and methods. We'll use a `Customer` type object for our example. We'll be providing a custom definition of all the members (properties and methods) that a `Customer` object will have.

```
var init = function(name) {
    this.name = name;
    this.status = "ACTIVE";
    this.makeInactive = function() {
        this.status = "INACTIVE";}
    };
```

```
dojo.declare("Customer", null, init);
```

In the preceding code the object d1 contains the following properties and methods:

```
{
"name": "Tom Jones",
"status": "ACTIVE",
"declaredClass": "Customer",
"preamble": null
}
```

This constructor will create a new object with some object specific properties and functions. Unfortunately, there is still a problem. The function makeInactive will exist in each new object that is created. A better way to define the function would be to put it on the prototype for the constructor. This could be done inside the init function by using a reference to "this.constructor.prototype", but Dojo provides a simpler method. The following code illustrates how to add members to the prototype by using the props parameter.

```
var init = function(name) {
    this.name = name;
    this.type = "REGULAR";
    this.status = "ACTIVE";
    };
```

```
var props = {
    makeInactive: function() {this.status = "INACTIVE";}
    };
```

```
dojo.declare("Customer", null, init, props);
```

Now the object is correctly created with the method definition ensconced safely on the prototype object sharing the single copy of the function among all the instances of Customer objects. The props parameter contains an object that has members (both properties and functions) that will be added to the prototype of the constructor only if the member is not already defined in the object.

12.3.1 Superclasses and Inheritance

One of the most important features of an object orientated language is the ability to implement inheritance. Think of inheritance as the power to define a new class by extending an existing class. The existing class is called the superclass, and the new class is called the subclass. We can implement a hierarchy of classes by continuing to extend the subclass by defining its own subclass! The benefit is that we can reuse code that we've already written. In the next example, we'll see how to create a new type of Customer class called `RetailCustomer` by using our existing `Customer` data type. Retail Customers have some additional properties to identify the state that taxes them and the discount percentage that we'll offer them as a special type of customer.

```
var props = { discountPercent: 0};

var init = function( name, taxingState ) {
    // "name" parameter is used by superclass constructor
    this.type = "RETAIL";
    this.status = "ACTIVE";
    this.taxingState = taxingState;
    };

dojo.declare("RetailCustomer", Customer, init, props);

c1 = new RetailCustomer("ABC Photos", "IL");
```

When a new `RetailCustomer` object is created, the constructor for `superclass` runs first, and then the `init` function for the subclass runs. So `init` can override values provided by `superclass`. The `superclass` function is named so because it acts as an inheritance mechanism that can be overridden in the subclass. This provides reuse of the code from the `superclass`. The `init` function contains arguments for all the arguments required by the `superclass` constructor in addition to any it needs for its own work. Why not put the property `discountPercent` in the constructor and assign it to 0 there? That way would work, but by convention we reserve the constructor for properties that are dependent on what parameters are passed to the constructor when the object is created. So to be more correct, we should really move the assignment of type and `status` from the `init` function to the `props` object.

12.3.2 API for `dojo.declare`

The following table describes the arguments used when calling the `dojo.declare` method. The method signature is: `dojo.declare(className, superclass, init, props)`.

Table 12.1   **Description of** `dojo.declare` **Function**

Parameter Name	Parameter Data Type	Description and Usage of Parameter
`className`	String	Class Name.
		The name of the constructor (loosely, a "class"). All classes are concrete. Abstract classes are not supported.
`superclass`	Function or Array of Functions	Superclass.
		If it is an array, the first element is used as the prototypical ancestor, and any following functions become `mixin` ancestors.
		Specify `null` when there is no superclass. Using `null` is the equivalent of the `no-args` default constructor in Java.
`init`	Function	Constructor Function.
		An initializer function called when an object is instantiated from this constructor. Properties can be added in this function by using the `this` keyword. Since all members are added directly to the new object, use this function primarily for properties and add functions using `props`. Methods could also be added to the prototype using "`this.prototype.functionName`" reference, but that is not preferred.
		This parameter is not required. If the `init` parameter passed is not of type Function, it is treated as the `prop` parameter instead (the `declare` function rearranges the properties), and then `prop` is not required.
		Why use `init`? Use `init` to run some code when the object is created. This is most like the constructor method in Java. This function can also take parameters that would be passed into it when the constructor is called—i.e., new `Customer("Tom", 100)` would pass two parameters into init function.
		When using `init` with superclasses, be sure and repeat the parameters for the superclass `init` function as the first parameters to the subclass `init` function.

Table 12.1   **Continued**

Parameter Name	Parameter Data Type	Description and Usage of Parameter
props	Object or Array of Objects	Properties object.
		An object (or array of objects) whose properties are copied to the created prototype. The created object doesn't directly have these properties.
		The properties are added to the instance of the object created. Any functions are also added to the instance. To add functions to the prototype, add the functions to the array superclass passed as the second parameter.
		These are like the member declarations in Java. Properties and methods are declared but not executed when the object is created.
		A form of interfaces can be supported by adding properties for other object types here.

12.3.3 Other Dojo Functions

In addition to the dojo.declare function, Dojo also provides some other useful functions for working with objects. If you ever read the source code for the dojo.declare method (and you should), you'll see that many of these functions are used internally to implement the declare function. But there is nothing to prevent you from using them directly, and they are so useful that you'll probably find many opportunities to do just that.

Dojo Function: dojo.mixin

Table 12.2   **Description of** dojo.mixin **Function**

Method Signature:	dojo.mixin(obj, props)
Summary:	This method adds all of the properties and methods of one object to another object. Only members that are actually in the source property are copied. In other words, members in the prototype are not copied. Also if the target object already has the member, then it is not copied, even if the value in the source object is different.
Parameter: obj	The object that is to be augmented with additional properties and methods.
Parameter: props	An object containing properties and methods that will be added to the object referenced by obj.

Dojo Function: `dojo.extends`

Table 12.3   **Description of `dojo.extends` Function**

Method Signature:	`dojo.extends( constructor, props)`
Summary:	This method adds all of the properties and methods of one object to the prototype of constructor function. The members are immediately available to any objects already created from the constructor and all future objects to be created from that constructor.
Parameter: `constructor`	The constructor function whose prototype is to be augmented with additional properties and methods.
Parameter: `props`	An object containing properties and methods that will be added to the object's prototype referenced by `obj`.

12.3.4 Object Graphs and Dot Notation

The next group of Dojo functions are needed to make dot notation easier to use. So we'll have to discuss dot notation first. And to discuss dot notation, we have to talk about *object graphs*. Some of the following will be review for many of you, but it never hurts to reinforce the concepts of objects.

As has been said before, in JavaScript applications "Everything Is An Object" (EIAO). For all of us who have drunk of the Object Oriented Kool-Aid (and if you have not, I can get you some!), we believe that everything in the world can be described as an object. Leaving the larger existential question alone, we can probably at least agree that everything in memory during the running of an object oriented application is an object. And that certainly applies to JavaScript. We can think of our page running within the browser as consisting of a large number of objects interacting with each other.

Each object is distinct. This is important as it satisfies one of the primary pillars of object orientation: encapsulation. Encapsulation is the characteristic of allowing a thing to be separate from all other things. Each object exists as its own capsule (that is, it is encapsulated). But encapsulation should only go so far. If objects were so perfectly trapped within their capsules that nothing could get in or out, that they could not see the properties of other objects or that those other objects could not see their properties or run their methods, then our application would be pretty useless. It would be like a box of rocks. Existing in their perfect solid state but not interacting with each other—and nothing useful could come of it.

To achieve some purpose, the objects must interact with each other, and one way of doing this is to refer to each other. Think of object A as having a reference to object B. These references are contained in the properties of objects.

For example, an object representing a Customer may have a property named `orders`, which would contain a list of references to Order objects. Although each of the Customer objects and each of the Order objects are independent instances of objects, they are related through their references to each other. Imagine the objects as round spheres floating in the application memory space and the properties as cords connecting various objects. Now, in this thought experiment, grab an object and pull on it. What happens? Not only do you retrieve the object you grabbed, but it pulls along all the objects that it references, and they in turn pull various other referenced objects along with them. This bundle of objects you have retrieved is called an *object graph*. And the single object you grabbed is the *root Object*. In an object oriented application, there are as many object graphs as there are objects. And each object graph is "like a box of chocolates—you never know what you're gonna get." When you pull on an object, you may just get that single object—or that one and a few others. Or maybe every object in the system is somehow connected.

Object graphs can be large, complex, and even self-referential. What happens when an object deep within the graph references an object within its chain or even the root object? But we've gone a bit too far. Let's return to somewhat simple object graphs that aren't too large and don't have circular references. How do we use object graphs within a program? How do we reference an object or property deep within the object graph? Let's answer these questions with an example.

```
c1 = new Customer("Tom Jones");
c2 = new LargeCustomer("ABC Photo");
c2.subsidiary = c1;

subName = c2.subsidiary.name;
```

In this example, the reference `c2.subsidiary.name` is used to refer to the `name` property in the `subsidiary` object referenced by object `c2`. This is valid syntax, and this example works in JavaScript. However, the problem with using dot notation directly in JavaScript is that if any reference in the chain fails, an error occurs because of a null reference. In other words, the reference to `name` will fail if the `subsidiary` property has not yet been assigned. And it fails badly, causing a syntax error and ending execution of any additional JavaScript code.

The fix provided by Dojo for this is to test each reference to make sure an object is there, and when there isn't, to return a null immediately. The following functions, which make use of dot notation, can now be described.

Dojo Function: `dojo.getObject`

Table 12.4 **Description of `dojo.getObject` Function**

Method Signature:	`dojo.getObject(name, create, context)`
Summary:	This method returns a property value from an object graph using dot notation. It is useful for long reference chains where it is not certain that each property has a value.
Parameter: `name`	Path of property in the form "a.b.c".
Parameter: `create`	This parameter is optional and may be true or false.
	If true, an object is created for each item referenced in the chain where an object does not already exist.
Parameter: `context`	Optional. When specified, this is an object to be used as the root of the object graph; otherwise, `dojo.global` will be used as the starting point for the reference.

Dojo Function: `dojo.setObject`

Table 12.5 **Description of `dojo.setObject` Function**

Method Signature:	`dojo.getObject(name, create, context)`
Summary:	This method sets a property value in an object graph using dot notation. It is useful for long reference chains where it is not certain that each property has a value.
Parameter: `name`	Path of property in the form "a.b.c".
Parameter: `value`	This is the value that the property specified by `name` will be set to.
Parameter: `context`	Optional. When specified, this is an object to be used as the root of the object graph, otherwise `dojo.global` will be used as the starting point for the reference.

Dojo Function: `dojo.exists`

Table 12.6 **Description of `dojo.exists` Function**

Method Signature:	`dojo.exists(name, object)`
Summary:	This method returns a boolean value based on whether the object referenced by the `name` parameter using dot notation exists or not. If the object exists, this method returns true otherwise it returns false.
Parameter: `name`	Path of property in the form "a.b.c".
Parameter: `object`	This parameter is optional. When specified, it is used as the starting point for the `name` reference. Otherwise, `dojo.global` is used.

Dojo Function: `dojo.isObject`

Table 12.7   **Description of** `dojo.isObject` **Function**

Method Signature:	`dojo.isObject(anything)`
Summary:	This method returns a boolean value based on whether the reference passed to the method points to an object. A reference to any object, array, or function will evaluate as true. If the reference is "undefined," this method will return false.
Parameter: `anything`	Any reference.

Summary

JavaScript is a fully object oriented language. Wrap your mind around that fact and take advantage of it!

The function `dojo.declare` is used to define classes that can be used to create new objects using the standard JavaScrip keyword `new`.

Dojo also provides some additional useful functions for working with objects such as

`dojo.mixin`...Merges the properties of one object with another

`dojo.extends`...Merges one objects properties with another objects prototype

`dojo.setObject`...Sets a property within an object graph

`dojo.getObject`...Gets a property within an object graph

`dojo.exists`...Tests a property in an object graph for existence

`dojo.isObject`...Tests a reference to see if it is an object

In the next chapter we'll discover how to work with Strings, one of the most common data types used in most applications.

Strings and JSON

Few can touch the magic String, and noisy Fame is proud to win them...

—Oliver Wendell Holmes, 1809–1894

13.1 Text Strings

The manipulation of strings is one of the most common processes performed by most computer applications. By some estimates, over 30% of the typical program is devoted to working with strings. Hopefully whatever language you might choose to write your programs in will provide many varied and robust string manipulation functions and methods. In this aspect, JavaScript will not disappoint you. JavaScript provides over 20 methods associated with the string object. However, even this seemingly abundant functionality will usually turn out to be not quite enough.

Remember, a good API will allow a programmer to express his programming goals in as small a coding idiom as possible, usually a single function call. For example, your goal may be to make sure that a string is of a certain fixed length. Using JavaScript alone, you could achieve this goal in a small number of lines of code. However, there is no single function in JavaScript that will let you do this in a single statement. It turns out that this would be a pretty useful function to have. So Dojo provides it for us with the `dojo.string.pad` function. Dojo also provides another string function, `dojo.string.substitute`, which will allow you to change a string by substituting some part of the string for another.

We could imagine lots of additional Dojo functions that could help us achieve string manipulation goals in a single statement, but the team that developed Dojo also had some other objectives in mind. They wanted to keep Dojo as small as possible so that it would load faster and be easy to learn. Dojo has to support objectives that are, at times, at cross purposes with each other. It should be big enough to be useful (because of its breadth) and yet should also be small enough to be useful (because of its small footprint). In the category of string manipulation, Dojo supports both objectives by depending on the existing string primitives supported by native JavaScript to be sufficient for most cases. And for those additional special cases, Dojo provides a few string primitives, the already mentioned pad and substitute. Let's now dive more deeply into these Dojo string functions.

The Dojo string functions are part of "core" not "base." What this means is that they are not automatically available when you include the Dojo on your page. They must be imported using the dojo.require function. This is easy to do by just adding the following code to your page:

```
dojo.require("dojo.string")
```

13.1.1 Dojo Function: dojo.string.pad

This function is used to add leading or trailing characters to a string and to ensure that the string is at least a minimum length. Although it certainly would be possible to achieve this goal using the existing JavaScript String functions, the dojo.string.pad function allows us to do it in a single step, resulting in much more readable code. One of the typical uses for this function is to provide leading zeros on numbers when supporting the display of currency, dates, and other specialized number formats.

Following is the API for the dojo.string.pad function:

Table 13.1   **Description of** dojo.string.pad **Function**

Method Signature:	dojo.string.pad(string, size, char, end)
Summary:	Ensure that a string is of at least a specified size by putting characters at either the beginning or end of the string.
Parameter: string	String to be padded.
	The string will not be modified. Instead, a new string will be returned.
Parameter: size	Length of the string to be padded.
	If the length of the string is already greater than or equal to "size," the return string is the same as the original string.
Parameter: char	Character used to pad the string.
	Optional. If "char" is more than one character in length, it will still be padded onto the string that would result in a new string with a length greater than "size."
	Default is 0.
Parameter: end	Flag to put padding at beginning or end of string.
	Optional. If end is true, padding will be applied to the end of the string; otherwise, the string will be padded at the beginning.
	The default value is false.

This function does not change the string that it is evaluating. Instead, it returns a new string. Remember, in JavaScript, strings are "immutable." That means they can't be changed, rather a new string must be returned. The Dojo string functions take a string as a parameter, but they leave that string unchanged. The function returns a new string instance. This is also the way that the standard JavaScript string functions operate so Dojo strives to be consistent.

13.1.2 Usage Example for `dojo.string.pad`

Because the string functions are not included in `dojo.js`, it is necessary to import them using the `dojo.require` function.

```
dojo.require("dojo.string");
fractional = 27;
pad = 4;
valueParts = dojo.string.pad(fractional, pad, '0', false);
```

This code takes a string `fractional` and pads it to a length `pad` with leading zeros. Remember, the final parameter `false` causes the padding to be put at the beginning of `fractional`. The string `fractional` is not modified. The variable `valueParts` will now have a value of `0027;`. Notice the integer "27" is being automatically converted to a string.

13.1.3 Dojo Function: `dojo.string.substitute`

As Murphy said, "If anything can go wrong, it will," and that is certainly as true in computer applications as in many other of life's endeavors. A common feature of our code will be to search for things that go wrong and notify the user with error messages. Error messages can be both general and specific. For example, if some user input is required but missing, the user may get a general error message such as "Field missing." However, it is usually more helpful to get a specific error message like "Last name is missing." The drawback to having very specific error messages is that the number of them can multiply very quickly, which can be an especially serious problem in JavaScript when we are trying to minimize the size of the page sent to the browser. Storing lots of possible error messages in the HTML file could cause its size to grow quickly.

Specific error messages often have a common form. Imagine some possible error messages that might occur in a typical Customer entry form:

```
Last name required.
        First name required.
        City required.
```

All these can be replaced with an error message in the more general form:

```
        ${0} required.
```

Where ${0} is a token that can be replaced with the specific field name when appropriate. This allows the page to display specific error messages that can be very helpful to the user, while at the same time minimizing the amount of space taken up by JavaScript code. The 0 in the token represents the first parameter that can be substituted into the message. Additional tokens could be used to allow more parameters to be substituted into the message.

```
File '${0}' is not found in directory '${1}'.
```

In this case, ${0} would be replaced with a file name, and ${1} would be replaced with the name of a directory.

```
File 'George.jpg' is not found in directory 'c:\Pictures'.
```

Dojo provides a simple string function to make these kinds of parameter replacements easy. That function is dojo.string.substitute. It not only allows a string to have parameters injected into it, but it can perform processing on those parameters before the injection to provide extra formatting. Dojo also makes the token easier to read by using meaningful strings instead of just numbers as in the following example:

```
${fieldName} required.
```

The new token identifier fieldName is more meaningful then 0.
Following is the API description for the "substitute" function:

Table 13.2   **Description of** dojo.string.substitute **Function**

Method Signature:	dojo.string.substitute(template, map, transform, thisObject)
Summary:	Performs parameterized substitutions on a string.
Parameter: template	String containing tokens to be replaced.
	Parameter tokens will be represented in template by text in the form of the form ${key} or ${key:format}. The later form specifies the name of a formatting function, which can be applied to the parameter. The name of the formatting function should correspond to the name in the token.
Parameter: map	Object or Array containing values to be substituted into template. The properties in the object should have names corresponding to the token values.
Parameter: transform	Function used to process the values before they are substituted into template. The transform function will be run after any formatting functions.
Parameter: thisObject	Object containing the formatting functions to be used for tokens that are in the form ${key:format}.
	Optional. If this parameter is not used, the global namespace will be used for the location of the formatting functions.

A little more needs to be said about formatting functions. These are custom functions created to perform various kinds of formatting before the value is substituted into the template string. The types of formatting functions are completely up to you. You write them and give them whatever name you wish. Just be sure that the name you give the function corresponds to the value in the token. For example, `${lastName:upperCase}` would run the `upperCase` function on the `lastName` parameter to be substituted into the `template`. Formatting functions should take a single unformatted value and return a formatted value.

13.1.4 Usage Example for `dojo.string.substitute`

We'll start with a simple example first. Our template string will provide an error message for fields that require a dollar amount of at least a certain value.

```
${fieldName} must be less than ${dollarAmount}
```

Imagine that a field called "Credit Limit" must have a value less than $1000.00. Following is a code example for using the `substitute` function to inject the right values into this string to get an appropriate error message.

```
template = "${fieldName} must be less than ${dollarAmount}"

map = new Object();

map.fieldName = "Credit Limit";
map.dollarAmount = "$1000.00";

errorMessage = dojo.string.substitute(template, map);
```

Notice the correspondence between the key name in the template and the name of the property in the map object (i.e. `${fieldName}` and `map.fieldName`). The variable `errorMessage` will now have a value of "`Credit Limit must be greater than $100`";

The `dojo.string.substitute` function is fairly complicated, so to fully explain it, we'll work with a more complex example. Imagine that we have a template string containing two parameters to be replaced. The first parameter will be a field name, and the second parameter will be a dollar amount, just as before. Now we also want to apply a function (which we will call `ucFirst`) to the first parameter to make sure the first letter is capitalized. We also want to apply a function (which we will call `showMoney`) to the second parameter to make sure it is in the form of a dollar amount with two trailing decimal digits. Additionally, we want to apply a function (which we will call `trim`) to remove any leading or trailing spaces in either of the parameters to be injected into our template.

Following is the template string for the messages:

```
${fieldName:ucFirst} must be greater than ${dollarAmount:showMoney}
```

We'll have to define a few functions and then make the correct call to dojo.string. substititue. Let's see what the code will look like. We'll focus on the code related to the Dojo function call and leave out some of the detail code for the formatting functions.

```
dojo.require("dojo.string");

// Define functions

ucFirst = function(value) {
    // This function will take a string and make sure the first letter
    // of the string is upper case and the subsequent letters
    // in the string are lower case.
    var newValue = … // this is left as an exercise for the reader
    return newValue;

dollarAmount = function(value) {
    // This function will take a number and put a dollar sign in front
    // of it and ensure that two decimal digits are at the end
    var newValue = … // this is left as an exercise for the reader
    return newValue;
}

stringTrim = function(value) {
    // This function will remove leading and trailing
    // spaces from a string
    var newValue = … // this is left as an exercise for the reader
    return newValue;
}

template = "${fieldname:ucFirst} must be less than
➡${dollarAmount:dollarAmount}"

map = new Object();

map.fieldName = "  Credit Limit  ";
map.dollarAmount = 1000.00;

errorMessage = dojo.string.substitute(template, map, stringTrim);
```

The value for errorMessage is "Credit Limit must be less than $1000.00".

13.2 JSON

JavaScript allows us to manipulate strings of generic text, but it also provides for a special type of text string called JSON, which is an acronym for JavaScript Object Notation. Now wasn't that helpful? No? We'll let's describe it another way. JSON is a technique for representing JavaScript objects as text strings. After we convert a JavaScript object to text, we can transfer that text around the Internet using HTTP, which only allows plain text to be transmitted. In general, we'll use JSON to transfer objects back and forth between the browser to the server. Another use for JSON is to create JavaScript objects using a more concise format than we get using methods calls. Let's see an example. We'll create two objects using both JavaScript and JSON.

First we'll view the code for creating an object using JavaScript and the standard Object Oriented technique.

```
// create a new object using JavaScript command

object1 = new Object();
object1.id = 100;
object1.name = "ABC Customer";
```

Now let's review the code for creating an equivalent object using JSON.

```
// create a new object using JSON

object2 = {id:100, name:"ABC Customer"};
```

Both objects are equivalent. They both have the same properties. After the object is created, there is really no way to tell they were created using different methods. Because we have two different but seemingly equivalent techniques, which one should you use? If you want to "be like Mike" and adhere to the conventions used by Dojo, you should use the JSON technique. Not only is JSON preferred by Dojo users, but it is also the preferred technique for most JavaScript programmers.

We can choose to use JSON or not when creating objects in JavaScript. But what options do we have when we want to send those objects to the server or get objects back from the server? When the browser builds an HTTP request to send to the server, data can either be sent in the URL (using the GET message type) or within the body of the request (using the POST message type). However, in either case, the data is sent as plain text. So we must find a way of converting a JavaScript object from the browser's internal format into a plain text string that can be sent using HTTP.

JSON is the perfect solution for this problem. We can represent the object as a JSON text string and transmit it between the browser and the server. We've already seen that JavaScript provides a syntax for creating an object with JSON, but what about the corresponding syntax to take an object and convert it to JSON? As popular as JSON is within the JavaScript community, you would expect there would be an easy way to do that. But you would be wrong. JavaScript does not provide any native function for producing the JSON equivalent of an object. There is no toJSON method defined for JavaScript. So someone has to write one. Fortunately, for us, that "someone" is Douglas Crockford. He's the source for all things JSON and a fount of general wisdom in his role as an industry guru. Dojo has taken advantage of his work by providing a few JSON functions based on his work.

13.2.1 Dojo Function: `dojo.toJson`

The Dojo function `dojo.toJson` will create a text string representing an object in the form of a JSON string. This process is called *serializing* the object, and the resulting string is the "serialization" of the object. *Serialization* is the computer science term for converting an object to a series of bytes that can be saved to a file or transmitted across some connection.

Following is the API for the `dojo.toJson` function:

Table 13.3   **Description of** `dojo.toJson` **Function**

Method Signature:	`dojo.toJson(it, prettyPrint)`
Summary:	This function will return a string containing the JSON representation of an object.
Parameter: `it`	Object to be serialized as JSON.
Parameter: `prettyPrint`	Flag to force the JSON text string to be formatted for easier viewing.
	If prettyPrint is true, objects and arrays will be indented to make the output more readable. The variable `dojo.toJsonIndentStr` is used as the indent string. To use something other than the default (tab), change the variable before calling `dojo.toJson()`.

Sometimes you would like to provide your own serialization method for turning an object into JSON. That is supported in Dojo by allowing you to add a function to your object (or its prototype) called either `json` or `__json`. It should take no parameters and return a string representing the JSON serialization of the object. There is no need to call the method directly; just use the `dojo.toJson` function, and it will check to see if you've provided your own custom method and will run it.

13.2.2 Usage Example for `dojo.toJson`

Let's create an object and see what the JSON string looks like.

```
// create a new object using JavaScript command

object1 = new Object();
object1.id = 100;
object1.name = "ABC Customer";
object1.toString = function() {
   return "Customer: " + this.name + ", (id: " + this.id + ")"; }

jsonStr = dojo.toJson(object1);
```

The variable `jsonString` will now have a value of

```
{
   "id": 100,
```

```
        "name": "ABC Customer",
        "phone": [
            "630-555-1212",
            "630-555-0000"
        ],
        "address": {
            "line1": "123 Main St",
            "city": "Chicago",
            "state": "IL",
            "zipCode": "60540"
        }
    }
```

Notice the special syntax for the `"phone"` array and the included object for `"address"`.

Notice that even though the object contained a function, `toString`, it was not serialized. Functions are not serialized by this `toJson`, although it is perfectly acceptable to create your own custom `json` method, which would serialize the functions.

Another "gotcha" when using this function, is to try to serialize an object that has a reference to itself. You'll end up causing `toJson` to fall into an infinite recursion that will eventually fail by running out of memory.

A final reminder, `dojo.toJson` is part of Dojo "base," which means you don't need a `dojo.require` statement to use it.

13.2.3 Dojo Function: `dojo.fromJson`

Ajax applications submit requests to the server for data. There are many available forms in which the data may be returned: plain text, name/value pairs, XML, and so on. One of the most desirable formats for many developers is to have the data returned as a JSON string, which can then be used to create JavaScript objects in the browser. As suggested before, you might think that turning a JSON string into JavaScript object would be a native feature of JavaScript. But you'd be wrong. There is a special technique we need to use to turn JSON into objects. We can't just assign the string to a reference. It would be treated as a string. We need to actually execute the JSON string as JavaScript. Review the following example:

```
jsonString = '{"id": 100, "name": "ABC Customer", "phone":
➡["630-555-1212", "630-555-0000"], "address": {"line1": "123 Main St",
➡"city": "Chicago", "state": "IL", "zipCode": "60540"}}';

var cust = eval( '(' + jsonString + ')');
```

The variable `"cust"` now points to an object containing an `"id"`, `"name"`, `"phone"`, and `"address"` property. Additionally, the `"address"` property references an object containing properties for `"line1"`, `"city"`, `"state"`, and `"zipCode"`.

Simply assigning the string to an object (`jsonString`) did not result in a creation of a new object. We have to use the native JavaScript `eval` function to actually execute the

JSON string. The problem with this approach is that there is a possible security problem when we execute arbitrary JavaScript code. So you should first make sure that the string really is JSON and not some other JavaScript code returned by the server. The technique for doing that check is a bit involved, and fortunately, not necessary for us. Dojo has done this for us by providing a function to turn a JSON string into JavaScript objects and checking the code beforehand. The `dojo.fromJson` function performs this magic for us!

Following is the API for the `dojo.fromJson` function:

Table 13.4   **Description of** `dojo.fromJson` **Function**

Method Signature:	`dojo.fromJson(json)`
Summary:	This function takes a string in JSON format and builds new JavaScript objects from the string.
Parameter: `json`	JSON string
	This string must be a properly formatted JSON string. The string will be evaluated to confirm that it is JSON and then will be executed as JavaScript to create new objects.

Note that if the JSON string contains a function definition, the function will be properly created in the new object.

Usage Example

```
jsonString = '{"id": 100, "name": "ABC Customer", "phone":
➥["630-555-1212", "630-555-0000"], "address": {"line1": "123 Main St",
➥"city": "Chicago", "state": "IL", "zipCode": "60540"}}';

var cust = dojo.fromJson(jsonString);
```

The variable `"cust"` now points to an object containing an `"id"`, `"name"`, `"phone"`, and `"address"` property. Additionally, the `"address"` property references an object containing properties for `"line1"`, `"city"`, `"state"`, and `"zipCode"`.

Summary

In an effort to maintain a small footprint, Dojo does not provide many additional string functions. Developers should use the native string functions available in JavaScript. However, there are a few string functions that Dojo does provide:

> `dojo.string.pad`—Pad a string with extra characters
>
> `dojo.string.substitute`—Inject parameters into a string template

JSON (JavaScript Object Notation) is a compact method for representing JavaScript objects as text strings. Use it to send data between the browser and the server when making XHR requests.

> `dojo.toJson`—Serialize an object into a JSON string
>
> `dojo.fromJson`—Create new objects from a JSON string

Events and Event Handling

Stuff Happens…Just Handle It

—Unknown

Yes, stuff happens, both in life and in web applications. Users click page elements, enter data, move the mouse around, and perform myriad other activities. In a more formal way, we refer to the stuff that happens as "events." And our response to events can't be passive. Our pages must do things to handle the events. Events and event handling and how Dojo can help are the topics of this chapter.

14.1 Description of the Event Model

In this chapter we examine events and event handling in Dojo. But as we delve into the Dojo specifics, it is also important to review the techniques for identifying and responding to events in the standard browser programming model and JavaScript. That way, Dojo extensions will make more sense. To summarize, we'll discuss the main topics related to events and describe the techniques first in plain JavaScript and then using Dojo. I'll cover the following topics:

- What are events?
- What are event handlers and how are they assigned?
- How are events represented?

14.1.1 What Are Events?

The common meaning of events is "stuff that happens." And this definition can be applied to the browser programming model as well. There are two primary categories of events—things that happen to the DOM and things that happen outside the DOM. The first category of events is known as DOM events. The second category of events is Browser events.

DOM events include things done to the DOM as a whole or to individual DOM elements. The classic DOM event occurs when a user clicks a DOM element such as a button or a link. But there are many other possible events. The browser can detect various types of user interaction coming from the keyboard or the mouse. And the user may interact with any of the DOM elements on the page, even those that don't appear to allow user response such as paragraph text or image files.

For example, when a user moves the mouse over some paragraph text, a number of events are generated. First, when the cursor passes into the area of the screen where the text is displayed, an onfocus event is generated for that DOM element. As the user continues to move the mouse, the cursor passes over the text. For each discernable movement of the cursor, the browser generates an onMouseMove event. And when the cursor moves outside of the boundaries of the paragraph element, an onblur event is generated by the browser. It is possible to create responses to each of these events.

> **Note**
>
> All events generated by the browser have a name by which they can be identified. For example clicking an element creates an event named "onclick."

The situation becomes more complex when we recognize that DOM elements can be stacked on top of each other and appear in the same space on the web page. The following HTML snippet demonstrates how two different DOM elements can be created in the same space:

```
<div id="div1" >
   <p>Here's some text</p>
</div>
```

When the cursor is placed over the paragraph text, it is also over the <div> element, its parent. As the cursor is moved over the paragraph text, events for both the paragraph and the <div> are generated. And you can cause the page to respond to either or both.

To complicate things further, we should recognize that there is a wide variety of possible user interactions that the browser can detect in addition to the ones we've already discussed. These include the following events:

- Pressing the mouse button
- Releasing the mouse button
- Pressing a key
- Releasing a key
- Moving the mouse wheel

And this is still only a subset of the possible events. How many different events might a web page have? Let's do a quick and dirty calculation. Imagine a page with 200 DOM events (not a large page by any means). There are at least 50 types of user interactions possible with each DOM element. So there are more than 10,000 possible events that could be identified by the browser that we could write event handlers for. And that doesn't include the Browser events.

Aside from DOM events, what other events can be identified? One of the most well known is the onLoad event, which is triggered when the browser has finished building the web page from the HTML file received from the server. This event is generated internally in the browser and is not based on any user input at all. Another type of event, window.onresize, is created when the user changes the size of the browser window itself. Although it is based on user activity, it isn't associated with any specific DOM element.

The task of responding to events might now seem immense. But there is some good news. Even though the universe of possible events on a typical web page might be quite large, the number of events that we need to respond to is usually rather small.

14.1.2 Additional Dojo Events

Dojo can recognize all the events already described, but it also adds a few events of its own. The most interesting of these is an event that occurs when a JavaScript function is executed. This allows developers to use a new programming model called *Aspect Oriented Programming (AOP)*—more on this later in the chapter.

Dojo also provides enhancement to some of the standard Browser events such as onload. In standard JavaScript, the onload event is triggered when the browser has completed the loading of the web page. But often, you don't want your code to run until the page is loaded and Dojo has done all of its setup work, including loading of the various Dojo packages and the execution of the Dojo page parser. If you simply attach an event handler to onload, your handler may run before Dojo setup is complete. Dojo provides a special function for assigning event handlers so that they don't get executed until Dojo setup is complete. This is the dojo.addOnLoad function.

The following example shows two techniques for using dojo.addOnLoad. The first line of code shows how to attach an existing function called eventHandler as an event handler for the Dojo onload event. The subsequent code shows how to attach a line of code inside an anonymous function, which is then associated with the Dojo onLoad event.

```
dojo.addOnLoad(eventHandler);

dojo.addOnLoad(function() {
    console.log("Dojo setup complete");
});
```

Now that we understand the events that can occur in a web page, we need to explore how to respond to them.

14.2 Defining and Assigning Event Handlers

If a tree falls in the forest, does it make a sound? Or more apropos: If an event triggers no action, is it really an event? Philosophy aside, identifying events is only important because we want to associate some action with them. These actions are known as *event handlers*. They're the JavaScript functions that execute in response to events.

Let's explore a simple example. The following function displays a message on the screen:

```
function showAlert() {
    alert("Hello World");
}
```

Is this code an event handler? Maybe, but only if it is used to handle an event. Although that sounds like circular logic, let me explain what I mean. An event handler can be any function, and the example code certainly is a function. What makes a function into an event handler is that we tell the browser to call that function when it detects a certain event. Let's see how we do that.

Imagine that we would like the `showAlert` function to run whenever a button on the web page is clicked. We need to create the DOM element for the button and then assign an event handler to the event that is generated when the user clicks the button. The following code shows one technique for creating the element and assigning the event handler:

```
<button id="btn1"
    onClick="showAlert" >
</button>
```

Dojo lets us assign event handlers programmatically using JavaScript.

14.2.1 Using `dojo.connect` to Assign Event Handlers

The dojo.connect method allows us to assign an event handler by naming the DOM element, the event, and the event handler and passing them as parameters to `dojo.connect`. Table 14.1 describes this function in more detail.

Table 14.1   `dojo.connect` **Function for Standard Browser Events**

Method Signature:	`dojo.connect (domNode, event, handler)` or
	`dojo.connect (domNode, event, context, method)`
Summary:	This function binds an event handler to an event on a DOM node.
Parameter: domNode	Reference to the DOM node.
Parameter: event	A string containing the description of the event. These are the same as the standard event properties such as `onclick`, `onblur`, `mouseover`, and so on.

Table 14.1   **Continued**

Parameter: handler	This is a reference to the globally scoped function that is called when the event is triggered. No parameters for the handler can be specified because Dojo provides the parameters itself when it makes the call to the handler.
	This property can be either a string naming the function or a reference to the function.
	When Dojo calls the handler, it passes the Dojo event object, which is described in Table 14.2.
Parameter: context	Reference to an object containing the handler function.
Parameter: method	A function within the scope of the context object. When context isn't specified, global becomes the default scope.

14.2.2 Usage Example for Assigning Event Handlers

Let's start with a simple example of how to assign an event handler to the `onclick` event for a DOM element. First we must have a DOM element. The following code creates a DOM element for a button:

```
<button id="button1">
    Click Me!
</button>
```

Next we create an event handler that writes a log message containing the type of the event:

```
function handle(event) {
console.log("Running event handler for event type:", event.type);
}
```

The event handler code has a few interesting features. It takes an argument referencing the normalized event object created when the event is generated. This is the Dojo event object, not the raw JavaScript event object. The advantage of using the Dojo version is that it is the same regardless of the browser that is being used to run the page. Another important feature of the event handler function is that it doesn't return anything. Any data that it returns is ignored.

Next we assign the event handler to the `onclick` event for the button using the `dojo.connect` function:

```
dojo.connect(dijit.byId('button1'), "onclick", handler);
```

This code should only be executed after the DOM is fully loaded, Dojo has been

installed, and the DOM has been parsed by Dojo. This is easy to do by using the
`dojo.addOnLoad` function and calling `dojo.connect` with an anonymous function
containing the following code:

```
dojo.addOnLoad(function() {
    dojo.connect(dijit.byId('button1'), "onclick", handler);
});
```

There are a couple of comments I'd like to make concerning this code. First, when
assigning handlers to DOM events, always use `dijit.byId`, not `dojo.byId`. The reason
for this is that the Dojo parser might add additional DOM elements to the base DOM
element defined in the HTML. It might be one of those child elements that the event is
triggered on. Don't try to figure this out; just let Dojo pick the right one by using
`dijit.byId`.

The second point is that we have a choice when specifying the DOM event name.
We can use the "on" prefix or leave it off. For example, `click` and `onclick` are equivalent events. Choose whichever you prefer. I like using `onclick` just so I can be consistent with the DOM element property names.

To add additional event handlers, just run additional `dojo.connect` functions. You
can attach an unlimited number of handlers to an event.

```
dojo.connect(dijit.byId('button1'), "onclick", handler2);
```

To remove the event handlers, use `dojo.disconnect` with the same parameters.
Each handler must be removed separately.

14.3 Representing an Event as an Object

A developer doesn't write code to call the event handlers; the browser does that automatically when an event is generated. That means you can't control the arguments passed
to the event handler or whether any arguments are passed at all. When an event handler
is called in Firefox, an event object is passed as the parameter. This isn't true for Internet
Explorer, which requires the event handler function to look up the event object. Also,
the event object itself is slightly different between the two major browsers.

The Dojo event system provides two major benefits over JavaScript. First, it ensures
that an event object is always passed to the handler, regardless of the browser. And second, it provides a standard event object that is always the same. This is sometimes
referred to as a "normalized" event object.

Although event handlers receive only a single parameter, the event object, that object
contains multiple properties and methods. The primary purpose of the event object is to
be a wrapper around the event itself, capturing information about the event such as the
DOM element that triggered it and the coordinates of the cursor at the time the event

occurred. Table 14.2 describes the important properties and methods of the event object.

Table 14.2   **Dojo Event Object**

Summary:	The Dojo event object provides an object wrapper around the event exposing its important properties and methods.
Property: `target`	DOM node on which the event was triggered.
Property: `currentTarget`	DOM node that is assigned to act as the target DOM node for the event object. It is usually the same as the target node but may be assigned to a different node by Dojo. This is the element you should reference in event handler code.
Property: `layerX`	This is the X coordinate of the cursor relative to `currentTarget` DOM element.
Property: `layerY`	This is the Y coordinate of the cursor relative to `currentTarget` DOM element.
Property: `pageX`	This is the X coordinate of the cursor relative to the viewport at the time the event was created. The viewport is the area in the browser in which the document content is viewed. This doesn't include sidebar menus or status lines. It is the space that is available to the page.
Property: `pageY`	This is the Y coordinate of the cursor relative to the viewport at the time the event was created.
Property: `type`	The name of the event such as `click` or `mouseover`. This string will not have `on` at the beginning.
Property: `relatedTarget`	For certain events such as `onmouseover` and `onmouseout` this property references the object that the mouse moved from. This would be different than the DOM element on which the event was triggered.
Property: `charCode`	Contains the keycode for key press events.
Function: `stopPropagation`	The JavaScript event model allows event processing to bubble up to overlapping DOM elements. In other words, the same event is triggered on the parent element. Running this function stops that from happening.
Function: `preventDefault`	Some DOM events have a default behavior (such as a "submit" button submitting the form). Running this method on an event prevents the default behavior from occurring.

14.4 Using Aspect Oriented Programming in Dojo

Aspect Oriented Programming (AOP) is a programming technique available in some languages that allows certain types of program execution to be treated as events to which event handlers may be applied. For example, let's define two functions, `foo` and `bar`, which simply write a message to the console as shown in the following code:

```
function foo() {
  console.log("Running foo");
}

function bar() {
  console.log("Running bar");
}
```

Now we need to make sure that every time `foo` executes, `bar` is also executed. A simple way to do this is to add a line of code to the `foo` method that executes `bar`, as shown here:

```
function foo() {
    console.log("Running foo");
    bar();
}
```

Although the solution just provided would work, we've hard-coded it. What if we wanted to make this assignment dynamic? Dojo provides a solution. Dojo can treat the execution of a function as an event to which we can associate another function as an event handler. The following version of `dojo.connect` provides this association:

```
dojo.connect(null, "foo", null, "bar");
```

Now whenever we run `foo`, the function `bar` automatically runs next.

We've now implemented a simple example of AOP. But if you're new to AOP, you may be asking: Why in the world would I want to do this? The standard usage of this approach allows us to dynamically add features that apply to many object types. For example, if we wanted to add logging to functions, we could do it after the functions were already written by assigning a log method to each of the functions using AOP instead of having to add code to each function.

The AOP approach can be better because it doesn't hard code the logging method to the target factions and no target function code has to be modified. After all, if you believe the industry benchmarks, every time you touch code, there is a 5% chance that you will break something. So if you can avoid modifying the methods, you're better off.

In the preceding examples, we used the `null` parameter. This parameter defines the scope of the method for either the event or event handler. The `null` parameter defaults to the global object so we would be executing globally scoped functions. It is also possible to watch and execute methods within specific objects. In that case, the `null` parameters would be replaced by object references.

The following table described the special form of the dojo.connect function needed to assign AOP advice methods to target methods.

Table 14.3   `dojo.connect` **Function for AOP**

Method Signature:	`dojo.connect (object, method, object, method)`
Summary:	This function associates an event handler with the execution of a method.
Parameter: `object`	Object containing the method whose execution will be treated as an event. This property contains a reference to the object.
Parameter: `method`	Method whose execution is treated as an event. The method name is a string.
Parameter: `handlerObject`	Object containing the method that will act as the event handler. This property contains a reference to the object.
Parameter: `handlerMethod`	Method that will act as the event handler. The method name is a string.

Summary

Dojo provides numerous enhancements to the standard browser Event model.

Dojo provides a normalized event object and event handler call.

The `dojo.connect` functions allow assignment of event handlers. Multiple event handlers can be assigned to a single event.

The dojo.disconnect function allows event handlers to be removed.

The `dojo.addOnLoad` function allows assignment of additional event handlers to the standard browser `onload` event with the assurance that the event handlers won't be called until Dojo is fully loaded and it has parsed the DOM.

Dojo can provide a simple AOP model through the use of `dojo.connect` to associate one function with another.

We've now concluded our discussion of events. Next we cover one of the biggest Ajax events of all—calling the server using the `XMLHttpRequest` object. We use a slightly friendlier name for this process: *remoting*.

Ajax Remoting

A fair request should be followed by the deed...

—Dante Alighieri (1265–1321)

When most developers think about Ajax, they are thinking about the XMLHttpRequest object—the special object that allows JavaScript to make requests of the server without refreshing the entire page. After the server returns the request, the response data can be used to manipulate the page in some way. It is this object that is the key to creating Ajax-enabled web pages. And as you might imagine, Dojo provides powerful functions for creating and working with request objects. This chapter describes those functions and their uses.

15.1 Remoting

To set the context for this chapter, let's remind ourselves of the technique used by pre-Ajax web pages to provide new content. The user clicks a link or a button or maybe even enters a URL in the address area of the browser. Then the browser sends a request to the server, possibly even passing some data along, and the server responds with a brand new web page, which completely replaces the first page. Often, the new page is very similar to the replaced page. It may have the same heading, footer, and navigation controls. But some part of the page will be different, else why a new page? Wouldn't it be more efficient to just replace the part of the page that changed and leave the rest of the content alone? Of course it would. However, the technique for achieving this wasn't widely understood until Jesse James Garret published his article on Ajax back in the day (February 2005 to be precise[1]).

---

1. "Ajax: A New Approach to Web Applications," by Jesse James Garrett, February 18, 2005,
   http://adaptivepath.com/publications/essays/archives/000385.php.

Garret described a technique for making a server request from inside the web page. The request will return some small amount of data or html rather than an entire new page. And, even better, this request could be made at the same time that the page is working, without holding up the operation of the page. In programming terminology, the request ran in a different thread than the displaying page. The server request was made "asynchronously" and didn't interfere with the operation of the page. When the server returned the response, it could be handled by a local JavaScript function, the "request handler." Data returned from the server could be used to update the Document Object Model (DOM), which resulted in the user seeing something new on the page without the necessity of the entire page being replaced.

Now we can give a better definition. "Remoting" is the creation and execution of an asynchronous server request that can be processed without doing a page refresh in the browser.

15.2 Review of `XMLHttpRequest` (or `XHR` for Short)

JavaScript supports Remoting by providing a special constructor, `XMLHttpRequest`. By creating a new object of this type, you can make requests of the server that can provide data back to you. The following code shows how you can create an XHR request using JavaScript.

```
var XHR = new XMLHttpRequest();

XHR.onreadystatechange = handleResponse;

XHR.open('GET', 'getData.html');

XHR.send(null);
```

This request will run asynchronously. There are two implications of this. First, you must anticipate what to do as the user continues to use the page while it waits for a response from the server. And second, you must provide a handler function to run after the server returns its response.

We'll ignore the first consideration for now and focus on handling the response from the server. After the response is returned from the server, the browser interrupts whatever it is doing and calls the JavaScript function named as the handler for the response. In this case, we've named the event handler `handleResponse`. Following is a typical example of what a response handler would look like. Notice that we are checking to make sure that a complete response has been returned (`readyState == 4`), and we are verifying that the response was successful (`status == 200`). The data received from the server is in the `XHR.responseText` property. Although we're using the data to update the DOM in this example, there is no limit to what you could do with the data.

```
function handleResponse() {
  if (XHR.readyState == 4){
   if (XHR.status == 200) {
      document.getElementById('dataArea').innerHTML = XHR.responseText;
   }
  }
}
```

I've ignored a few potential problems with this code. For instance, what happens if we've got multiple XHR requests outstanding at the same time? Our globally scoped XHR object would have conflicts if we used it for two concurrent requests. Also isn't the idiom for checking the status and readyState a little verbose? And because a typical response handler just updates a DOM element, is there a standard idiom we can apply to do that, too?

These and other issues are addressed by the Dojo functions used as wrappers around the raw JavaScript XHR object. Let's review those now.

15.3 The `dojo.xhrGet` Function

The Dojo function `dojo.xhrGet` wraps the XMLHttpRequest calls and the creation of the XHR object just introduced. Under the hood, it does nothing more than we could do ourselves by coding JavaScript manually, but the amount and the complexity of the code that it hides is certainly worth the small effort to understand its use.

The first use case for this function we'll consider is the need to make a request for some data from the server and use that data to manipulate the DOM. We'll make an HTTP request of type GET and ask for a resource on the server called getData.html. After the response is returned, we'll use it to update a DOM element called, whose id is dataArea.

```
dojo.xhrGet( {
    url: "getData.html",
    handleAs: "text",
    load: function(response) {
        document.getElementById("dataArea").innerHTML = response;
    }
 );
```

A few things you'll notice right way. We're only passing a single object as a parameter to the function call. However, this object contains a number of properties. The object, in effect, acts as a series of parameters. Instead of passing each parameter individually, we're passing them as properties within a single object. The method signature is simple given that it only takes a single object as a parameter. But knowing what properties to define in that object and how the properties interrelate can be a bit more difficult.

In this simple use case, the `url` property contains the name of the resource on the server that we are requesting with the XHR request. We don't specify the HTTP request type (i.e., GET) because this is already built into the name of the function. For other HTTP request types, different function names will be used (i.e., `xhrPost` for POST requests). The `load` property contains the function to be called by Dojo when handling the request. The real request handler is an internal Dojo function assigned when it creates the XHR object. That handler calls our `load` handler. The `load` handler only gets called once `readyState ==4` and `status == 200` so we don't have to perform those checks ourselves. Our `load` handler is called by Dojo, which passes `response` into our function. The parameter `response` is the `XHR.responseText` property from the XHR object. The `handleAs` property describes the format of the data returned from the server.

Let's look at the API for `dojo.xhrGet` and then look at the properties for the passed parameter in more detail.

Table 15.1   Description of `dojo.xhrGet` Function

Method Signature:	`dojo.xhrGet(args)`
Summary:	This function will create, send, and handle an `XMLHttpRequest` object of HTTP GET request type.
Parameter: `args`	Object containing properties used to configure the XHR object to be created by Dojo.

To really understand this function we need to look at the possible properties within the `args` parameter in more detail.

Table 15.2   Description of Arguments for `dojo.xhrGet` Function

Property	Description
`handleAs`	Describes format of data returned by the request. Acceptable values are `text` (default), `json`, `json-comment-optional`, `json-comment-filtered`, `javascript`, and `xml`.
`sync`	Indicates whether the request should be a synchronous request, which blocks additional execution until the request returns or whether the request should occur asynchronously so that execution can continue while the request is being processed by the server. The default is "false," which makes the request asynchronous.
`header`	Object containing HTTP header values. The properties of the object should correspond to the name of the HTTP header item, and the value in the property will be the value of the corresponding header item. These values will be added to the actual HTTP header sent to the server.
`form`	DOM node for a form. Used to extract the values of the form elements and send to the server.

Table 15.2   **Continued**

Property	Description
url	String URL representing resource requested on the server.
content	Object containing properties with string values. These properties will be serialized as `name1=value2` and passed in the request.
timeout	Milliseconds to wait for the response. If this time passes, the `error` callback function is executed.
preventCache	If "true," then a `dojo.preventCache` parameter is sent in the request with a value that changes with each request (timestamp). Useful only with GET-type requests. Default is false.
load	Function to be called on a successful response. The signature of the function should be `function(response, ioArgs){}`.
error	Function to be called when the response fails. The signature of the function should be `function(response, ioArgs){}`.
handle	Function to be called when the response returns in the case that neither `load` nor `error` has been called. The signature of the function should be `function(response, ioArgs){}`.

For the `load`, `error`, and `handle` functions, a function is provided that takes response and ioArgs as parameters. The `ioArgs` parameter is complex enough that it deserves its own table to explain its various properties. The table below explains the ioArgs properties.

Table 15.3   **Description of `ioArgs` Property for `dojo.xhrGet` Function**

`ioArgs` **Properties**	**Descriptions**
args	The original object argument to the IO call.
xhr	For `XMLHttpRequest` calls only, the `XMLHttpRequest` object that was used for the request.
url	The final URL used for the call. Many times it will be different than the original `args.url` value.
query	For non-GET requests, the query string parameters (i.e., `name1=value1&name2=value2`) sent up in the request.
handleAs	The type of response data from the server. This designates how the response should be handled.
id	For `dojo.io.script` calls only, the internal script id used for the request.
canDelete	For `dojo.io.script` calls only, indicates whether the script tag that represents the request can be deleted after callbacks have been called. Used internally to know when cleanup can happen on JSON requests.
json	For `dojo.io.script` calls only: holds the JSON response for JSON requests. Used internally to hold on to the JSON responses. You should not need to access it directly. The same object should be passed to the success callbacks directly.

15.3.1 Parameters in Detail

Some of the parameters are so interesting and invoke such useful functionality, that it is worthwhile to consider them in more detail. Let's review the `handleAs` parameter.

15.3.1.1 `handleAs` **Argument to XHR**

The `handleAs` property of the `args` object tells Dojo what kind of data will be returned by the XHR request. And not only that, depending on the type of data, Dojo will perform some processing on it before it is returned to our response handler. The following table describes the valid `handleAs` values and explains how Dojo treats each type of data.

Table 15.4   **Description of** `handleAs` **Types**

`handleAs` type	Description
`text`	The data from the server will be a string of text. When the callback function is called, this will be the first parameter (response).
`json`	The data from the server will be returned as a JSON string, which will be used to create the object described by the string. The object will be the first parameter to the callback function.
	Note: There are actually two additional `handleAs` types called `json-comment-optional` and `json-comment-filtered`, which may be used to prevent JavaScript Hijacking—a security flaw introduced by allowing the page to `eval` arbitrary JavaScript coming from the server. It potentially exposes other objects on the page.
`javascript`	The data returned from the server will be JavaScript. Dojo will execute the JavaScript using the `eval` function.
`xml`	The data returned from the server will be in XML format. The XML will used to create a DOM object. The object will be the first parameter to the callback function.

15.4 `dojo.xhrPost`

The `dojo.xhrPost` can be used, in many respects, the same way as `dojo.xhrGet`. That is, the parameters are almost the same, and the behavior of the function is also almost the same. The major difference is that the data being sent to the server is handled differently. In `xhrGet`, the data is passed back as name/value pairs in the URL itself.

```
http://www.mydomain.com/getPage.jsp?id=100&name=Joe
```

In this case, the values for id and name are passed as part of the URL and are known as the *query string*.

In `xhrPost`, the data is passed within the body of the HTTP request itself. It is not visible in the URL. This is a much more secure approach in that the browser user can't see passed data merely by using the forward and backward keys to see what URLs the browser has been sending. Also there is no limit to the amount of data that can be passed within the body of the request. The URL itself is usually limited to about 4000 characters, usually more than enough but insufficient for some of the edge cases.

Because of this difference in how POST and GET work, there is an additional property that can be set in the argument object passed in the call to `xhrPost()`. The `postData` property is a string that contains the data to be submitted in the body of the HTTP POST request built by the XHR request. This is an important property because it must be set before the `xhrPost()` function is called. This is something new for many developers who have become accustomed to the browser automatically formatting and sending the data when a form is submitted. The following code is typical for submitting form data through the `xhrPost()`.

```
dojo.xhrPost( {
    url: "getData.html",
    handleAs: "text",
    postData: "id=100&name=Joe",
    load: function(response) {
        document.getElementById("dataArea").innerHTML = response;
    }
} );
```

Let's explore a more complicated use case. Imagine that you are responsible for developing a registration page for users of your web site. Along with the typical demographic information like name and address, you would also like your users to choose a user name for future logins to the system. However, because of the popularity of your site, many common user names have already been taken. In a pre-Ajax implementation of this page, the system would check the user name when the form was submitted. Submitting a user name that had already been taken would cause a page to be sent back to the browser with the appropriate error message. And also sent back would be the values that the user had already entered so that the user didn't have to re-enter everything else just to choose a new user name.

The user would probably still be a little aggravated given that they had already forgotten the other user names they had considered at the time.

Wouldn't it be better to notify the user of the problem with user name as soon as they entered the value in the field instead of after submitting the request? Of course! By making an Ajax request to the server right after the user enters their choice for user name, the server could return an error message that could be displayed on the form right away. Following is the HTML that demonstrates how JavaScript could trigger the Ajax request immediately after the user enters the user name:

```
Make up a user name and enter it here:
<input type="text" name="username"
    onchange="checkUserName(this.value)"
/>
```

Notice the event we're using—onchange. This event is triggered when the user enters some value in the field and focus moves from the username field to another field. This is better than using the onblur event because we are sure that the value has changed and we're not making unnecessary Ajax requests. This example assumes that there is a local JavaScript function called checkUserName, which contains the code to create the XHR request along with an event handler to interpret the response from the server. There is an even better way to assign an event handler function to the event using Dojo. We discuss that technique later in Chapter 14, "Events and Event Handling."

Now let's look at the event handler function itself. This is the code that gets called when the browser detects the onchange event. The following code uses dojo.xhrGet to perform an Ajax request.

```
function checkUserName(value)
    var query = "username=" + value;
    query = encodeURIcomponent(query);
    dojo.xhrGet( {
        url: "checkUserName.jsp" + "?" + query,
        handleAs: "text",
        load: function(response) {
            // process server response
            // intentionally left empty for now!
        }
    );
```

We first create the query string to be sent to the server. If we use POST instead of GET, we'll pass the query string as a parameter. The following code uses dojo.xhrPost to make the Ajax request.

```
function checkUserName(value)
    var query = "username=" + value;
    query = encodeURIcomponent(query);
    dojo.xhrPost( {
        url: "checkUserName.jsp",
        postData: query,
        handleAs: "text",
            load: function(response) {
            // process server response
            // intentionally left empty for now!
        }
    );
```

Now, what about processing the response from the server? The prior code examples did not provide the details on how to manage the response. We need to consider what kind of responses we can get back from the server. One of the following must be true: Either the user name is already taken, or it isn't. We could display a short error message when the user name is taken. Seems simple enough. However, error processing involves many edge cases. What about the following issues:

- What if there is a network problem when we submit the request and we never receive a response from the server?

- What if we are able to reach the server, but the database on the server is temporarily down? The server responds with a status code such as 500.

- What if the user name is available when the Ajax request is made but is then grabbed by another user before the first user completes his registration by submitting the registration form?

- How do we notify the user of these various error conditions?

These issues can be divided into two broad categories: How do we programmatically detect error conditions? And how do we notify users of error conditions after they are detected?

Let's consider the issue of identifying error conditions first. Dojo has defined different callback functions to handle various types of responses from the server. Table 15.5 summarizes the callback functions and the error conditions that cause them to be executed.

Table 15.5   **Possible Error Conditions for Remoting Requests**

Response Condition	Callback Function
Server does not return a response, either it times out or can't be reached.	`error`
	The function assigned to `error` will be called if it has been assigned, otherwise `handle` will be called.
Server responds but with a status code of other than 200 indicating some sort of server error.	
Server responds with a status code of 200.	`load`
	The function assigned to `load` will be called if it has been assigned, otherwise `handle` will be called.

Table 15.5   **Continued**

Response Condition	Callback Function
Any server response.	`handle`
	If `error` or `load` have been assigned, one of them will be called. Otherwise, `handle` will be called. If neither `error` nor `load` is assigned, `handle` can be used to handle all of the server responses.

When deciding which callback functions to use, keep the following in mind:

- Dojo will only execute a single callback method for each request.

- You must provide the implementation for the callback function. Dojo calls your implementation but doesn't really handle it itself.

- You assign the callback function by setting a property in the xhr method parameter object, either `load`, `error`, or `handle`.

- The objects passed to the callback function are the same, regardless of type of handler.

15.4.1 Usage Example—Error Handling

In this use case, certain kinds of failure are more serious than others. If the Ajax request that verifies the user name should fail, the validation can simply be done again when the full form is submitted. So it may not even be necessary to notify the user that the validation failed. Also if the validation should succeed, again it is not necessary to notify the user because no action is required. He or she can just go on happily entering additional data. Although, it would be possible to reserve the user name on the server so no other user can get it, which might cause some scalability problems.

But what happens when the validation fails and the user name is not valid? We should present the user with an error message. But should we return the cursor to the user name field, interrupting whatever other work the user is then doing? What are the details of the server's response that tells the browser that the validation failed? The Ajax request returns data from the server, but there is no standard for how exactly to show a validation failure. We're only limited by our imagination. Following are some of the possible responses from the server when using Ajax Remoting:

- The server could return a string of data container either the value `success` or `failure`.

- The server could return a value of `failure` along with a descriptive error message.

- The server could return a value of `failure` along with a descriptive error message and some suggestions for available user names similar to the one entered by the user.

Which is the right approach? Well, that is up to you. Neither Ajax nor Dojo proscribes your actions. However, later when we study Dojo widgets, we'll see that widgets have a more standard (but still flexible) way of handling error messages.

15.5 Working with Forms

Many of the pages in a typical business application collect data on forms and send that data to the server for some kind of processing. So working with form data in JavaScript is very common. How does the use of Ajax and Dojo influence how we work with form data? Developers may think that because they are using Ajax to submit data to the server instead of using the standard form submit that they don't need to use forms anymore. This is incorrect for a number of reasons.

Forms will still be used because even though the application may be making Ajax Remoting requests prior to form submission, the form will usually still be submitted as the final step of entering data on a page. This reduces the amount of new development on the server since the service used to process form submission without Ajax has probably already been coded.

Another reason to continue to use forms in Ajax applications is that forms are just a darn good way to organize data in the browser. Related data elements can be grouped together by keeping them within a form tag. Multiple forms can reside on the same page to separate groups of data. Also the browser gives us some convenient shortcuts for referencing data fields that are within forms. For example, review the following HTML snippet that follows. It defines a simple form with two data fields and a submit button.

```
<form action="submitForm" name="userInfo" method="POST">
    First Name:  <input type="text" name="firstName"/> <br/>
    Last Name:   <input type="text" name="lastName"/> <br/>

    <input type="submit">

</form>
```

When the DOM is built for these fields, they can be referenced by the following shorthand. Notice how the browser builds a DOM that contains elements with names corresponding to the existing form and form data elements. Remember, upper/lower case is important!

```
firstName = document.userInfo.firstName;

lastName = document.userInfo.lastName;
```

And, finally, another good reason to continue to use forms in your application (rather than just using the `<input>` tags alone) is that Dojo provides many useful functions for working with data held in forms, which we discuss now.

15.5.1 Dojo Function dojo.formToObject

Because JavaScript is an Object Oriented programming language, as developers, we naturally want to work with our data as objects. Dojo provides a function (`formToObject`) for converting the data in a form to an object so that we can work with it more easily. Let's look at the API for `dojo.formToObject`.

Table 15.6   **Description of** `dojo.formToObject` **Function**

Method Signature:	`dojo.formToObject(formNode)`
Summary:	This function will return an object with properties corresponding to the form fields in the form specified in `formNode`.
	The function returns the values encoded in an HTML form as string and number properties in an object. Disabled form elements, buttons, and other non-value form elements are skipped. Multi-select elements are returned as an array of string values.
	The names of the form elements will be the same as the property names in the returned object. Upper and lower case will be maintained in the property names.
Parameter: `formNode`	DOM form element used to extract form element names and values.
	The `formNode` may be a reference to a form DOM element. It may also be a string containing the id of the form element.

One of the most useful features of this function is that the form node can be identified by either a reference to a DOM node or by the id of the node.

Usage Example

This example assumes the existence of the following form.

```
<form action="submitForm" name="userInfo" id="form1" method="POST">
    First Name:   <input type="text" name="firstName"/> <br/>
    Last Name:    <input type="text" name="lastName"/> <br/>

    <input type="submit">

</form>
```

Notice how we are now using the id attribute in the form tag. The following function call returns an object representing the form.

```
var userData = dojo.formToObject("form1");
```

The object `userData` looks like this:

```
{"firstName": "Jim Bob", "lastName": "Jones"}
```

Notice that there is no property for the "submit" button when using `dojo.formToObject`.

15.5.2 Dojo Function `dojo.objectToQuery`

When using XHR to make a server request, it is typical to send some data along. We've already discussed ways of doing this using `xhrGet` and `xhrPost`, which both allow query strings to be passed along either in the URL or the body of the request. Because the program is probably working with this data in the form of an object, it would be useful to be able to convert the properties in the object to a query string so they can be easily used for the XHR functions. Dojo provides a function to do this called `dojo.objectToQuery`. Let's review its API in Table 15.7.

Table 15.7   **Description** of `dojo.objectToQuery` **Function**

Method Signature:	`dojo.objectToQuery(map)`
Summary:	This function will return a string containing the properties of an object as name/value pairs in the form of a URL query.
	The query string will be URL-encoded, which means that special characters will be converted to their URL values (i.e., a space will be converted to `%20`).
Parameter: **map**	Object to be copied as a query string. The object should only contain properties than can be represented as a number of a text string.
	Array properties will get translated to a series of name/value pairs with the same name corresponding to the name of the property.
	Properties that refer to other objects will be ignored.

Following is an example of an object to be converted along with the conversion:

```
qObject = new Object();
qObject.id = 100;
qObject.name = "John Smith";
qObject.type = "RETAIL";
qObject.active = true;
qObject.setStatus = function(status) {this.status = status};
qObject.owner = qObject;

var queryString = dojo.objectToQuery(qObject);
```

The resulting query string looks as follows:

```
id=100&
name=John Smith&
status=RETAIL&
active=true&
setStatus=function (status) { this.status = status; }&
owner=[object Object]
```

Notice a few things about the output. We've added line breaks after each name/value pair to make it easier to read. Also the URI encoding has been removed, again for readability. One of the properties of the object is a function, `setStatus`. It is converted to its equivalent string, probably not very useful to send back to the server, but sent it will be. Also another property, `owner`, is a reference to an object (in this case, itself). It is converted to a string, `owner=[object Object]`, which is the default string used to describe an object. Again, this is probably not very useful information for the server. In general, objects to be converted to query strings should be maps containing properties that are either strings, numbers, or booleans.

15.5.3 Dojo Function `dojo.formToQuery`

When the user clicks a "submit" button on a standard HTML form, the values of the form elements are automatically converted to a string containing name/value pairs, and that string is sent to the server either at the end of the URL (for GET requests) or as part of the HTTP body (for POST requests). However, when creating an Ajax request, this conversion of form elements does not occur automatically and must be done manually with JavaScript. Dojo provides a function to do the conversion: `dojo.formToQuery`. Following is the API for this function.

Table 15.8   **Description of** `dojo.formToQuery` **Function**

Method Signature:	`dojo.formToQuery(formNode)`
Summary:	This function will return an string containing name/value pairs corresponding to the form elements and values in a form from the DOM.
	The string will be URL-encoded, which means that special characters will be converted to their URL values (i.e., a space will be converted to %20).
	The names of the form elements will be the same as the property names in the returned object.
Parameter: `formNode`	Form whose elements will be copied to a string.
	The `formNode` may be a reference to a DOM element, which is a form. It may also be a string containing the id of the form element.

Let's review the following HTML form and see the resulting query string.

```
<form action="submitForm" name="userInfo" method="POST">

    First Name:
    <input type="text" name="firstName" value="Jim Bob"/><br/>

    Last Name:
    <input type="text" name="lastName" value="Jones"/><br/>

    <input type="submit">

</form>
```

The following code would be used to create the query string representing the form:

```
query = dojo.formToQuery("userInfo");
```

The value of the query string would be `firstName=Jim%20Bob&lastName=Jones`. Notice that the space in `Jim Bob` has been replaced with `%20`. That is URL encoding. Also notice that the query string does not being with `?`. When adding the query string to the end of a string with a URL, you will have to manually concatenate the `?` as in the following example:

```
query = dojo.formToQuery("userInfo");

URL = "submitform.jsp" + "?" + query;
```

When submitting the query data using an Ajax request, just set the `postData` property.

```
query = dojo.formToQuery("userInfo");

dojo.xhrPost( {
    postData: query,
    url: "getData.html",
    handleAs: "text",
    load: function(response) {
        document.getElementById("dataArea").innerHTML = response;
    }
);
```

15.5.4 Dojo Function `dojo.formToJson`

Because JSON is the *lingua franca* of the JavaScript world for representing objects, you'll find that you often want to use it for formatting data to be sent to the server. This function will take a form and produce the equivalent JSON object.

Table 15.9   Description of `dojo.formToJson` **Function**

Method Signature:	`dojo.formToJson(formNode)`
Summary:	This function will return an object with properties corresponding to the form fields in the form specified in `formNode`.
	Returns the values encoded in an HTML form as string properties in an object. Disabled form elements, buttons, and other non-value form elements are skipped. Multiselect elements are returned as an array of string values.
	The names of the form elements will be the same as the property names in the returned object.
Parameter: formNode	Form to be copied to an object.
	The `formNode` may be a reference to a DOM element, which is a form. It may also be a string containing the id of the form element.

15.5.5 Dojo Function `dojo.queryToObject`

Sometimes it is useful to take an existing query string and create a new object that contains properties corresponding to the name/value pairs in the query string. The `dojo.queryToObject` function does this. This may be useful when the server sends back name/value pairs as the XHR response.

Table 15.10   Description of `dojo.queryToObject` **Function**

Method Signature:	`dojo.queryToObject(queryString)`
Summary:	This function will return an object with properties corresponding to the name/value pairs in a query string. If the query strings contain multiple values for the name, an array property will be created for that name.
Parameter: queryString	Query string to be used to create a new object containing properties corresponding to the name/value pairs in the query.

Summary

Remoting is the submission of an HTTP request by the browser without refreshing the page when the response comes back. It is accomplished using the `XMLHttpRequest` (XHR) JavaScript Object.

Dojo provides two functions that wrap the creation of an XHR request to make it easier to use:

> `dojo.xhrGet`...submit an HTTP Get request
>
> `dojo.xhrPost`...submit an HTTP Post request

Submitting data captured on HTML forms is a typical use for Dojo Remoting. It is typical to convert the form data into name/value pairs. Dojo provides a number of useful functions for working with form data and query strings:

> `dojo.formToObject`...Create an object containing properties from form elements
>
> `dojo.objectToQuery`...Create a query string from object properties
>
> `dojo.formToQuery`...Create a query string from form elements
>
> `dojo.formToJson`...Create a JSON string from form elements
>
> `dojo.queryToObject`...Create an object from name/value pairs in a query string

Once we've used Dojo's excellent remoting capabilities to retrieve some data from the server, we'll probably want to update some elements on the page with the new data. The next chapter shows us how to work with DOM elements.

16

Working with the DOM

You look mahvelous.

—Billy Crystal (his *Saturday Night Live* impression of Fernando Lamas)

A web site is defined as much by how it looks as by what it does. And Ajax raises the bar in the area of user interface and visual design. There is very much an expectation today that your site should look "mahvelous." So any good Ajax library worth its salt should provide us lots of ways of improving the look of a site. Not only does Dojo provide many full-blown widgets, as we explored in Part II, "Dojo Widgets," but it also provides techniques for working with individual DOM elements that may not even be part of a widget. This chapter explores ways of identifying DOM elements and then manipulating them in some way—usually by changing some visual aspect.

16.1 Finding Needles in the DOM Haystack

Dojo widgets, which we've already discussed in Part II, are certainly part of the DOM. But what about DOM elements that aren't associated with widgets? They require some attention also. Let's do a quick review to remind us what the DOM is. It stands for Document Object Model and is the browser's internal representation of the web page. We think of a browser as a piece of software that takes an HTML file and displays the page to the computer monitor. This is known as *rendering* in display terminology. However, that understanding of the browser is actually not quite correct.

What a browser really does is take an HTML file and convert it into an internal representation of the file called a Document Object Model and then renders the DOM. Each HTML tag is converted to one or more DOM elements. This may sound like a distinction without a difference, but it is actually quite important in the Ajax world. After the DOM is built, it doesn't have to be static. We can manipulate elements in the DOM, and the browser will instantly rerender the DOM and change the display that the user sees. Now, not all DOM changes necessarily cause the display to change, but that is most typical. Because Ajax applications rely so heavily on manipulating the DOM, it is important for developers to be able to identify DOM elements and to manipulate them. It is possible to do that using JavaScript alone, but we'll use Dojo to make it easier. Let's talk first about how to find DOM elements.

16.2 Dojo Query

The DOM for a typical page can easily contain hundreds and sometimes even thousands of elements, also known as *element nodes* or just plain *nodes*. If we need to perform some operation on a subset of elements, we need a way to quickly identify those elements. The DOM provides us a technique for iterating through itself that involves getting all the child nodes for each node (beginning with the root node) and looping through them. When a node also has children, we can iterate through those as well. Eventually we could walk through the entire DOM tree, testing each element node for whatever properties we are looking for. This brute force method isn't very elegant and doesn't perform very well. Are there any alternatives?

One technique is to provide direct access to a DOM element by specifying its id within the HTML as shown below here:

```
<div id="target"></div>
```

We can then use the `document.getElementById("target")` function to reference the specific DOM element. However, this technique is limited because we can only find a single element. What about when we want to find a group of elements that possess some common property? There is another DOM method available to us, `document.getElementsByTag()`, which returns an array of the elements for a specific HTML tag such as `<p>` for paragraph elements. But this function is limited to only allowing us to specify a tag. What if we want all the elements that use a particular CSS style?

Cascading Style Sheets (CSS) already provide a method for finding DOM elements by using a technique it calls *selectors*. Selectors are strings that identify DOM elements that styles should be applied to. The selector syntax is very rich and can be used to find elements based on a variety of properties. Following is an example of a very simple selector that might be part of your CSS style sheet:

```
h1 {color: blue}
```

This rule finds all the DOM elements for the `<h1>` tags and sets their `color` style property to blue, making the text within the element blue. The "h1" part of the rule is the selector, which tells the browser which set of DOM elements that the rule applies to. Selectors are very powerful, but they can only be used when applying styles in CSS.

Wouldn't it be nice if we could somehow use the CSS selector syntax to retrieve a list of elements to be used for other purposes? Yes, it would be nice, but that is not part of the JavaScript language. However, it turns out that Dojo can give us that capability.

The `dojo.query()` method takes a selector string as an argument and returns a list of unique DOM elements that match the string. Although this is an extremely powerful technique, the function call is very simple. But there is a little problem. You need to understand the selector syntax to use `dojo.query()`. So even though it isn't formally a part of Dojo, let's spend some time getting to know the selector syntax. This will be a valuable exercise given that we'll not only be able to use our knowledge in `dojo.query()`, but we'll also be able to better use CSS selectors for their original purpose—applying styles in style sheets!

16.2.1 CSS Selectors

There are many types of selectors, and the syntax can be somewhat challenging for the more advanced ones. But it isn't important to understand every type of selector. We'll get tremendous power by just knowing the basics. So let's start our review of selectors with the simplest types and work our way upward from there.

16.2.1.1 Simple Selectors

Let's review some simple CSS selectors just to get a feel for them. The most basic selectors correspond to HTML tags, such as in the following example:

```
p {color: blue}
```

Remember, this selector is just the "p" that begins the line, not the rest of the style definition. This selector finds all the elements in the DOM created from the `<p>` tags in the HTML. If additional elements of type `<p>` were added to the DOM using JavaScript, they would be found also.

16.2.1.2 Selector Grouping

Selectors can be put together by separating them with a comma. This is the equivalent of combining the two sets of elements identified by each individual selector. Any overlap between the sets would be removed. The new set would not repeat an individual DOM element even if it had been identified in each individual selector. The following example shows selector grouping:

```
p, h1, h2 {color: blue}
```

This would identify a set of all `<p>`, `<h1>`, and `<h2>` DOM elements.

16.2.1.3 Element ID Selectors

Selectors may identify DOM elements by the id of the element. Place the "#" character in front of the element id as in the following example:

```
#target {color: blue}
```

This example would find the DOM element whose id is "target," which could be specified in the HTML sample shown here:

```
<div id="target"></div>
```

16.2.1.4 Class Attribute Selectors

Style properties are often grouped together and named. The following example defines a class called "plainText," which can be applied to any element associated with that class. Use the "." character at the beginning of the class name.

```
.plainText {color: blue}
```

This example would find the DOM element whose class is "plainText" that could be specified in the HTML sample shown here:

```
<div id="target" class="plainText"></div>
```

It is also possible that the class might have been assigned programmatically using JavaScript.

16.2.1.5 Structural Selectors

Sometimes it is useful to only select an element if it is part of some other element or element branch. These are called structural selectors. Just list the types separated by spaces with the highest level element type first. For example, you may want to find paragraph elements but only if they are part of a div element. The following example shows how you would do this.

```
div p {color: blue}
```

This example would find the DOM element of type p but only if it is a child or descendent of a div type. In the following HTML code, the first <p> element would be found, but not the second.

```
<div><p>Hello</p></div>
<p>Good-bye</p>
```

16.2.1.6 Attribute Selectors

Element nodes in the DOM can have attributes associated with them. Sometimes you may want to find all the elements that have a particular attribute or have a particular value for an attribute. The technique for creating attribute selectors is to include the attribute name in square brackets:

```
[height] {color: blue}
```

This example would find all DOM elements that have a height attribute regardless of the actual value assigned to height.

One of the most common uses for this selector is to find all the DOM elements that need to be converted to Dojo widgets. Remember, when we want to replace an element with a widget, we assign the attribute dojoType to the widget as the following code demonstrates for a dijit.form.ValidationTextBox widget.

```
<input type="text" id="firstName" name="firstName"
    dojoType="dijit.form.ValidationTextBox"
    required="true"
/>
```

The `dojo.parser` needs to find all the elements containing an attribute of `dojoType`. The following code is taken from the Dojo source code for `dojo.parser` and shows the use of an attribute selector to find all the elements that need to be transformed to Dojo widgets.

```
var list = d.query('[dojoType]', rootNode);
```

16.2.1.7 Other Selectors

There are many additional selectors available to us. I've included a table from the specification to give you a flavor of them. Some of the selectors allow a style to be applied to a specific part of an element (such as the first line). These don't apply to `dojo.query` because it is used to find the element and not to apply the style.

The specification describes more complex selectors, and I'd recommend that you read the specification for more detail.[1]

Table 16.1   **Other CSS Selectors**

Pattern	Meaning	Type of Selector
*	Matches any element.	Universal selector
E	Matches any E element (i.e., an element of type E).	Type selectors
E F	Matches any F element that is a descendant of an E element.	Descendant selectors
E > F	Matches any F element that is a child of an element E.	Child selectors
E:first-child	Matches element E when E is the first child of its parent.	The :first-child pseudo-class
E:link E:visited	Matches element E if E is the source anchor of a hyperlink of which the target is not yet visited (:link) or already visited (:visited).	The link pseudo-classes
E:active E:hover E:focus	Matches E during certain user actions.	The dynamic pseudo-classes
E:lang(c)	Matches element of type E if it is in (human) language c (the document language specifies how language is determined).	The :lang() pseudo-class
E + F	Matches any F element immediately preceded by an element E.	Adjacent selectors
E[foo]	Matches any E element with the "foo" attribute set (whatever the value).	Attribute selectors

1. http://www.w3.org/TR/REC-CSS2/selector.html Copyright © World Wide Web Consortium, (Massachusetts Institute of Technology, Institut National de Recherche en Informatique et en Automatique, Keio University). All Rights Reserved.

Table 16.1   **Continued**

Pattern	Meaning	Type of Selector
E[foo="warning"]	Matches any E element whose "foo" attribute value is exactly equal to "warning."	Attribute selectors
E[foo~="warning"]	Matches any E element whose "foo" attribute value is a list of space-separated values, one of which is exactly equal to "warning."	Attribute selectors
E[lang|="en"]	Matches any E element whose "lang" attribute has a hyphen-separated list of values beginning (from the left) with "en."	Attribute selectors
DIV.warning	*HTML only*. The same as DIV[class~="warning"].	Class selectors
E#myid	Matches any E element id equal to "myid."	ID selectors

Dojo also provides support for the CSS 3 Specification that includes some additional selector types that are beyond the scope of this discussion. Again, more information can be found in the specification.[2]

16.2.2 Using Selectors in `dojo.query`

The technique for using a selector to find a set of DOM elements using Dojo is straightforward. Just pass the selector as a string to the `dojo.query` function. For example, to find all the `<h1>` elements, use the following code.

```
elementList = dojo.query("h1");
```

More complex selectors require a more complex selector string, but the syntax for getting the elements is still the same. To find all the `paragraph` elements that are descendents of a `div` element, use the code shown here:

```
elementList = dojo.query("div p");
```

And the syntax doesn't get any more complicated—although the selector strings do! Here's another example. This one uses the class attribute selector just described to find all the elements that are associated with the class "plainText."

```
elementList = dojo.query(".plainText");
```

The `dojo.query` function is part of base Dojo. This means that you don't need to include a `dojo.require` statement to bring the function into your page. Just call the function from your code.

2. The CSS 3 Specification can be viewed at the following link: http://www.w3.org/TR/2001/CR-css3-selectors-20011113/.

16.2.3 Using DOM Elements Found by `dojo.query`

What can you do with the elements from the DOM after you find them using `dojo.query`? The short answer is that you can do anything with them you want. Typically though, you would probably want to change some style property, move the elements, make them visible, hide them, or perform some kind of special effect. All these things can be done using some special features of Dojo known as *animation and effects*.

16.3 Animation

For me, the term "animation" brings to mind Saturday mornings as a child, being glued to the television, watching hour after hour of cartoons. And actually, in terms of explaining animation in Dojo, this may be an apt metaphor. Thinking about cartoons will help us understand some things about animation.

16.3.1 Understanding Animation

A cartoon is a series of fixed images that when, presented in sequence, provide the illusion of movement or action. It turns out that this is exactly the same process used by Dojo. Let me give you an example. A well-known web design company in Chicago, 37signals, developed a method of highlighting DOM elements whenever they changed due to an Ajax request. The method requires that the background color of the element be changed to yellow and then the background color should slowly fade back to white (or whatever the original background color was). They called this the Yellow Fade Technique (YFT) for obvious reasons.

Exactly how is the effect performed? We simply set the background color of the element to yellow. The following code shows how we would do this for an element whose id is "div1":

```
document.getElementById("div1").style.background = #FFFF00;
```

To fade the background color back to the original background color, we just have to do a little math. Remember that the Red/Blue/Green (RGB) color scheme used by the web consists of hexadecimal representations of each of the colors. So yellow is represented in the values in Table 16.2.

Table 16.2   **Selected RGB Hex and Decimal Values Comparison**

Color	RGB Hex Value	RGB Decimal Value
Red	FF	255
Green	FF	255
Blue	0	0

We'll use the decimal values instead of hexadecimal. So the three colors are represented by the range of numbers from 0 (no color at all) to 255 (full color). I like to think of each color as a flashlight with 256 different power settings.

It never strikes me as intuitive, but in the world of computer monitors, red and green mixed together is yellow! Let's say the original background color was white (RGB value: 255,255,255). To produce the fade, we simply need to iterate through a series of fixed values for color until we reach the value we are looking for.

For example, starting with the color yellow and fading back to white, we would loop through the following values for background color:

    255, 255, 0
    255, 255, 1
    255, 255, 2

And so on and so on, all the way to 255, 255, 255.

At each iteration we would set the new background color and pause for a bit before moving on to the next value. Think of the browser as showing us 256 distinct images, each having a different background color for the element we're working with. We'll call each image a frame (as Dojo does), and by iterating quickly through the frames, it would appear as through the background is fading from yellow to white. So we might use the following code to perform out looping:

```
for (i = 0; i < 256; i++) {

    color = "rgb('256, 256",  + i + "')";
    document.getElementById("div1").style.background = color;


}
```

The problem with this code is that the frames will go by so quickly that we won't even get a chance to see them. It will look like the last frame just suddenly appeared. In other words, the yellow background will appear for only a few milliseconds or not at all. Also while the JavaScript is performing the loop, no other code execution is possible. This could be a more serious problem when we use a different property that might include many more iterations.

Using a special JavaScript function called setTimeOut can solve both these problems. It allows us to specify a function to be executed and a delay before that function is run. This allows other JavaScript to run while the browser is waiting for the time-out function to run again. We'll modify our code to use this new function:

```
var FADE_BLUE = 0;

function yellowFade() {
    el = document.getElementById("fade_target");
    color = "rgb("255, 255, " + FADE_BLUE + ")";
    FADE_BLUE = FADE_BLUE + 1;
    el.style.background = color;
    if (FADE_BLUE >= 256) {
        return;
```

```
    } else {
        setTimeout(yellowFade, 1);
}
```

The function `yellowFade` would have to been called from somewhere the first time, but once it starts it runs for a single value of `FADE_BLUE` and then kicks off another iteration by calling the `setTimeout` function, which will run one millisecond later. If you run this code you'll find that the effect is rather slow because the browser doesn't run the code right away; it takes a little longer than a single millisecond to start the next iteration. A better approach would be to lengthen the delay and to increase the increment size for changing the color. Not too complicated, but more than we really want to deal with every time we create some kind of visual effect. Isn't there an easier way? We'll see shortly that Dojo provides a wrapper around this technique in the form of the `dojo.animateProperty` function. It hides the details of changing the property values and running the `setTimeout` function. Let's explore how we can use this new Dojo function to simplify the creation of animations.

16.3.2 Dojo Animation Function

Certainly it is possible to use JavaScript to create very complex visual effects just by using the technique of changing a style property value repeatedly over a period of time. So we already have in our hands the tool we need to build wonderful special effects. However, Dojo can make this technique much easier to use by providing a simple function call to do all the necessary coding for us. Dojo provides a function, `dojo.animateProperty`, which does this all for us.

Table 16.3   **Description of** `dojo.animateProperty` **Function**

Method Signature:	`dojo.animateProperty( node, properties, duration, rate)`
Summary:	This function will iterate over values of a property on a DOM element beginning with the current value (or a stated value) of the property and extending to the specified ending value in the arguments. The effect of the iteration is to produce a visual change to the element.
	This function doesn't perform the animation. It actually returns an object that represents the animation. To run the animation, execute the `play()` method of the returned object.
Parameter: node	Id of a DOM element or a DOM node reference.
Parameter: properties	An object containing properties with names corresponding to actual properties within the DOM element's style object. For example, this object could have a property called `background`. Additionally, each of the properties would reference an object containing beginning and ending values for the property along with any unit of measure for that property.
	Each property object may have a `start`, `end`, and `unit` property.

Table 16.3   **Continued**

Parameter: duration	The time in milliseconds the animation will take to run. This parameter is optional.
Parameter: rate	The time in milliseconds to wait before advancing to next frame. This parameter is optional.

Following is an example of its use.

```
var animation = dojo.animateProperty({
    node: dojo.byId("target"),
    duration: 1500,
    properties: {
            backgroundColor: { end: "white" }
    }
});


animation.play();
```

This example iterates over a color property from whatever the current background color is to the color "white," spanning a time of 1.5 seconds. To the user it looks like the element's background color slowly fades to white. The preceding example achieves the same effect as we built manually in section 16.3.1 by iterating the `style.background` property ourselves. However, I think you'll agree that using the Dojo function simplifies the code that we have to write.

And although our example is fairly simple, we can use `dojo.animateProperty` to provide more complex animations that cycle through multiple style properties at once. Following is an example from the Dojo documentation that shows just that:

```
dojo.animateProperty({
    node: node, duration:2000,
      properties: {
            width: { start: '200', end: '400', unit:"px" },
            height: { start:'200', end: '400', unit:"px" },
            paddingTop: { start:'5', end:'50', unit:"px" }
      }
}).play()
```

This more complex effect will vary three different properties over a period of two seconds. We now have the tool to create almost any visual effect we can think of but, even better, Dojo has pre-packaged some standard effects for us.

16.3.3 Standard Animation Effects

Some animations are so common that Dojo provides shortcut functions to create them. They could be built by running one or more complex `dojo.animateProperty` function calls and a varying a number of properties at the same time, but by having a simple Dojo function with a descriptive name, we can achieve the same goal more directly. For example, it is often useful in an Ajax application to move a DOM element from one position on the page to another. We could do this by using `dojo.animateProperty` and varying the `top` and `left` properties, but instead we can use the `dojo.fx.slideTo` function and specify only the final position rather than the starting and ending values of each property. This and other common effects are contained in the `dojo.fx` package. Let's discuss these functions now.

16.3.3.1 `dojo.fx.slideTo`

This function allows you to "slide" a DOM element around the screen. Rather than just redrawing it in a new location, this effect shows the element at intermediate locations so that it appears to move.

Table 16.4   **Description of `dojo.fx.slideTo` Function**

Method Signature:	`dojo.fx.slideTo( node, left, top, unit)`
Summary:	This function returns an animation object that will move a DOM element from its current position to a new position specified by the arguments.
Parameter: node	DOM element to be moved.
Parameter: left	The left position to which the element should be moved. This represents the value of the `left` style property of the element. Don't include the unit of measure.
Parameter: top	The top position to which the element should be moved. This represents the `top` style property of the object. Don't include the unit of measure.
Parameter: unit	The units that the left and top properties are specified in (i.e., `px` for pixels).

Following is an example of its use.

```
dojo.fx.slideTo({
    node: dojo.byId("target"),
    left:"100",
    top:"50",
    unit:"px" }).play()
```

This example moves a DOM element whose id is "target" from whatever its current position is to a new position where the element's upper left corner is 50 pixels from the top border of the browser window and 100 pixels from the left border of the browser window. Remember that this function simply returns an animation object. To run the animation you, must execute its `play` method as shown in the example.

16.3.3.2 `dojo.fx.wipeOut`

This function may sound like it has something to do with riding a surfboard, but it does not. However, like a surfer who "wipes out," the DOM element that this effect operates on also disappears beneath the waves. Think of this effect as causing the DOM element to disappear beginning from the bottom of the element to the top. Another way to picture this effect is to imagine what would happen if you placed an eraser at the bottom of the element and "wiped up." You would be wiping out the element.

Table 16.5 **Description of** `dojo.fx.wipeOut` **Function**

Method Signature:	`dojo.fx.wipeOut( {node, duration, onEnd})`
Summary:	Returns an animation that will shrink the element from its current height to 1px and then hide it.
Parameter: node	DOM element on which the "wipe out" effect will be performed.
Parameter: duration	Length of time in milliseconds over which the effect will occur.
Parameter: onEnd	Function to be executed after the effect is run.

Following is an example of its use.

```
dojo.fx.wipeOut({
    node: dojo.byId("target"),
    duration: 500
}).play()
```

This code causes the DOM element to disappear over a period of half a second (500 milliseconds). The way that it works internally is that the element's height is changed from the original height to a new height of zero over the duration of the effect and then hidden. The original element takes up no space on the page after it is hidden so any elements below it are moved up as it disappears.

16.3.3.3 `dojo.fx.wipeIn`

This function is the inverse of the previous function. It causes an element to reappear after it has been wiped out using the `dojo.fx.wipeOut` function. However, the resulting look might not be exactly what you imagined. The resulting element might have a smaller height than it did originally. The reason for this is that there are two ways to set the height of an element. The first uses the `height` style property and is used to explicitly set the height. The second technique is to let the browser figure out what the height should be based on the content of the element. The Dojo documentation refers to this as the "natural" height. After the element's height is set to zero using `dojo.fx.wipeOut`, Dojo doesn't remember the original height, so it allows the browser to recalculate it using the "natural" method, which may be different than the original height.

Table 16.6   **Description of** `dojo.fx.wipeIn` **Function**

Method Signature:	`dojo.fx.wipeIn( {node, duration, onEnd} )`
Summary:	Returns an animation that will expand the node defined in "node" to its natural height and make it visible.
Parameters: node	DOM element on which the effect will be performed.
Parameters: duration	Length of time in milliseconds over which the effect will occur.
Parameters: onEnd	Function to be executed after the effect is run.

Following is an example of its use.

```
dojo.fx.wipeIn({
    node: dojo.byId("target"),
    duration: 500
}).play()
```

This causes the DOM element to reappear over a period of half a second.

16.3.3.4 `dojo.fadeOut`

This effect causes the element to gradually disappear. It is similar to `dojo.fx.wipeOut` in that by the end of the effect the element is no longer visible, but the technique for achieving that end is different. In this effect, the element becomes less and less opaque until it is completely invisible. However, it still takes up room on the page so that surrounding elements don't get rearranged. It uses the `opacity` style property of the element that can range from 1 (completely opaque) to 0 (completely transparent). Notice that this effect is in Dojo base and not the `dojo.fx` package, so no `dojo.require` statement is necessary to make it available.

Table 16.7   **Description of** `dojo.fx.fadeOut` **Function**

Method Signature:	`dojo.fadeOut( {node, duration, onEnd} )`
Summary:	Returns an animation that will increase the opacity of the specified element until it is completely transparent.
Parameter: node	DOM element on which the effect will be performed.
Parameter: duration	Length of time in milliseconds over which the effect will occur.
Parameter: onEnd	Function to be executed after the effect is run. This parameter is optional.

Following is an example of its use.

```
dojo.fadeOut({
    node: dojo.byId("target"),
    duration: 500
}).play()
```

This example will fade the element specified in `node` over a period of half a second.

16.3.3.5 `dojo.fadeIn`

This effect is the reverse of the `dojo.fadeOut` effect. It causes an element that is currently invisible to gradually become visible. It uses the reverse technique that `dojo.fadeOut` uses. It changes the opacity style property of the element from 0 (fully transparent) to 1 (fully opaque). The element, even when invisible, still takes up space on the page, so no rearranging of surrounding elements is necessary. Notice that this effect is in Dojo base and not the `dojo.fx` package, so no `dojo.require` statement is necessary to make it available.

Table 16.8   Description of `dojo.fx.fadeIn` **Function**

Method Signature:	`dojo.fadeIn( {node, duration, onEnd} )`
Summary:	Returns an animation that will decrease the opacity of the specified element until it is completely visible.
Parameters: node	DOM element on which the effect will be performed.
Parameters: duration	Length of time in milliseconds over which the effect will occur.
Parameters: onEnd	Function to be executed after the effect is run.

Following is an example of its use.

```
dojo.fadeIn({
    node: dojo.byId("target"),
    duration: 500
}).play()
```

This example will gradually make a transparent element visible over a period of half a second.

16.3.3.6 `dojo.fx.chain`

This function is not an effect in itself. But it does allow you to use multiple effects together. Given a series of effects, this function will execute each one in order. The effects are executed one at a time until the last effect is complete.

Table 16.9   Description of `dojo.fx.chain` **Function**

Method Signature:	`dojo.fx.chain( animations)`
Summary:	This function will run a series of animations one at a time, starting a new animation only after the prior animation is complete.
Parameters: animations	An array of animation objects to be executed serially and in order.

Following is an example of its use.

```
dojo.fx.chain([
      dojo.fx.wipeOut({ node:node }),
      dojo.fx.wipeIn({ node:otherNode })
]).play()
```

This example will hide thefirst element and then show the second element.

16.3.3.7 dojo.fx.combine

This function allows you to combine multiple effects. But while dojo.chain runs the effects serially, this function runs the effects in parallel so they are executing at the same time. This function starts each effect in the order specified, and then they run essentially in parallel.

Table 16.10   **Description of** dojo.fx.combine **Function**

Method Signature:	dojo.fx.combine(animations)
Summary:	This function will execute multiple animations concurrently.
Parameters: animations	An array of animation objects to be executed at the same time.

Following is an example of its use.

```
dojo.fx.combine([
      dojo.fx.wipeOut({ node:node }),
      dojo.fx.wipeIn({ node:otherNode })
]).play()
```

This example will hide the first element and show the second element at the same time.

16.3.3.8 dojo.fx.Toggler

Many visual effects have a sort of "equal and opposite" effect that can be associated with them. For example, dojo.fadeOut makes a DOM element disappear, and dojo.fadeIn brings it back. We can think of one function as hiding the DOM element and the other function as showing the element. This is such a common idiom that the Dojo team decided to encapsulate it in a function, dojo.fx.Toggler. You provide an effect that "shows" the element and a separate effect that "hides" it. The Toggler object has two methods, show and hide, which you can run to execute the associated effect. These effects don't have to work on the same style properties. The "show" effect could change the background color property while the hide effect could change the height property.

Table 16.11   **Description of** dojo.fx.Toggler **Function**

Method Signature:	dojo.fx.Toggler({node, hideFunc, showFunc})
Summary:	This function will toggle effects on a single DOM element. The arguments are passed as a single object with properties. As with the other effects, this function returns an animation object. To run the effect, the play() method of the animation object must be executed.

Table 16.11   **Continued**

Parameters: node	DOM element on which the effect will be performed.
Parameters: hideFunc	Function to be executed that will "hide" the element.
Parameters: showFunc	Function to be executed that will "show" the element.

Following is an example of its use.

```
var t = dojo.fx.Toggler({
    node: dojo.byId("target"),
    hideFunc: dojo.fx.wipeOut,
    showFunc: dojo.fx.wipeIn
});
t.hide();
t.show();
```

This example will hide the element and then show the element—usually these wouldn't be done together.

Summary

The hallmark of most Ajax applications is their ability to manipulate DOM elements to provide special visual effects.

Dojo provides a powerful function called `dojo.query`, which lets a developer use CSS selectors to find DOM elements.

Dojo provides a function, `dojo.animateProperty`, which can be used to change the style properties of a DOM element over a specified interval, producing a variety of visual effects.

Besides providing a generic function for animation, Dojo also provides a number of standard visual effects including

`dojo.fx.slideTo`...move a DOM element

`dojo.fx.wipeOut`...make a DOM element disappear

`dojo.fx.wipeIn`...make a DOM element reappear

`dojo.fadeOut`...make a DOM element gradually fade out

`dojo.fadeIn`...make a DOM element gradually fade back in

Dojo provides a way of running multiple effects together. Use `dojo.chain` to run effects in serial and `dojo.combine` to run effects in parallel.

We've reviewed many of the building blocks for Dojo applications in the past chapters. After we put them all together into a complete application, we might find that we have a few errors. The next chapter will discuss tools and techniques in Dojo for finding these errors and debugging our applications.

Testing and Debugging

Manager: Did you test that program?
Programmer: Well, it compiled.

—Both the Manager and Programmer chose to remain anonymous
(but you know who they are).

We've probably all made a program change that was so small and so straightforward that we really didn't need to test it. And then we lived to regret that decision. Why do developers often avoid testing? One of the reasons is that it isn't always easy to do. By providing tools for making testing easier, Dojo encourages developers to do what they know they should—test, test, and test. We test to find errors, and after we find them, we must fix them. In this chapter we explore some special features that Dojo provides to aid in finding errors and fixing them.

17.1 Testing

It is more important to build quality into our programs than to inspect them for quality after the fact. We should write our code in such a way that we don't introduce errors. Easier said than done, of course. And because of that we still need to inspect our programs for errors. The classic pattern for inspection testing consists of the following steps:

- Select the thing to test
- Prepare test input
- Prepare expected results
- Execute code
- Compare the actual results to the expected results

An historic difficulty with this approach was that the pieces of our application that we could easily execute were usually quite large—often entire programs. That meant that they required lots of input and generated lots of results. Creating a set of expected results for a single execution pass and then comparing those results with the expected output was difficult and time-consuming. Fortunately, a real paradigm shift occurred in understanding how to do testing that we still benefit from today. What if our program "pieces" were much smaller? Then they would require less input and generate fewer results. An important additional benefit is that when the smaller pieces failed, it would be much more apparent what went wrong because we would be dealing with a much smaller amount of code. So a testing approach- was developed that focused on the smallest pieces of executable code possible. These small pieces were called units, and the approach became knows as *unit testing*.

17.1.1 Unit Testing

In the JavaScript world, the best candidate on which to perform testing are object methods. Methods usually contain a relatively small amount of code (or at least should), and they return a single object for a set of input parameters. A single unit test should execute a single method for a given set of parameters and can then be compared to a single result. By testing at this fine-grained level we can make our output comparison very simple, and the test either fails or succeeds. Understanding the results of the test becomes straightforward.

17.1.2 DOH—The Dojo Unit Testing Framework

All right, so unit testing is a good thing. But how do we do it? Remember, we're from Dojo, and we're here to help. Dojo provides an excellent framework for helping us define and run unit tests. This framework is named "doh." It is pronounced like Homer Simpson's famous exclamation: Doh! (often accompanied by a smack to the forehead). The Dojo team "eats their own dog food." That is, in industry parlance, they use doh for testing. Dojo is delivered with an entire suite of unit test scripts that were run on the various components of Dojo using doh. And we can also use the doh testing framework to test custom JavaScript code that we write ourselves.

17.1.2.1 Create a New Unit Test

Unit tests typically follow a pattern. Following are the steps that occur inside almost all unit test methods:

- Create the object whose method is to be tested.
- Execute the method under test with appropriate parameters and get back a result.
- Compare that result to an expected result.

Sometimes these separate steps are combined together in a line of code, but we can still think of them as distinct. Let's see an actual example of creating a unit test. First we need an object and method to test. We'll create an object called `StringUtils` that has a method `countLetters`, which can count the number of occurrences of a letter within a given string. Following is the code to create the constructor for this object:

```
function StringUtils() {

    this.countLetters = function( string, char ) {
        var count = 0;
        for (i=1; i<=string.length; i++) {
            if (string[i] == char) count++;
        }
        return count;
    }

}
```

This code could be included within the `<script>` tag of a page or in an included JavaScript file. To create an instance of the object, we would use the new keyword on the constructor.

```
var su = new StringUtils();
```

We can now test the utility method by running it and seeing what results we get.

```
result = su.countLetters("hello","o");
```

The value of result should be "1" because there is one occurrence of the letter "o" in the string `"hello"`. We could just display the result using an alert box. But instead of using this informal approach to testing, we'll create the test as a doh unit test.

```
var testCase = { runTest: function() {
    var su = new StringUtils();
    result = su.countLetters("hello","o");
    doh.assertEqual(1,result);}
}
```

We've created a new object called `testCase` that contains a function called `runTest`. Note that a unit test in doh is actually a JavaScript object itself. The object must contain certain properties, one of which must be a function called `runTest`. This is the function that will be run by doh and contains the test case itself. There are also other possible properties such as `setUp` and `tearDown`, which are run before and after the test methods, respectively, and can create and remove objects and other resources that the test method might need.

The last line of code in the preceding example is especially interesting. This is known as an `assert` method and is a standard unit test function that compares the output to the expected results. For the test to succeed, the assert method must evaluate as `true`. Sometimes this results in tests that might appear backwards at first. For example, imagine that our string utility also has a method called `hasLetter` that returns a `true` or `false` depending on whether a given letter is in a string. Not only do we want to test for the `true` condition when looking for a letter we expect to find, but we also want to test for the `false` condition when the function looks for a letter that it should not find. In that case, we use the `assertFalse` method as shown here:

```
doh.assertFalse( su.hasLetter("cat","z"));
```

Now we can verify that the function works when it doesn't find the letter. In the given example, the function `hasLetter` returns false, but because the assert function `assertFalse` expects a `false` result, the assert method then returns `true`, which designates that the test succeeded!

Use the assert functions to compare values returned or created by your functions against the values you expect—that is, the values you expect if the function operates properly. You can then make changes to your JavaScript code and run the tests again. If all the tests still pass, your change has not introduced any new errors. (Or at least your changes have not introduced errors for the behavior you test, which may be another matter entirely.)

There are additional assertion methods, including the following:

- `assertEquals`...compares expected to actual results
- `assertFalse`...verifies that argument is false
- `assertTrue`...verifies that argument is true

17.1.2.2 Register Unit Test

We've created the test as an object with a `runTest` property containing the test case. You might think that the next step would be to run the test, but we first have to let the doh unit testing framework know about the test. This is done because often we want to add lots of tests together before we start running them. To register the test, use the `doh.register()` function.

```
doh.register( testCase );
```

There are a number of variations of this function. They mostly deal with assigning this test to a group of tests that can be run together. A group is just a collection of unit tests identified by a single name. For example, to add this test to a group called `"StringUtilsTest"` use the following code.

```
doh.register( "StringUtilsTest", testCase );
```

17.1.2.3 Run Unit Test

Now we need to run the test case. We can use the `doh.run()` method to execute all the tests that have been registered with the framework.

```
doh.run();
```

The doh framework will execute all the tests that have been registered and disply the results.

17.1.2.4 Review Results of Test

The results of the test will be displayed to the console. If you are using Firebug, the results will display to the Firebug console; otherwise, they will display at the end of the web page. Following is a screen shot of the test for the countLetters method in StringUtils.

```
1 tests to run in 1 groups
------------------------------------------------------------
GROUP "StringUtils Tests" has 1 test to run
PASSED test: Count Letters
WOOHOO!!
------------------------------------------------------------
| TEST SUMMARY:
------------------------------------------------------------
        1 tests in 1 groups
        0 errors
        0 failures
```

Figure 17.1   Example of unit testing output

These results show that no errors have been detected. What is the difference between errors and failures? Failures occur when an assert method has returned a false value. Errors occur when the test is not able to run.

So we've created a unit test, run it, and reviewed the expected results. And it worked! So we're done, right? Not quite. Not only are there other types of tests we can perform, but we're not even finished with our unit testing. Let's review the test condition we're checking for. Study the code that is in bold type in the example below.

```
var testCase = { runTest: function() {
    var su = new StringUtils();
    result = su.countLetters("hello","o");
    doh.assertEqual(1,result);}
}
```

We're checking to see if the countLetters method in StringUtils counts the correct number of occurrences of the letter "o" within the string "hello". And even though it worked, the method is not fully tested. We may also want to check boundary conditions. For example, does our method still work if the letter is at the beginning of the string? Or at the end? What about if the letter is capitalized in the string? Or when the letter doesn't occur at all? Now we can see why doh allows us to register tests within groups—because we're going to need more then a single test to feel confident that our method is correct. And we'll need a group of tests for each of the other methods in our object to be tested.

How much testing do we need to do? Dojo provides us with a framework to do unit testing but does not provide us with actual tests to perform. Creating tests is up to us, and we have to decide when enough is enough. Testing every possible combination of inputs for a method usually isn't practical. Remember the 80/20 rule—most of the benefit of testing can be achieved with a relatively small number of test cases.

17.1.3 Other Types of Testing

Unit testing alone is not enough. Just because a method seems to perform correctly for a given input doesn't mean that we are done testing. We need to perform other types of tests to ensure the validity of our system. Let's briefly discuss some of the additional types of testing you need to do.

Integration testing determines if objects are working well together, not just alone as in the case of unit testing. *Functional testing* is used to verify that the object actually performs the function that the user expects it to. *Stress testing* shows us how our system performs under the stress of a heavy user load or large number of transactions.

Certainly all these types of testing are important and must be done. However, Dojo doesn't provide any specific support for these are kinds of testing methodologies, so we won't say any more about them here.

> **Note**
>
> Although I said I wouldn't talk about any other testing tools, I can't quite help myself. There is a Firefox plugin called Selenium that is excellent for testing user interaction with a web application. You can get more information and download the plugin at http://selenium.openqa.org/.

Next let's discuss what happens when unit testing shows us that our program is failing in some way. Does Dojo provide any techniques for debugging our application after a problem is discovered?

17.2 Logging

When good programs go bad it is helpful to know what they were doing when they crossed the line. A simple debugging technique is to have the program display some output showing the value of a variable. In JavaScript, this can done by using the `alert` method. The following line of code could be put into any function to display the value of x at the time that the `alert` method runs.

```
alert("Value of x: " + x);
```

This code would create a dialog box that would appear on top of the web page. An example of an alert box is shown in Figure 17.2. This example assumes that x is used in the program and has the value 7 at the time the alert statement is executed.

Figure 17.2   Example of `alert` message

This technique is sometimes described as "the poor man's debugger." It gets the job done, and it works in all browsers—but there are a few problems. One problem is that you must be sure to remove the code when deploying the application. Your users certainly don't want to see these messages and have their work interrupted.

So our dilemma is that we'd like to write some messages to display the internal state of our code and have those messages be separate from the output of our page. Also, just to be greedy, we'd like it if we didn't have to touch any code to turn the messages off when we move the program out of development. After all, if we believe the benchmarks, every time we touch code, there is a 5% chance that we unintentionally break something, so we need to minimize code changes.

17.2.1 Basic Logging

The solution to our problem is to use logging. You may be familiar with logging in other environments. For example, Java provides a number of logging frameworks such as the open source log4j or the new logging framework built right into the JDK. Dojo can give us some of the same functionality of these existing logging frameworks but within in the JavaScript environment.

To implement logging, Dojo allows us to write messages to a separate area on our page called the *console*. The console will appear at the end of the web page. However, if we happen to be using Firebug, which is a plug-in for Firefox, Dojo will write log messages to the Firebug console instead. To add logging to your page, set the `isDebug` attribute to `true` in the `<script>` tag, which references Dojo as shown in the code here (the attribute is in bold):

```
<script type="text/javascript"
src="../dojo-release-1.1.0/dojo/dojo.js.uncompressed.js"
djConfig="parseOnLoad: true, isDebug: true"></script>
```

Now you can write log messages whenever you want. Insert a call to `console.log` anywhere in your JavaScript where you'd like to display the internal state of the program.

```
console.log("Value of x: ", x);
```

Now, whenever your program executes the `console.log` method, output will be sent to the console. When using Internet Explorer or when using Firefox without Firebug, the console is attached to the end of the page. Figure 17.3 provides an example of what the console output would look like in IE.

Figure 17.3   Example of console logging

You can display as many objects in the log message as you like. Simply pass any additional objects as parameters to the `console.log` method call.

```
console.log(a, b, c);
```

You can easily turn logging off by setting the isDebug attribute to `false`.

```
<script type="text/javascript"
src="../dojo-release-1.1.0/dojo/dojo.js.uncompressed.js"
djConfig="parseOnLoad: true, isDebug: false"></script>
```

Although this is a change to your code, it is certainly small and less invasive then having to remove or comment out all the various log messages in your code. And turning logging back on is a snap. Just set the property back to `true`.

17.2.2 Advanced Logging

Dojo logging provides some additional methods and configuration options that can be quite useful.

17.2.2.1 Timer

A very useful feature of the logging mechanism allows us to measure how long it takes to execute some JavaScript code. We can use a timer that we can turn on using the `console.time()` method and then turn off using the `console.timeEnd()`. Be sure to pass the name of the timer to the function. By naming the timer, you may have multiple timings running at one time. The name is arbitrary and is just used to identify the timing. An example of a simple timer is shown here:

```
console.time("Timer 1");
// ... some code to be timed
console.timeEnd ("Timer 1");
```

The amount of time in milliseconds since the timer was started is shown in the console (see Figure 17.4).

Figure 17.4   Example of timer logging

Using a timer can sometimes be useful, but be careful about certain issues. Don't include any user input within the code being timed. Also because of the speed of JavaScript, single executions of a block of code may not take very much time—often you'll see timings of zero as in the preceding example. So repeated executions are usually necessary before slower code blocks become obvious.

17.2.2.2 Logging Message Types

There is an interesting variation of the logging framework that allows us to write out different types of logging messages. Instead of using console.log for all messages, we can use any of debug, info, warn, or error as the logging method that will write the message to the console in a different color. This makes viewing a lengthy log file in the console much easier. Your eyes are immediately drawn to the more important messages first. Following are examples of writing each of the various types of log messages:

```
console.error("This is a log message written using console.error()");
console.warn ("This is a log message written using console.warn()");
console.info ("This is a log message written using console.info()");
console.debug("This is a log message written using console.debug()");
console.log  ("This is a log message written using console.log()");
```

The log messages will display in the console as shown in Figure 17.5.

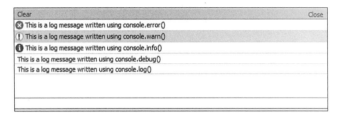

Figure 17.5   Example of different logging message types

The different types of log messages are in different colors. Also there are icons assigned to some of the types to make them stand out even more. In some logging frameworks, it is possible to set an option that allows only certain types of messages to display—this is not yet a feature of the Dojo logging framework.

Summary

Dojo provides a unit testing framework called doh that allows unit tests to be created as objects that contain a `runTest` method.

Doh unit tests must be registered using `doh.register()` and executed using `doh.run()`.

The console is used to display the results of the unit test execution or in the Firebug console when using the Firebug plugin for Firefox.

Dojo provides a logging mechanism that will work in most browsers.

The primary logging method is `console.log("...log message...")`.

We've now completed our tour of Dojo. Now start developing. Good luck!

A

D

E

S

BOOKS ONLINE

ENABLED

THIS BOOK IS SAFARI ENABLED

INCLUDES FREE 45-DAY ACCESS TO THE ONLINE EDITION

The Safari® Enabled icon on the cover of your favorite technology book means the book is available through Safari Bookshelf. When you buy this book, you get free access to the online edition for 45 days.

Safari Bookshelf is an electronic reference library that lets you easily search thousands of technical books, find code samples, download chapters, and access technical information whenever and wherever you need it.

TO GAIN 45-DAY SAFARI ENABLED ACCESS TO THIS BOOK:

- Go to **informit.com/safarienabled**
- Complete the brief registration form
- Enter the coupon code found in the front of this book on the "Copyright" page

If you have difficulty registering on Safari Bookshelf or accessing the online edition, please e-mail customer-service@safaribooksonline.com.